MEDIEVAL GENTLEWOMAN

Man's life is well comparëd to a feast
Furnished with choice of all variety:
To it comes Time; and as a bidden guest
He sets him down in pomp and majesty;
The three-fold age of man, the waiters be;
Then with an earthen voider (made of clay)
Comes Death, and takes the table clean away.

Richard Barnfield (1598)

'Don't stand chattering to yourself like that', Humpty Dumpty said, looking at her for the first time, 'but tell me your name and business.'
'My name is Alice, but –'
'It's a stupid name enough!' Humpty Dumpty interrupted impatiently. 'What does it mean?'
'Must a name mean something?' Alice asked doubtfully.
'Of course it must,' Humpty Dumpty said with a short laugh: 'my name means the shape I am – and a good handsome shape it is too. With a name like yours, you might be any shape, almost.'

Lewis Carroll, *Alice Through the Looking Glass*

MEDIEVAL GENTLEWOMAN

LIFE IN A GENTRY HOUSEHOLD IN THE LATER MIDDLE AGES

ffiona Swabey

ROUTLEDGE
NEW YORK

Published in the United States of America and Canada in 1999 by
Routledge
20 W 35th Street
New York, NY 10001-2299

First published in 1999 by
Sutton Publishing Limited · Phoenix Mill
Thrupp · Stroud · Gloucestershire · GL5 2BU

Library of Congress Cataloging-in-Publication Data available upon request.

ISBN 0-415-92511-8

Typeset in 11/15 pt Ehrhardt.
Typesetting and origination by
Sutton Publishing Limited.
Printed in Great Britain by
WBC Ltd, Bridgend.

To the memory of my mother Elisabeth von Westhoven
4 October 1907–16 September 1974

and her twin brother Rüdiger von Westhoven
4 October 1907–27 September 1944

Contents

List of Plates and Illustrations

Picture Credits

COLOUR PLATES

Alice de Raydon's Book of Hours (MS Dd.4.17 f. 19r), by permission of the Syndics of Cambridge University Library.

Lord Lovell's Lectionary (MS Harley 7026 f. 4v) and agricultural workers in the manor fields (Royal 1 E ix f. 62v), by permission of The British Library.

St Petronella (MS 349 f. 56v), with the kind permission of the Provost and Fellows of The Queen's College, Oxford.

The Gough map, of London and the Home Counties (MS Gough Gen. Top. 16, detail), marriage (MS Canon Misc. 110 f. 23r), Astrological and Prognostic Almanac (MS Rawl. D. 939, part 3), women dancing (MS Bodl. 264 f. 97v) and cooking (MS Bodl. 264 f. 170v), by permission of The Bodleian Library, Oxford.

Old Wardour Castle, by permission of English Heritage Photographic Library.

Stained-glass window with Bryan arms, by courtesy of Jo Atkins.

BLACK AND WHITE ILLUSTRATIONS

The Banqueting Hall, Penshurst, by courtesy of Viscount De L'Isle, Penshurst Place.

Aerial view of Acton Hall, by courtesy of David Johnson.

Page from the Household Book of Alice de Bryene (PRO, C47/4/8b) and page from the Letter-book of Alice de Bryene (PRO, SC1/51/24), held at the Public Record Office, Kew.

Steward's account for Acton (PRO, SC6/1249/4) and Bailiff's report for Oxenhall (PRO, SC6/1247/3), Crown Copyright material in the Public Record Office is reproduced by permission of the Controller of Her Majesty's Stationery Office.

Sir Robert de Bures' brass, by courtesy of The Monumental Brass Society.

Woodsford Castle, Dorset, by courtesy of the Landmark Trust © Richard Hayman.

Lord Bryan's tomb, Tewkesbury, by kind permission of the Vicar and Churchwardens of Tewkesbury Abbey © Lionel Pitt.

Wheel of Fortune (MS Douce 203 f. 103v), '*Concordiam in populo*' (MS Rawl. D. 939 part 3), St George slaying the dragon (MS Liturg. 104 f. 88v), Heron (MS Auct. F.4.15 f. 5v), Friar (MS Douce 104 f. 46r), labourer (MS Douce 104 f. 39r), knights (MS Bodl. 264 f. 149v), 'Of a feast we sing' (MS Arch. Selden. B. 26 f. 15r), by permission of The Bodleian Library, Oxford.

Adam and Eve (MS CCC 161 p. 7) and calendar page for February (MS CCC 285 f. 3v), by permission of Corpus Christi College, Oxford.

Labourers at harvest time (MS, Royal 2B vii f. 77v), Richard II delivered to London (MS Harley 1319 f. 53v), shepherds with flocks (MS Royal 2Bvii f. 74), cowherds (MS Royal 2B vii f. 75), woman shearing a sheep (MS Harley 1892 f. 27v), St John of Bridlington (MS Royal 2A xviii f. 7v), man asleep in a cornfield (MS Royal 10E iv f. 7v), women riding (MS Royal 2B vii f. 152v), lady dictating to a secretary (MS Royal 10E iv f. 307), Christine de Pisan presenting her book to Queen Isabel (MS Harley 4431 f. 3) and old age (MS Harley 4425 f. 10v), by permission of The British Library.

Encaustic tile with the Bryan arms, by courtesy of the Friends of Shaftesbury Abbey.

Rokewode Mazer (Mus No. M. 15-1950) and Swinburne Pyx (Mus No. M. 165-1914), by permission of the V&A Picture Library.

Richard II's Livery Badge, by courtesy of the Musée des Beaux-Arts et d'Archéologie de Troyes, France © National Gallery, London.

Arms of Sir Guy Bryan, by courtesy of Edsel & Eleanor Ford House, Grosse Pointe Shores, Michigan.

Alice de Raydon's Book of Hours (MS Dd. 4.17 f. 6r), by permission of the Syndics of Cambridge University Library.

St Sytha, John Lacy Hours (MS 94 f. 9), by courtesy of the President and Scholars of St John the Baptist College in Oxford.

Alice de Bryene's personal seal (Bacon Collection MS 2270), by courtesy of the Department of Special Collections, the University of Chicago Library.

Alice de Bryene's brass, All Saints', Acton, by kind permission of Dr J.M. Blatchly, MA, FSA.

Acknowledgements

My greatest debt of gratitude is to Dr Caroline Barron who has been a constant source of encouragement and support throughout the writing of this book. I am also indebted to Professor Joel Rosenthal for his continuing interest and advice.

I also thank the following people who have seen parts of my manuscript at its conception and offered their comments, or who have answered specific queries: Dr Helen Bradley, Professor Christopher Dyer, Dr Christopher Given-Wilson, Professor Christopher Harper-Bill, Dr Ruth Harvey, Professor Richard Marks, Professor Colin Richmond, Professor Ian Short, Dr Anne Sutton, Dr Jennifer Ward and Dr Christopher Woolgar.

Thanks are due to the Rt. Hon. William Waldegrave for permission to quote the extract on page 92 from the book of his mother Mary, the late Countess Waldegrave.

Some of the expenses incurred in my research and funds towards the cost of reproducing illustrations were covered by two grants from The Scouloudi Foundation in association with the Institute of Historical Research. An award from the Isobel Thornley Bequest Fund gave me further assistance in meeting the cost of supplying illustrations. I am most grateful to both trusts for their generosity.

Notes and Abbreviations

I have kept French and Latin quotations in the original in some instances with a translation in the footnotes where necessary. Certain words and phrases such as *materfamilias* (literally mother of the family) and *domina domus* (lady of the household) cannot be accurately translated since they relate to medieval concepts of society and authority. I have also retained the medieval spellings for certain surnames such as Boteler for Butler, since that is how they appear in *The Household Book*, but have included modern forms in the Index. For the same reason Alice de Bryene's surname is given as Bryene, while other members of the family are referred to as Bryan. *Sir* in italics denotes a member of the clergy rather than a knight.

Cash

£1 = 240*d* or 100p
1*s* = one shilling, 12*d* or 5p
1 mark = 13*s* 4*d*

Linear

1 yard = 0.9 metre

Liquid

1 gallon = 8 pints or 4.5 litres

Weight

1 lb. = 1 pound, 16 ounces or
0.45 kilograms.
Grain was measured by dry weight, hence:
1 quarter = 8 bushels or 35.3 litres;
1 bushel = 50 lbs

ABBREVIATIONS

CCR	Calendar of Close Rolls
CFR	Calendar of Fine Rolls
CIM	Calendar of Inquisitions Miscellaneous
CIPM	Calendar of Inquisitions Post Mortem
CPR	Calendar of Patent Rolls

Introduction

Alice de Bryene was born in about 1360, the only child of a prosperous Suffolk knight and his lady. Her father, Sir Robert de Bures, died in 1361 and two years later her mother remarried Sir Richard Waldegrave, another prominent knight from Northampton who settled in East Anglia. In about 1375 Alice married the eldest son of Lord Guy Bryan, a wealthy member of the minor aristocracy, by whom she had two daughters. Widowed in 1386, she remained single and sometime within the next ten years moved from the West Country, where she and her husband had owned property, to those estates in Suffolk that were her patrimony.

By the early 1400s she had established her home at Acton, near Sudbury in Suffolk, where she lived until her death in 1435. From here she managed her estates of over 6,000 acres, half in East Anglia and the rest in Dorset and Gloucestershire. In common with other estate owners at this time, annual records were drawn up for her by the various officials she employed to help her in this task: bailiffs who managed her farms, receivers who accounted for a group of manors and stewards who recorded the household expenditure. Some of these records have survived, including a single set of annual accounts for her household at Acton.

When I first looked at the household accounts for 1412–13 I was particularly impressed by the horses. The number fed in her stables appears to bear little relation to the movements of those guests who visited Alice at the Acton manor, except for the merchant's: his visits can always be detected because his horse was rewarded with a special ha'penny loaf whenever he came to deliver goods. On some occasions the steward accounted for fodder for nineteen horses, at other times for only four. Nor do the figures help us predict with any certainty when Dame Alice went visiting herself, but they do indicate a continual traffic to and from her Suffolk manor. Like an inquisitive neighbour watching the cars arrive and depart at the silent house next door, I wanted to find out more: who owned the horses, why had they come, how long were they staying, where were they going next? Predictably I could find no answer, but it was the horses that carried me forward on my quest to discover something about the life, familial ties, social networks and estates of Alice de Bryene.

The household accounts were translated by Marion Dale and edited by Vincent Redstone in 1931.[1] Though they have frequently been used to analyse consumption, marketing and gentry lifestyles, most notably by Christopher Dyer,[2] no work has yet been published which focuses on Alice de Bryene herself, nor attempts made to describe her social and business relationships by identifying the numerous named and unnamed visitors mentioned in the daily accounts as guests at Acton. Besides these accounts, nearly eighty bailiffs' reports still exist, together with three receivers' reports and a few stewards' accounts. There are also various deeds in a number of archives that relate to her estates and the copies of eight letters made for her, which were transcribed by Edith Rickert in 1927.[3] Although Dame Alice's will is lost, the trust deed setting up her chantry has survived.

ALICE DE BRYENE'S WORLD

Political and Economic Background

Alice de Bryene's grandfather died in 1360 and her father the following year. It is possible that both were victims of the second epidemic of the Black Death, which first ravaged the country in 1348–9. The plague is generally believed to have reduced the population in England by about one third to a half. The immediate effect, apart from the visual image of deserted villages and empty fields, was a shortage of agricultural labour which helped to accelerate the demise of the manorial system. Though there still remained at the turn of the century some bonded tenants who provided labour services in return for their accommodation and smallholdings, the majority were waged workers who paid rent for their land. This was to have a profound effect on both the social structure and farming practices, as well as providing further impetus to the growth of a monetary system.

The hierarchical framework was also altered by the gradual decline of the chivalric ideal. Military service, which had once been the linchpin of feudalism and hence of the nobility and monarchy, was increasingly contracted out to mercenaries: the last feudal host was summoned in 1386. Military prowess may no longer have inspired as much glamour and prestige: many men no longer bothered to answer the call to knighthood and the days of chivalry, troubadours and tournaments were drawing to a close. The peerage was becoming a hereditary rather than an elected class, as is demonstrated by the claims of the four litigants to the Bryan estate *and* barony on the death of Alice's great-granddaughter in 1457. But even if the heroic image of the knight and the romantic ideal of the lady were beginning to fade, chivalric principles found expression in the concept of gentility.[4] Alice de Bryene's 'gentility' lay in her status as 'lord' of the manor and in her 'service' to her dependants.

The rise of lay literacy resulted in an increase in the appointment of lay ministers and officials. Though ecclesiastics still held positions in government, their high profile in the civil service was diminishing. Powerful on the chessboard, a popular medieval pastime, knights and bishops were no longer such important props of the monarchy. Laymen with legal training increasingly held high positions, and the assembly of the House of Commons was becoming a force to be reckoned with. There was an increasing interest in local government, and Members of Parliament forged strong links between the capital and the provinces, between the king's Court and household and his subjects in the localities.

When Alice was born, Edward III's reign had reached its zenith. In 1360 he had ruled for over thirty years, having wrested power from his mother and her lover who had deposed and disposed of his father Edward II. Mindful always of his peers on whose support his authority rested, he successfully pursued the war with France, which brought prosperity, glamour and occupation to the English nobles and their followers. But fortunes change: in 1370 Edward III was in his dotage and the enemy in the ascendancy. His son and heir, the Black Prince, died a year before him in 1376, leaving a ten-year-old boy, Richard, to succeed to the throne. No regents were appointed and Richard's council governed rather ineffectually, divided by jealousy and competition and driven by the dual desire to continue the now unprofitable war with France and to curb the influence of John of Gaunt, Duke of Lancaster and uncle to the boy king. This factionalism flared up once again in the following century, occasioning that spasmodic and bloody conflict known as the Wars of the Roses.

Richard II was not made of the same metal as his grandfather. Like his great-grandfather, Edward II, he relied on a handful of close friends and attempted to exercise personal authority without the support of his peers. Finally in 1399 after an ill-conceived bid for autocracy, he too was deposed and murdered. Henry IV's early years were understandably troubled after this *coup d'état*, his position challenged by aggrieved supporters of the dead king. By 1408 the most serious rebellions had been crushed, but he had few years left to enjoy his throne before his premature death in 1413. During his son's reign there was a brief revival in the fortunes of the war with France, notably at Agincourt, but it was an impossible heritage that Henry V left in 1422 to his heir, a nine-month-old boy. Regents were appointed in both England and France, and the Crown was plagued by financial troubles.

These were the kings who reigned while Alice de Bryene was alive. She would have heard the news of Henry VI's coronation in France in 1431, two years after he was finally old enough to be crowned king of England. Also in 1431 Joan of Arc was tried and immolated in France. But Alice did not live long enough to reflect on England's loss in 1450 of all the French territory, with the exception of Calais, that had been held by Edward III since she was a baby. Five kings had ruled in her lifetime: two ascended the throne as minors and one was deposed and murdered. It is difficult to assess the impact these events may have had on individuals, but they must certainly have helped to shape the environment in which they lived; indeed some of Alice's relatives suffered from the vicissitudes of political upheavals and paid with their lives for their miscalculated affinities. Other incidents may have had just as dramatic an effect. The Peasants' Revolt in 1381, sparked off by the third imposition of a poll tax in four years, was especially violent in East Anglia and at Bury St Edmunds, only 20 miles from Alice's estates. The rebellions were swiftly and decisively quelled but may have lingered long in local memory.

Religion

During Alice's lifetime we can observe elements of the transition from the high days of thirteenth-century Catholicism to the Reformation of the sixteenth century. By 1400 the concept of the universe had started to fragment into two separate spheres, the religious and the secular: Church and society were no longer co-terminous. Dissatisfaction with corrupt practices in the Church, accentuated by the Great Schism of 1378 and the ensuing spectacle of two Popes vying with each other, gave voice to men like Langland whose *Vision of Piers Plowman*, written in the mid-1360s, described the metaphorical journey of an individual to reach salvation. Though theologically orthodox, the poem was fiercely anti-clerical, as were the writings of his contemporary John Wyclif. Greater introspection, triggered perhaps by a psychological reaction to the Black Death, found its niche in Lollardy, the only heresy in medieval England for which the death penalty was prescribed. The translation of the Bible into English in the 1380s, inspired by Wyclif, may not have presaged Protestantism but helped to shape a new and less egocentric sense of piety and spirituality in favour of social justice. The bell that pealed at Alice's baptism was the same that tolled at her funeral, but it rang with a different pitch.

Culture and Society

Also significant at this time is what we might term the rise of nationalism, most evident perhaps in the use of English as the lingua franca. Although in 1350 everyone would have spoken some English, Alice's first syllables were quite possibly Norman French, the language of the ruling class. French was the idiom used in written communications, for personal letters and occasionally wills and legal records, though most official documents, whether government directives or bailiffs' reports, were still in Latin. But with the French war, the growth of the mercantile class particularly in London and the development of a Court culture, English became the language of the educated, who, if they had not actually read *The Canterbury Tales*, would have heard recitations of them in the vernacular. The use of English even for private conversations among the nobility would have been the norm in Alice's old age, and though it may not have helped to break down social barriers it would have provided people with a form of common identity. It also reflected a move away from the cultural influence of the clerical and noble class.

Otherwise Alice's England was not one of special cultural innovation. The great cathedrals had already been built – this was the era of the parish church, with square tower and wide nave. Decoration consisted of wall paintings, finely carved wooden screens and stained-glass windows. A Court culture flowered briefly in Richard II's time with an emphasis on the exaltation of anything new, a reaction perhaps to the traditionalism of the nobles' households. The young king was apparently fastidious about personal cleanliness; his royal palace at Sheen was equipped with baths and latrines and he is also credited with having invented the handkerchief. Such polite fashions were soon to be adopted by the nobility and new gentry class, and domestic architecture was developing to provide greater privacy in both the bedchamber and at table. Living conditions were still comparatively harsh, but diets began to improve with greater consumption of meat and legumes. The introduction of the iron cooking-pot at about this time is believed to have resulted in a longer life expectancy especially for women, as the trace mineral released in cooking helped counteract the chronic anaemia suffered by many as a consequence of constant childbirth.

But it was in social relations that perhaps there was the greatest transformation in Alice's time. The manorial system had enabled the lord and lady of the manor to dispense patronage for their households and estates were, like the monarchy, little kingdoms. Life was centred around agriculture and the production of food, and in many ways the lord in his manor and his workers and servants in his fields and household were mutually dependent. Though such patronage remained an important feature of local life in the next couple of centuries, the growth of the independent yeoman paying rent for his land, selling his own produce, sending his children to learn a skill or a trade, created a decisive shift in the social structure. When military considerations had been paramount women of the propertied class had had a significant role to play, as wives or widows, in the defence and management of property for their families, in the upkeep of social contacts and dispensation of patronage. That power was gradually whittled away and with it the interdependence of landlord and tenant.

The household based around the monarchy, castle or manor had long been the pivotal centre of the community. Change of emphasis was eventually to result in the emergence of the family as the significant social unit. Such transition was very gradual and it is unlikely that Alice was aware that she was living in a period of change. Few of us in our journey through life are able to travel in complete concert with the times. In any event she had to adapt to her own changing circumstances – childhood, adolescence, marriage, motherhood, widowhood, old age and that ultimate certainty, death. But nor could she live in total isolation from the outside world, any more than we can today. It is in this period of transition and occasional turmoil that we must view her life.

* * *

It is often said that it is not possible to write medieval biography but only the history of social ideas. This is valid even today for we are all to a certain extent creatures of our contemporary culture. However, by focusing on one woman I hope to provide an exemplar from which to trace the pattern of other women's lives; and other women do appear in this book, not only to highlight similarities and differences but also to provide information that is unavailable for Alice. There are just too few surviving records to make an attempt to write a biography.

Another reason for the lack of material is that there are fewer records relating to women than men in the Middle Ages because in most instances married women were barred by law from holding land or office independently and were not entitled to initiate legal proceedings. Often women just do not figure in legal deeds even though they may have been party to them. Alice, as a widow, enjoyed *femme sole* status and since she owned several large estates one might expect her to be more visible. But there is still much missing and so I shall sometimes invite you to speculate with me about Alice de Bryene's private world in the hope that it will provide a looking-glass in which to view the lives of both men and women of her time.

Or to put it another way, since some aspects of Alice's life appear obscure I have occasionally turned to Lewis Carroll's 'Alice' for inspiration, though I do not think in this instance we need look to the realm of dreams for guidance. Carroll has two nice fables to illustrate the dangers that confront the historian. When Alice and her animal companions are soaking wet after swimming in a wonderland pool of tears, the Mouse proposes to tell them a tale to dry them out. He proceeds to deliver a factual account of the history of England from the time of William the Conqueror. But it brings no one any comfort and they are *not* amused. Factual though my study is at times, I hope it will also entertain and not be too dry. Later on, in a looking-glass world, Alice meets Humpty Dumpty, an individual who believes that ordinary words mean whatever he wants them to mean.

Both tales encapsulate the caveat given by E.H. Carr in his discussion on the historian and his facts:[5] the necessity to beware the nineteenth-century propensity to concentrate on facts in the belief that such objectivity would 'show it how it really was', and a later, more pragmatic view, that puts emphasis on subjective interpretation. There is a further peril in the tendency to project contemporary values of institutions like marriage and ideas about individual self-determination on the medieval *mentalité*.

My work has been influenced by the development of women's history and subsequent debates. Eileen Power, writing at the time one might consider the conception of women's history, described a breed of historians who 'foolishly imagined that Kings and Parliament and the jury-system were history'.[6] Yes they were and so also, as we have learned to acknowledge, were women. More specifically it has recently been argued that the traditional view of 'a great divide' between the Middle Ages, the Early Modern period and the present day, particularly in terms of socio-economic change and the position of women, is a fiction.[7] This argument lays stress on the continuing domination of women especially in the field of their productive work (that is economic, not biological or social reproduction) by enduring patriarchal attitudes. Challenging this is the hypothesis that there was a 'golden age' in the later Middle Ages when unique economic circumstances, especially in London, gave women opportunities in the labour market, thereby enabling them to enjoy some autonomy and exert some influence, opportunities that were eroded in the following centuries.[8]

By their very nature these arguments with their concentration on the effect of patriarchal ideals, economic roles and the public sphere, while pertinent, undervalue the contributions made by women in all historical periods in their less visible roles. The distinction drawn between public and private spheres anyhow seems untenable, if what is envisaged is two completely separate worlds, especially when one considers the medieval household as a social institution. The concept that men worked in the fields and women at home provides a framework, but its boundaries are too rigid. We shall find plenty of evidence of women's activities outside the home, and most of the domestic work in a large household was done by men.

Alice de Bryene *had* a public role: a widow and member of a privileged class, she was able to wield considerable influence through her patronage and social networking as *Domina* of the manor. However, as a woman, she may also have brought a different and more feminine type of influence to bear in her 'lordship' of the manor, as manager of her estates and in her social relationships with others, by the formation of strong emotional bonds. Uncovering these aspects of her life may help redress an imbalance where women's contributions are concerned – those activities in the household, at the dinner table, in relationships and in the realm of individual piety, activities that should be judged of value in their own right. This study does not deal with arguments about misogyny, nor does it focus on whether a woman's work was as highly esteemed as that of a man. It does however endeavour to illustrate that women had significant roles to play in the later Middle Ages, and undertook them with confidence and respect.

Women's history has contributed much to our wider understanding of the underlying tensions in the past and has shed light on important factors previously ignored, such as gender, sexuality, demography, the family and society. It is, however, an academic discipline and consequently is circumscribed by a style sometimes called the male discourse, which, if not exactly patriarchal, seems occasionally to contain elements of medieval scholasticism. As much as possible I have tried to avoid this type of focus, which seeks to count exactly how many angels could dance on the head of a pin. While it might be of interest to define the quantity of salt used to preserve red herrings and whether they should therefore be considered fresh or pickled, it does not really give us the flavour of life in a medieval household. Though I have been rigorous in my research, I have also occasionally felt the need to tell a story – it seems to me that this is partly what women's history is about.

I recall with some sadness my first history degree when much of my enthusiasm and curiosity dwindled under a plain diet of facts and figures. Like Lewis Carroll's 'Alice' I wanted to read books that also had pictures, conversation, images and people to whom I could relate. It took twenty-five years and another history degree before I recovered my appetite. Now more than ever it seems important that we connect to our past, to ordinary people and ordinary lives, for this is a significant part of our heritage. As you join me at Alice's table in her manor at Acton, I trust you will find something there to please your palate.

CHAPTER 1
The Medieval Household

Imagine it is mid-morning on Friday 7 October 1412. Make your way to the small village of Acton a few miles north of Sudbury in Suffolk. Coming from the south the first visible landmark you will see on the horizon is the bell tower of the church. A few minutes from there across the fields is Acton Hall. Quite probably you will be met near some sort of gate-house or bridge, for the house is protected by a moat. Once across you will find a large manor house with a tiled roof, numerous chambers, a chapel, great hall, kitchen wing, wash-house, brewhouse and bakehouse. Close by, near the kitchen, is a windmill and a small stream flowing through the gardens where there is a well. There are swans and heron on the moat, pigeons flying around the dovecot and geese, poultry and partridges in the yard. Various farm buildings, barns, animal pens and stables are situated close by.[1]

Here in the hall of Alice de Bryene's manor house you may be surprised by the bustle of activity. The tables have already been laid with freshly laundered cloths and silver goblets, salt cellars and spoons will soon be brought in and put at the appropriate places. Guests usually brought their own sheath knives. In the kitchens final preparations are being made for elaborate sauces of herbs, spices and dried fruit that will accompany the fish dishes, but no meat will be served for dinner today since Fridays, like Wednesdays and Saturdays, are fish not flesh days in Alice's household. There is a selection of salt fish and stock fish – that is dried cod – from the household stores, as well as the oysters, smoked herrings, merlings and haddocks that were purchased earlier in the day. Apart from the customary wine and ale to drink there is also the daily bread, some of which was freshly baked that morning, mostly white but a few brown loaves as well.

Outside some boys are holding the horses of those other visitors who arrived just before you, while another boy has gone to fetch sufficient fodder for all ten animals that will be stabled there. Wooden planks provide walkways across those areas of the yard which are muddy. Most of the guests have already assembled in the hall and are awaiting their hostess. While we cannot see exactly how the

Aerial view of Acton Hall today. The curved wall on the left and pond on the right may indicate the course of the original moat.

company is dressed, we do know that Dame Alice is a little over fifty and has been widowed for twenty-six years. Once she has arrived everyone will be invited to take their places at table and offered water in which to wash their hands, before grace is said and dinner may begin.

As many as 44 meals were served at Acton that day: 8 people for breakfast, 23 for dinner – the main meal usually taken before noon, though meal-times tended to fluctuate according to the seasons and demands of husbandry – and 13 for supper. Apart from a few members of her household, Alice de Bryene entertained her half-brother Sir Richard Waldegrave with two of his household and Agnes Rokewode, a close relative, with her son. Also present were the rector of Withersfield, who was a house guest, and four local labourers with their mates, who were variously employed on the farm and in the manor house – carting, looking after the cattle, laying tiles, thatching, mending the great oven and doing carpentry. Finally there were two friars from the nearby town of Sudbury who also brought a household member with them. The friars had been guests the day before and may have spent the night there.[2]

Many of these details come from Alice de Bryene's Household Book, the daily record book kept by her steward. It covers the accounting year from Michaelmas (29 September) 1412 to Michaelmas 1413. During this period Alice served over 16,500 meals at Acton, an average of 45 meals a day, though daily totals could vary greatly. A fragment of another daily account dating from 29 March to 30 April 1412 has also survived. It is very similar in content to the other account and only ten people are named in it who are not mentioned in the later annual one.

Friday 7 October was not an unusual day, for we can read a similar story throughout the year. But we should not presume that Dame Alice was a merry widow with an insatiable appetite for company, indulging in a perpetual round of entertainment. She was simply playing her part, fulfilling the traditional role of 'lord' of the manor. The hospitality of the household, providing meals for neighbours, friends, workers and occasional strangers, was an essential and fundamental part of medieval social behaviour. For kings, bishops, lords and ladies the household was also a political powerbase and hospitality was not merely a domestic affair. It was a means of dispensing patronage and reminding neighbours of the social hierarchy. More than that, one might see confirmation of community bonds in the ritual breaking of bread together. Most importantly perhaps and in a very practical manner, sharing a meal was one of the few ways that people could actually sit down together, gossip, conduct business, exchange views and discuss joint ventures, concerns, obligations and responsibilities. If breakfast meetings and business lunches are anathema to some people today, Alice and her contemporaries would have recognized them as an essential factor of daily life.

Sometimes, as at the New Year's feast, more than 300 people came to dine at Acton; at other times only three were invited to join Alice and those of her household who were present on that particular day. Some of her guests were eminent men whose wives and children visited as well. About three times a week the bailiffs of one of her adjacent manors came to eat, as did the maidservants and various estate workers. In addition there were also about 50 clerical and religious visitors, many of whom came several times during the year, hundreds of workers throughout August to help with the harvest (on one day alone 60 were provided with food), visits from more than a hundred assorted named casual labourers and 120 other unnamed guests.

Each daily entry in the Household Book is prefaced with the number of meals served and the date. This is followed by a list of guests, many of whom are named while others are described by their occupations or from where they came. A pantry account follows with the number of loaves delivered to the table. Note is made that wine and ale were served, though no quantity was specified, indicating that there was a separate *butterlaria* account for these items. Next there are details of meat and fish sent from the kitchens that originated from the manor's storehouse, followed by the daily purchases, when made, that supplemented these provisions. Provender supplied to the horses in the stables and the total sum of purchases complete each entry. Figures are also given of the household brewing and baking, which took place at least once a week. An aggregate total of purchases and food consumed is noted at the end of each month.

Household accounts are a rich source of information from which we can learn much about the social, domestic, religious and economic lives and relationships of the medieval community, information that cannot be easily gleaned from recorded activities in the public world of government, church affairs and warfare. Every lay or ecclesiastical householder of a large establishment kept such accounts. Their primary purpose was to record daily consumption of and expenditure on victuals by the steward or official in charge who had the overall responsibility for the management of the household. Keeping such accounts enabled the householder to detect corruption and mismanagement and budget for the future. They also served as a deterrent against theft and carelessness.[3]

These accounts were essential because such households were like small hotels with numerous staff catering for a wide variety of needs relating not only to the provision and service of meals, which was often an elaborate ritual, but also musicians to provide entertainment and clergy to sing masses and say prayers. There were young men to accompany their masters and mistresses on journeys, run errands and take messages, and scribes and clerks to deal with correspondence and records connected with the management of the estates and other business matters. Men were employed to look after the horses and traction animals, and other servants engaged to help with the daily maintenance of the living quarters, such as cleaning windows and floors and keeping the fires, candles and rushlights lit. A few close companions of the householder might also be resident and occasionally there would be staff to take care of the young and the elderly.

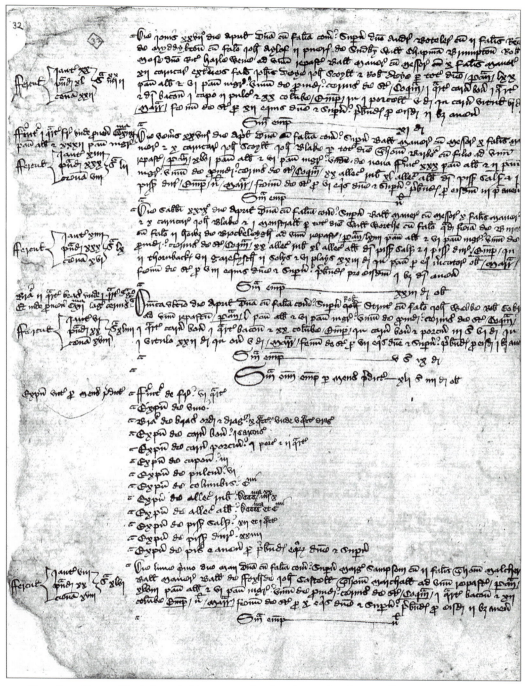

Page from Dame Alice's household accounts showing the total cash expenditure of 41s 4½d for the month of April 1413, followed by a list of victuals used from stock.

Among approximately 500 household accounts that have survived there is great diversity, for in some not only is the purchase of food itemized but details given of clothes, cloth, wax, wine, spices and jewellery bought, though often these were specified separately in a wardrobe account. Then there might be cash, corn and stock accounts, records of alms and gifts given, money spent on correspondence, travelling and supplying liveries. Separate accounts were sometimes drawn up for the expenses of maintaining children. Diet accounts – the word originates from *per dietas*, day rather than food – comprise the largest group, of which those of Elizabeth de Burgh, Lady of Clare, are among the most extensive. These run from 1325 to 1360 and include day journals, chamber, wardrobe, chapel and household accounts, as well as those of her goldsmiths and brewers and her travelling expenses.[4]

The Acton diet accounts are much more modest, reflecting a smaller and less formal household. There are also some extant stewards' reports from which we may estimate the size, composition and consumption of the de Bryene household. With these, the three receivers' reports and the numerous bailiffs' accounts relating to the estates it has been possible to identify many of those who visited Acton in 1412–13. Taken together, this information illustrates the special place households had in the later Middle Ages for they were not only like little kingdoms but simultaneously both private homes and public institutions, the nerve centres from which estates were managed, patronage dispensed and social networks maintained. Above all the household was an essential part of the fabric of society in which the life of the local community was contained.

The structure and functions of such households began to change in the later Middle Ages, reflecting development in agrarian practices. Previously, few large households had a fixed geographical location because it was common for estate owners to move with most of their staff from manor to manor, travelling with beds, silver and even, on occasion, with windows. Overseeing farms, which were often scattered over many parts of the country as a result of the accumulation of property through marriage, and living off the produce of these various manors was a fundamental feature of land ownership. A skeleton staff would be left at the main residence, while the rest of the household was on the move. But the fall in population after the plague epidemics made it difficult for landowners to find cheap or bonded labour to farm all their estates in return for small plots of land, and those estates that could not be managed directly were increasingly rented out for cash. People were becoming more settled and sedentary and for a woman on her own of Alice's age such an itinerant lifestyle may not have been particularly appealing or necessary.

Where a household was headed by a married couple, separate accounts were sometimes kept, which might be described as the inner and outer households. The inner account generally referred to the main residence, which usually meant that it was run by the lady, and the outer or foreign household, a smaller group that would go travelling with the husband. A noblewoman such as Anne Neville, Duchess of Buckingham might have both a great and an itinerant household of her own even when she was married.[5] In the case of a widow in sole control of her estates all these functions could be combined as a self-contained unit based in one place. What is then noticeable is the executive and administrative capacity of such women, their apparent autonomy, initiative and high status in the community and the significant influence they were able to wield as the head of a household.

Medieval household accounts were usually written in Latin. The word used for household was *familia*, from which the word family derives, but originally its root was *famulus/a*, meaning a servant. The hypothesis that there was little affection between parents and children in medieval families has now been challenged, although it is evident that the feelings were not expressed as they are in our contemporary society or acted out in the same way.[6] Similarly we need to be circumspect when we consider the role of the servant in the medieval household, for frequently there were strong emotional bonds between employer and employee. Beyond the affective relationship it is also clear that there was a mutual dependency: in many ways the *famuli* in the *familia* were part of the family and indeed the people in the household were the household.

While the household can be seen as a place, a formal institution, as well as the people connected with it, the word 'homely' was also in current use in the later Middle Ages. The term features in the writings for example of Margery Kempe, whose book about her pilgrimages and spiritual strivings is the earliest known autobiography of an English person. Margery was born in about 1370 in Norfolk and was therefore a contemporary of Dame Alice. For Margery 'homely' was a quality of a wife's relationship to her husband, as well as an individual's to God and permeates the account of her spiritual experiences.[7] Although there is little evidence to demonstrate how or where in the household such 'homeliness' might have been experienced, with its connotations of intimacy, comfort and informality as well as a sense of refuge and belonging, the ideal certainly existed. As landowners became less peripatetic they began to make those establishments that were their main residences more comfortable, and a small sedentary household like Alice de Bryene's may in fact have felt like a home.

Care for the well-being of servants and household members is often evident in provisions made for them in wills. When Alice's husband dictated his will in 1384, he expressed concern for his servants but, pleading poverty, stated '*ieo ne ay de quoy faire*' (loosely translated as 'I don't know what to do') and prayed that God would help and comfort them.[8] In fact, as in this case, it was often left to the surviving spouse to ensure that retainers and household members were well provided for. Where testators had more time to consider their responsibilities, gifts to servants were a common feature. Thus Alice's daughter Elizabeth Lovell remembered her household members, bequeathing money and chattels to her female retainers and generous sums to her other servants, such as 40*s* for John of the Chambre and a rather more modest 13*s* 4*d* for the kitchen John.[9]

The obligation of the householder to her *familia* was well recognized. Walter Hilton in his *Epistle of the Mixed Life*, a late fourteenth-century treatise written to assist members of the laity, who possessed both time and status, to achieve spiritual fulfilment, emphasized that combining the lives of Mary and Martha was an essential element of 'lordship':

> You should mix the works of the active life with spiritual works of the contemplative life and then you do well. For you shall sometimes be busy with Martha, to regulate and govern the household, your children, your servants, your neighbours and your tenants: if they do well, encourage them and help them; if they do badly, teach them to better themselves and chastise them. And you should also check and wisely ensure that your possessions and worldly goods are rightly cared for by your servants, organised and properly spent, so that you can use them more plentuously to perform the acts of mercy to your fellow Christians. At other times you shall, with Mary, leave the bustle of the world and sit down at the feet of Our Lord in humility in prayers and holy thoughts and in contemplation of Him, as he gives you grace. And so you shall profitably go from one to the other, deserving reward and fulfil both, and then you keep the order of charity well.[10]

The works of Martha were manifold. A description of Dame Alice's household and retinue gives us some idea of the different duties undertaken by household staff. As we have seen, the steward was responsible for the overall stock and at Acton, apart from the daily record, he accounted annually for all sales and purchases relating to consumption in the household, not only of food but of salt, spices, wax and wine, cleaning materials, rabbit skins, animal hides, empty vessels, kitchen and bakehouse utensils and miscellaneous payments made to workmen for general house repairs. He also accounted for money received periodically from the lady, although he noted that she actually paid various items herself including the wages of the household servants.

Just as Dame Alice personally paid the wages of the household staff, so too she paid for the household livery and many other household items. Her bailiffs frequently noted that the estate workers' clothes' allowances were a charge on the lady's wardrobe account. Women like Alice were not just nominal heads of households but actively engaged in matters where they could exercise their influence. We may imagine that it was she was summoned her *familia* once or twice a year when their livery cloth arrived and wages were due, to reinforce personal contact by having a private word with each, to congratulate, chivvy or maybe merely chat. These were after all her intimates in the sense that she saw them every day, people on whom she depended but for whom she was also responsible. We cannot conceive the degree of her intimacy with them, but the close physical proximity of their lives within a social hierarchy that created a distance must have called for skilful management.

The appointment of a steward was of crucial importance since he effectively had the responsibility for most of the financial arrangements pertaining to the household. In most medieval households stewards were clergymen or chaplains who would have had the necessary education and been considered trustworthy persons for the job. One such at Acton was *Sir* John Brook who had been a family retainer of long standing, having been a witness to various deeds when Alice was married and lived in the West Country, custodian of her grandmother's household in Suffolk, then steward of both Alice's London house and Acton manor and finally receiver for all her East Anglian estates.[11] In 1417 a layman, William Burgh, was given the post but eight years later she appointed another clergyman, *Sir* John Chetylbere, as her steward. By 1428 Chetylbere had ceded the position to a layman called Richard Andrew but it appears he remained in Alice's household as one of her chaplains. Both these men acted as trustees of the chantry foundation she set up before she died, an appropriate choice since while the steward was responsible for the management of the household during the lifetime of his employer, executors were expected to concern themselves with spiritual and material matters after their employers' deaths.

The election of household stewards to oversee wills or trust deeds was common practice among women: Eleanor, Duchess of Gloucester appointed her household steward as one of the executors of her will in 1399.[12] Margery Kempe was not prepared to take any chances when looking for a suitable person for the post. Dictating the story of her religious quest on pilgrimage abroad in Europe, the Holy Land, England and at her home in King's Lynn, Norfolk, she describes how she appointed God as steward of her household and executor of all her good works, an undertaking which she characteristically recorded, with her usual cheerful confidence and disarming lack of humility, God acknowledged he would fulfil as if for his own mother and wife.[13]

Not everyone approved of the appointment of ecclesiastics to lay positions, whether as steward or bailiff. John Gower writing between 1376 and 1379 thought that such men were 'fish out of water':

That monk is not a good cloisterer / who is made keeper or seneschal
Of some office which is outside; / for he must have horse and saddle
To run about the lands / and he spends with generous hands;
He keeps for himself the best of the grain, / and like a wretch leaves to others
The straw, and so like a lord / that monk becomes silly and vain.
With an empty grange and a full stomach / no account will be kept well balanced.
Of charity that is incomplete, / 'All is ours', says this monk,
When he is keeper of the manor. / This is part of the truth but not all;
For he with his mad appetite / would have more than seven others.
Such a keeper to speak the truth / the cloister had better drive out than keep,
Since he takes from others their profit. / St Bernard it is who tells us
It is an evil thing to see / a monk in a bailiff's habit.[14]

Apart from being honest, household stewards had to be good administrators. Providing the 16,500 meals that were served at Acton in 1412–13 must have required considerable organization, and so it is hardly surprising that the steward's records manifest all the niceties of a quarter-master's regime on military campaign. Figures for the annual purchase and consumption of victuals were remarkably constant as a visit to the Acton spice cupboard would show. In two annual accounts exactly the same quantity of almonds, raisins, rice, saffron, ginger, cinnamon, cloves and mace were bought, with little variation for figs, currants, dates, sugar, pepper, mustard seed, soda-ash and honey. Though it has been argued that there were many fictitious elements in medieval accounts, reflecting 'a bureaucratic instinct to make information conform to the Procrustean bed of accounting system',[15] Dame Alice's accounts do demonstrate methodical and careful supervision. Ultimately, however, the accounts were the responsibility of the householder who may even have checked the steward's accounts every night.[16]

The household chamberlain was occupied with the more personal side of domestic management and the safe-keeping of capital assets. Though the great hall was generally used for entertaining, lords, ladies and their guests did retire to their private chambers for more intimate conversation. Here was the fine bed with tapestries and intricately embroidered testers, silken cushions and furred coverlets. At the bottom of the bed stood the chest containing the family deeds and household money, which ultimately was in the chamberlain's safe-keeping. He also had the responsibility of seeing that the chamber was warm and comfortable and of looking after his employer's clothes. Mention is often made in women's wills of their gowns, which they frequently bequeathed to friends. These could be valuable items made of brocades and silks, trimmed with fur or even decorated with gems, and considered as capital assets. They were usually kept in the garderobe, a small room off the bedchamber where there was often a privy or basic toilet facilities. The air would have been sweetened with herbs and spices, which also acted as a deterrent against moths. There is no reason then why the chamberlain should not have been charged with the custody of these gowns as well, even if the lady's maid helped dress her mistress.

Once again there is evidence that Alice conformed to the accepted canons of medieval patronage by appointing one of her late husband's retainers as her chamberlain in Suffolk. In a practical way she was also rectifying the omission in his will to provide for his servants. This chamberlain was Robert Dynham who had been retained by her husband in the West Country and may even have been distantly related to him.[17] Other members of the family served her in different capacities: one of her chaplains was *Sir* Richard Dynham, and another Robert, probably the son of her chamberlain, was one of her valets or grooms.

Alice de Bryene frequently had dairy produce sent up to her chamber, indicating that she entertained her favoured friends there with special delicacies. Apart from these occasions, we can presume from the evidence of the Household Book that guests and the household generally enjoyed communal living and ate together in the hall, a tradition that was beginning to disappear in the late fourteenth century with the diminishing social importance of a large household. William Langland writing in the 1370s noted that customs were changing, a matter he considered distressing:

Banqueting hall in Penshurst Castle where Dame Alice visited her daughter in the 1390s. This view is from the dais end of the hall.

Elenge in the halle, ech day in the wike,
Ther the lord ne the lady liketh noght to sitte,
Now hathe ech riche a rule to eten by hymselve
In a pryvee parlour for povere mennes sake,
Or in a chambre with a chymnenee, and leve the chief halle
That was maad for meles, men to eten inne,
And al to spare to spille that spende shal another.[18]

When entertaining in the great hall, it was traditional for the hostess to sit at the centre of a table on a platform or dais with her social peers. Chairs or benches were placed along one side only. Dame Alice had one item of furniture called a *cathedra*, which more closely relates to a throne or at least to something of pomp and circumstance and which needed to be repaired by her smith.[19] Boards would have been set up on trestles at right angles to the high table and benches provided for the rest of the company lower down. Some guests may even have had to eat standing up.[20] Though some illuminated manuscripts depict dinner scenes with a high table on a raised platform, physical distance from the host was also an indication of 'lower' status. When Margery Kempe went on her first pilgrimage and irritated her companions by her refusal to eat meat and constant monologues at the dinner table about the love of God, they made her sit at the end of the table 'below all the others' and so she dared speak scarcely a word.[21]

While seating plans spatially emphasized the hierarchical order, manners dictated that the lower orders were acknowledged and included. In the mid-thirteenth century Bishop Grosseteste had advised his patron, the Countess of Lincoln, to sit in the middle of the high table for meals 'that your presence . . . is made manifest to all'. Although he exhorted her to forbid loud noises during dinner and to watch the service carefully for faults, he recommended she give rewards for good manners and polite behaviour, adding, 'order that your dish be so refilled and heaped up especially with light courses, that you may courteously give from your dish to right and left to all at the high table and to whom else it pleases you that they may have the same as you had in front of you'.[22]

Apart from a steward, chamberlain, chaplains and singing clerks, medieval households were staffed with squires, valets and boys: in 1421 Elizabeth Berkeley, Countess of Warwick, employed 9 gentlemen, 2 of whom were squires, 5 valets, 15 grooms or menial servants and numerous boys.[23] No 'gentlemen' are mentioned among the twenty-odd members of the Acton household, but there were squires, valets and boys. The squires were most likely men from the ranks of the gentry or lesser nobility, sons, relatives or friends of Alice's social peers, who formed part of her inner circle of companions or upstairs staff. They may have been long-term retainers or have come for a period of time to learn the manners and etiquette of the household. They would also have accompanied her when she went travelling or visiting and assisted her, together with the chaplains, in entertaining her guests.

The valets, who are sometimes called grooms in medieval accounts, were part of the downstairs staff. Some may also have been well born or at least men with a firm foot on the bottom rung of the social ladder. Their job was to ensure the smooth running of the household in a variety of ways. In the Household Book mention is made of a 'groom of the kitchen' who took two horses to Colchester every Sunday during Lent to purchase fresh fish. Besides marketing, these valets or grooms were involved with the preparation and service of food, and acted as the household butler, ewer (he who handed round the basin for guests to wash their hands), usher, and the server who was expected to know the ritual of carving as well as serving the meat.

In two of the Acton stewards' accounts money was spent on several yards of linen cloth bought for *naperounes* for various household members. But although they donned their aprons and carried their napkins, prepared and presented fancy pastries and confections and generally waited at table, a prestigious service in which high standards were expected, this was not their only task. For while the larger households of the aristocracy and lesser nobility were very complex and often divided into separate departments, in a smaller one like Alice de Bryene's a diversity of roles and greater flexibility would have been essential. Richard Mody, Alice's butler, was also employed to snare rabbits for the table and bred his own cattle and sheep. Another member of the household John Whyte, one of those who was awarded linen cloth in his capacity as pastry cook, bred stock as well and travelled to Stourbridge Fair with the steward to provision for the household.

The boys were the most junior and servile members of the household and employed to do a variety of jobs. At Acton it was probably these young men whose occasional labour, called a 'loving day' in the bailiffs' reports, was estimated to have been worth a shilling each. They were also paid extra to enquire or search for fish or find a stray animal. During the busy periods such as the harvest season many of the household were expected to work on the farm. But although they sometimes assisted with the harvest and laboured in the fields their privileged position as 'inhewys' staff, as they are described in one account, was acknowledged by the bailiff who, when accounting for gloves bought for the reapers, differentiated between those supplied to the servants of the manor and those for the household.

A glance at the Acton guest list for 7 October shows us that of the twenty-three guests only one was a woman. This was not unusual, with in fact less than 10 per cent of the total number of guests at Acton in 1412–13 being female, a phenomenon we shall consider more closely in Chapter 6. This imbalance is mirrored by the composition of medieval households, which were mostly male: the household of Elizabeth Berkeley consisted of about fifty members, only nine of whom were women.[24] In Alice de Bryene's household in the 1420s there were twenty-three men and just two women. While there would have been at least one maidservant in all gentry households who may have undertaken some domestic chores as well as attending to her mistress, the general household work with the exception of the laundry was usually done by men.

It seems unlikely that all these household members slept at the Acton manor house, and this must be true of other households. Some, like Robert Dynham, enjoyed rent-free accommodation on the estate in a partial return for their services and if those working in the kitchens or serving food did not always join the company for dinner, they would have helped themselves to something for breakfast and supper from the pantry as was customary. Numbers given in the Household Book for breakfast are consistently low, just three on special fast days when only the young, infirm or elderly would have been given a dispensation to eat, otherwise breakfast was usually provided for eight people. Breakfast was usually a light meal, just bread and ale or maybe some watered wine.[25] More were invited for supper but again the provision of this meal varied considerably depending on whether workmen had been engaged for the whole day or visitors invited to stay the night.

Beds were luxury items in the Middle Ages. Along with gowns and silver, they ranked high on the list of bequests in wills to favoured friends, relatives and servants. Lady Alice West, a contemporary of Dame Alice, left eight beds in 1395, three to her children and the rest to her servants. Her description of one, immediately after the preamble of her will bequeathing her soul to God and her body to be buried at a specific church, gives us an idea of how magnificent such beds could be: 'Also I deuyse to Thomas my sone, a bed of tapicers werk, with alle the tapites of sute, red of colour, ypouthered with chapes and scochons, in the corners, of myn Auncestres armes . . . the stoffe longyng therto, that is to seye, my beste fetherbed, and a blu caneuas, and a materas, and twey blankettys, and a peyre of schetes of Reynes, with the heued shete of the same, and sex of my best pilwes, . . . and a bleu couertour of menyuer [miniver], and a keuerlet of red sendel ypouthered with Cheuerons'.[26] Not all testators were so exuberant in the description of their material possessions: Alice's daughter Elizabeth left a red bed to her 'cousin' and servant Elena Borley. This bed was literally *unum lectum rubeum* with no frills attached, though no doubt it came with hangings, pillows, covers, sheets, featherbed and mattress and all the other necessary paraphernalia.

When travelling it was common for people to take quilts and bedding with them. Household members accompanying their lords and ladies would have bedded down at night on straw pallets by the fire in the great hall or in a servants hall if there was one. Guests of higher rank would have been offered a bed even if it meant doubling up. While no mention is made of beds at Acton, guests frequently stayed the night: on 23 May, for example, Sir Richard and Lady Joan Waldegrave arrived for a two-day visit with their son, a maidservant, squire and six household members. There appears to have been adequate private accommodation at the manor: John Reymes, one of Alice's chaplains, even had his own apparently well-appointed chamber and 12½d was once spent on repairing his window. Apart from sleeping accommodation, the Acton manor house was equipped with other essential amenities: repairs to a *seuera* (sewer) and work required for a *cloaca* (privy) suggest there was a rudimentary form of cesspool or drainage.

On the whole it appears that the Acton household was still geared to communal living even if customs were changing and Alice occasionally withdrew to her chamber. The existence of a chapel and presence of several chaplains and singing clerks in the household indicate that as well as a grace before meals there may have been daily prayers and mass on Sundays and important feast days, which all the household would have been expected to attend. Attending religious services and eating together helped bind the household in the sense of sharing a common identity. Simultaneously it also reminded members of the household of the hierarchical order, a necessity for people living in close proximity, even though medieval concepts of privacy must have been very different to ours. Essentially life in such a household was largely public.

Beyond the immediate staff living or working in a manor house, there were others connected with the household who strictly speaking were not *familia* but members of the householder's *consilio*, or council. Some of these may have been regular suppliers of luxury items like wine; others were local dignitaries and landholders of prominence occasionally employed for specific tasks, such as auditors, advisers, legal experts and trustees. Finally there were those involved with the day-to-day grass-roots organization of the farms: bailiffs, rent-collectors and the permanent agricultural workers – reapers, grangers, carters, smiths, ploughmen, shepherds, herdsmen and the manor maidservants. Employing and negotiating with such a large team suggests that any head of a household needed considerable managerial and supervisory skills.

While the records enable us to see Dame Alice and other widows in this role, women generally were engaged in a similar business. The legal position of married women, whereby all property was usually considered to belong to their

Labourers at harvest time.

husbands, conceals the reality of a woman's *de facto* executive role. Men heading such households usually had different affairs to occupy them – warfare, politics, the acquisition and protection of other property – but relied on their partners for support in the administration of their joint concerns. Since wealth lay mainly in landed property (the basis of the wider dynastic plan), maintaining it would have been a matter of mutual interest. Nor were married women without authority and financial independence.

An incomplete copy of a letter written to Alice de Bryene while she was still married is illuminating. It was addressed to Alice by a man called William Maldone, who had negotiated some business on behalf of her and her husband with John Waltham, a London tailor. Maldone advised Alice to contact Waltham in order to complete the matter to their mutual satisfaction. Arguably there is nothing unusual about this, wives doing business for their husbands and paying the bills, but it does demonstrate that despite a posse of male officials in the household, married women were approached and expected to deal with financial matters for their spouses.[27]

Another fragmentary letter from Alice's Letter-book, the purpose of which is discussed in Chapter 7, relates more specifically to the household. Internal evidence suggests it was written to Alice early in her widowhood by Richard Micheldever, receiver for her West Country estates. After effusive formal salutations, references to other letters he had written to her and apologies if he appeared unkind or disloyal in any way, the writer continues that he has discussed the matter about which she had consulted him with one of her household who would inform her more fully in person. Then he reflects on the supervision of her household, recommending that she govern it in accordance with her estate and, having decided what to do, to be consistent.[28] Rather vague advice perhaps, but evidence that running a household was like any business enterprise, details were discussed and advice sought and given.

The governance of the household was more generally addressed by Christine de Pisan, a contemporary of Alice de Bryene with some similar life experiences. She was born in Venice in 1365, moved to Paris where her father was retained by King Charles V, married at fifteen and had three children. Widowed ten years later, she started to write love ballads to support her mother and children and was soon enjoying international fame. She is often considered one of the first feminists: in 1399 she wrote *Letter to the God of Love*, which attacked the misogyny embodied in the allegory *The Romance of the Rose*. In two of her subsequent books, *The Book of the City of Ladies* and *The Treasure of the City of Ladies* she reinforced her argument that women were as capable and moral as, if not indeed superior to, men.[29]

The Treasure of the City of Ladies, written in 1405, can be considered a practical handbook advising princesses, courtiers, noblewomen, widows, wives and women in general how to conduct themselves and run their households. Didactic in nature and hardly innovative, it does however presume that women of all social classes would be knowledgeable about the various aspects of household and manorial administration, relating not only to husbandry but also fiscal and legal matters, accounting systems and labour relations. It was expected that such women would concern themselves with the overall supervision of households, estates and officials, even if they delegated the day-to-day management.

Alice could not have read Christine's book, which was not in circulation in England during her lifetime. Nor should we presume that all women had the requisite skills and inclinations to put her recommendations into practice, but if we take the text as an ideal it may suggest what some women did some of the time in some households. Also, both Christine and Alice were widows and may therefore have had more time for their chosen lifestyles. There is a deeper connection as well: in 1397 Christine's son Jean joined the household of John

Christine de Pisan presenting her book to Queen Isabel of France, Paris, early fifteenth century.

Montagu, Earl of Salisbury, who was Alice's cousin-in-law;[30] it is interesting therefore to speculate whether she and Christine might have corresponded or at least been aware of each other's existence.

Further advice on household management, particularly on domestic issues and relating more particularly to an urban situation, also came from France: the Goodman of Paris' compendium written at the end of the fourteenth century offered guidance to his new wife, some forty years his junior, on numerous matters ranging from morals to mosquitoes, gardening, cleaning, mending, shopping, viniculture, horse charms, cures for toothache, the engagement of servants and a special recipe for poisoning bears. His attitude towards women was ambivalent and he expected a wife to obey her husband as a dog would his master. She should put his comfort first so that when he came in from the rain he would be upheld in the hope of 'having his shoes removed before a good fire, his feet washed, and to have fresh shoes and stockings, to be given food and drink, to be well served and looked after, well bedded in white sheets and night–caps, well covered and assuaged with other joys and amusements, privities, loves and secrets'. A rainy day was obviously a godsend to the medieval husband. Though undoubtedly chauvinistic, the Goodman acknowledged that the burdensome task of running a household usually fell on women: 'some respit to husbands the weather may send, but huswives affaires have never an end'.[31] What is also apparent from his wide range of knowledge is that some men were just as *au fait* with basic housekeeping as women.

The household not only had a social impact on the community as a large organization where people might seek employment, cement friendships and maintain contacts, but also constituted a significant economic factor in the locality. It was the place where long–term or casual employment could be found and a market for buying and selling produce. Analysis of consumption and marketing in the late Middle Ages demonstrates that householders purchased different goods in different areas and just as consumers ranged in the social order, so commercial centres also formed a hierarchy.[32] The Acton household was basically static and provides a good example of how the local community might benefit when there was a large household in the area.

Much of the grain and meat needed for the Acton table was obtained from the demesne lands but the rest was bought by private treaty from employees and farmers such as John Ayloff of Sudbury who frequently sold Alice cattle. Tenant farmers sold her mutton and pork and delicacies like boar were acquired from neighbouring villages. Extra wheat also came from local suppliers, such as the rector of Stanstead, a visitor to Acton in 1412–13. Fresh fish was usually bought nearby in Colchester, and on every Saturday throughout the year a merchant called who may have been delivering fish for the midday meal along with other fresh produce for Sunday. Such a standing order must have made for greater convenience especially during the festive season when more provisions were needed: on 31 December 1412 the merchant brought an extra horse with him to Acton to carry the increased load. Preserved fish was purchased from a variety of sources, locally at Ipswich, Lavenham and Great Bricett and further afield from Stourbridge, near Cambridge. On occasion more expensive fish like salted salmon was obtained from London, though this was generally when other luxury items were needed, like dates and figs, which may not have been available nearby at that time.

Stourbridge was an important market that was held for three weeks in September and well patronized by Dame Alice. Both she and her steward provisioned there, buying a variety of goods like spice, rice, wax, coarse cloth for general kitchen and domestic use and pots and pans. Transport was expensive and her receiver John Pellican once charged 10*s* for this four-day trip. Occasionally wine was purchased there too, though more often it was acquired from Ipswich or London. Livery cloth and material for the lady's gowns seem always to have been purchased in London. Since she owned a town house there she would have been able to buy in bulk and store any surplus until it was needed in Suffolk, thereby reducing transport costs for large items. Other necessities for household use like building materials were obtained locally. Generally, apart from luxury goods, most of the produce needed for the household was purchased from neighbouring villages or towns, adding impetus to the economic life of the community.

The patterns of marketing and consumption in the households of the aristocracy, lesser nobility and gentry differed in the degree of the size of their expendable income. For those estate owners who still moved their households several times a year to different parts of the country where they had property, marketing was much more widespread. As noted earlier, the organization of the various domestic, managerial and accounting departments was more formal and specialized in these larger households, especially when several members of the family were resident. However, essentially the medieval household was a social institution with customs and traditions to maintain. Resources, marital status and idiosyncratic impulse also dictated the quality of the lifestyle, as we shall discover when we spend more time with Dame Alice.

CHAPTER 2
Marriage and the Family

A baby born in the mid-fourteenth century faced an uncertain future. Infant mortality was high, mothers often died in childbirth and the continuing wars with France left many children without a father. The two most serious outbreaks of the Black Death in 1348 and 1361 decimated numerous families, the latter epidemic being particularly fatal for young children. In some ways the infant Alice was fortunate: though her grandfather Sir Andrew de Bures died in April 1360 followed by the death of her father Sir Robert aged only twenty-seven eighteen months later, both her mother and grandmother survived and on their deaths she stood to inherit substantial landed property.

Focusing on the specific details of Alice's immediate family will help us unravel the complex threads of medieval family life in general – the diverse strands that entwined relatives who married and remarried, the knotty problems of property disputes and the numerous tensions and rivalries that ensued. Beyond these factors we will also find evidence of loyalties arising from shared interests, together with instances of deep attachments that were woven into the fabric of many relationships. Since so much of an individual's life was contained within the wider community, the political canvas cannot be ignored as many noble and gentry families suffered or profited from their allegiance to a particular faction: public life impinged upon private life and few well-born medieval women would have been spared the experience of a personal tragedy of either the death of a relative or a reversal in the family fortunes due to miscalculated loyalties.

THE BURES

The Bures took their name from the small Suffolk village 9 miles north of Colchester and 7 miles south of Acton. In the late thirteenth century Alice's great-grandfather Sir Robert de Bures appears to have been the first of the family to amass a fortune, from the rewards of military service in Scotland and Wales. He was also one of Edward I's yeomen attached permanently to the Royal Household's small standing army, a bailiff of Queen Eleanor and custodian of her castle at Haverford West. In 1300 he made a good marriage to a wealthy widow, as did many of his contemporaries, thereby consolidating his fortune. One of Hilary de Hodebovile's assets was the Acton manor later to become Dame Alice's permanent home. When he died in 1331 Sir Robert owned land in fifteen East Anglian villages, most of which was to become his great-granddaughter's patrimony.[1]

His son and grandson pursued similar careers profiting from service to the king and by their marriages to wealthy women. On their deaths the Bures' estates were temporarily divided between their widows, ultimately to be inherited by Alice.[2] Alice's mother Joan did not remain a widow for long. She was a local girl, the daughter of Sir Richard de Sutton of Navestock in Essex. In 1363 she married Sir Richard Waldegrave, bringing with her the income from her life interest in various Bures' manors. It was not as hasty a remarriage as those of some of her contemporaries and an understandable course of action for a young widow whose only child was an heiress. Though he had property in Lincolnshire and Northamptonshire, Sir Richard set up his residence with Joan in the manor he

Brass of Sir Robert de Bures, 1331, at All Saints, Acton, Suffolk.

acquired at Smallbridge in Bures St Mary, just a few miles from Acton. Within a short while they had children of their own, half-brothers for Alice: Richard, who remained a constant companion, and William.

Alice's paternal grandmother Alice de Bures was also born locally. She was the daughter of Sir John de Raydon of Overbury Hall in Layham, Suffolk. In about 1363 she too remarried. She did not have to look far, for her new husband was Sir John de Sutton, recently widowed and uncle of her daughter-in-law Joan. His sister-in-law by his previous marriage was married to Michael de Bures, a cousin of his new wife's first husband.[3] This network of relationships *is* complicated but the simplified family tree should make it clearer. Alice de Sutton retained a life interest in the residue of the Bures' estate as well as the income from her dowry, the manors of Raydon and Wherstead, though she and her new husband lived at Wivenhoe in Essex.[4]

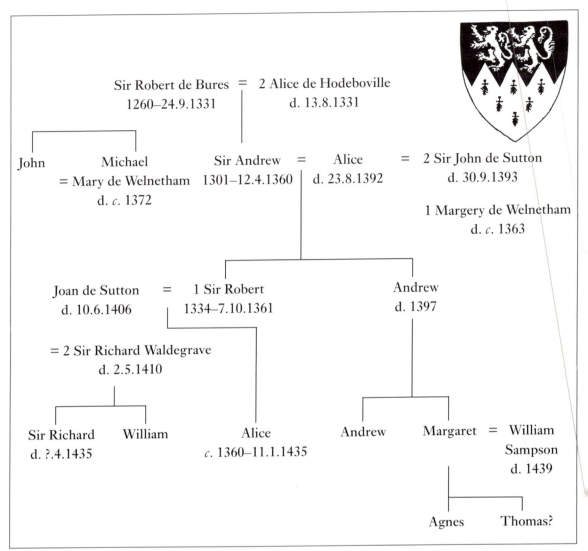

The Bures family tree and coat of arms.

CHILDHOOD

Although Alice probably spent her early childhood in her family's various East Anglian manors with her mother, grandmother, stepfather, stepgrandfather and half-siblings, it was customary for children of her class, particularly boys, to be sent away as young as seven to live in another household to learn basic household manners and management and make useful social connections. Girls were more likely to be kept at home until they were twelve years old and deemed to be adults.[5] However, the wardship of heirs and heiresses was often purchased by parents wishing to secure a wealthy spouse for one of their children, and the young ward might then join the household of her future in-laws until the wedding was celebrated. This seems to have been the case with Alice's own daughters, but then she was a widow and her two girls stood to inherit both the Bryan and the Bures' estates.

At a time when life expectancy was short and many people died before they reached thirty, it is hardly surprising that adolescent children were treated as adults. Yet the needs of an infant were recognized and only on rare occasions were wealthy heiresses likely to be sent away from home before they were seven. Alice's younger daughter Elizabeth was about six when her wardship was bought. In that same year Sir Richard Waldegrave was bound to the king for 1,000 marks to keep her 'a pure virgin, find her meat and raiment such as her estate requires and at the end of the year . . . deliver her, if required, sole and unmarried to John Lovell to whom the king has granted her marriage'.[6] While there is no evidence that Alice actually claimed the right of *nutriciam* (literally to nurture), which represented the *de facto* custody of an infant child,[7] it seems most likely that this was what she got, and that she was at least able to keep one of her little daughters with her while Waldegrave stood guarantee as her official guardian.

It does not appear however that Alice herself was made a ward. In any event her mother's remarriage would have guaranteed that she had the necessary protection and connections to make a good match. Her stepfather, Sir Richard Waldegrave, had had a distinguished military career on crusade as well as in the French wars, was an experienced courtier and had a high political profile. In his youth he had joined the household of William de Bohun, Earl of Northampton and was later retained by his son Humphrey, Earl of Hereford, Essex and Northumberland. On the earl's death in 1373 Sir Richard continued to serve his widow Joan Bohun, Countess of Hereford and remained in the Bohun affinity all his life.[8] If he was looking for education, patronage and a good marriage for his stepdaughter, then the Bohun household would have been an obvious choice. Alice was certainly acquainted with Joan Bohun, as we shall discover later. Marriage was socially endogamous in any case at this time and the choice of suitable partners within her social circle would have been limited. If Alice had spent some of her adolescent years in the countess's household, it is quite probable that she met her future husband there for the Bryans were also closely connected to the Bohuns.

THE BRYANS

Sometime in about 1375 Alice was married to Sir Guy Bryan, the eldest son of Lord Guy Bryan. The Bryans probably came to England from France with Henry II in 1154. The first Guy Bryan had settled in Devon where he held substantial property, the largest of which was Torre.[9] In 1238 Torre is mentioned in assize rolls as Torre Briane: Bryan had already become an eponym, but the family did not remain satisfied with their West Country estates for long. In 1307 another Guy Bryan is recorded as having estates in Pembrokeshire and West Wales, acquired no doubt as a result of his services to the king in the Welsh wars. One of the castles of which he was custodian was a few miles from Haverford West, so it is likely that this Guy Bryan knew Alice's great-grandfather.

Rewards may have included a wealthy spouse as well as castles, for the next Sir Guy was married to a lady called Welthenia, which was also the name of a daughter of Llewellyn, Prince of Wales.[10] Whether or not Sir Guy's wife was actually this Princess Welthenia, it appears she may not have much enjoyed her husband's company for the duration of their marriage. In an inquisition dated 1331 Edward III delivered the barony to Guy *le filz* since his father was apparently of unsound mind, '*navoit mye sen de luy meismes dassentir al dit accord, mes estoit hors de seine memoire*'.[11] In a further inquisition of 1349 it was recorded that a Guy Bryan had died holding the barony of Tallagharn, March and the castle. If this was the same deranged man of some twenty years previously then he was the father of Alice's father-in-law, Guy Lord Bryan.

Since marriage was of strategic importance in the Middle Ages a brief account of Lord Bryan's life may help shed light on the motives behind the Bures–Bryan alliance. Like many of his contemporaries, Lord Bryan chose the traditional way to increase his fortune, through military and political service. This he did by climbing steadily up the ladder as Edward III's valet, yeoman, knight, banneret, steward of the Royal Household and finally in 1377 as chamberlain to Richard II, the new boy king. He was also a seafaring man, an admiral of the westward fleet for twenty years and even kept his own ship. He was often sent on ambassadorial roles to sue for peace in France and at the Papal Court. A member of the king's close circle of friends, several of them such as the earls of Warwick, Arundel and Hereford appointed him as feoffee and executor of their wills. In 1369 he became a member of that most exclusive club, The Order of the Garter, the ultimate accolade for a medieval knight, though by this time he was probably rather long in the tooth.[12]

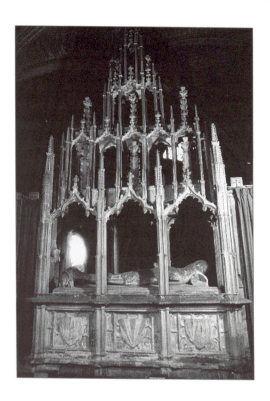

Lord Guy Bryan's tomb, 1390, opposite the Despenser chantry, Tewkesbury Abbey.

Despite these details, what can we say about Lord Bryan? It would be difficult to imagine him as a model of Chaucer's 'verray parfit gentil knyght'. Crusading and chivalry may have been the ideal in the fourteenth century, but the reality was the rise of members of the minor aristocracy through service to the king and opportune marriages to positions of social and material well-being. This he secured for himself, like others, not only from the profits of service in the king's wars, or chivalric banditry if you prefer, but also from the pay and perks as civil servant, diplomat, executor, financier, statesman, attorney and property-dealer. The list of properties held at his death is testimony to his success.[13]

Not all Lord Bryan's wealth was acquired through his own endeavours. In about 1350, when he was a widower with at least three daughters, he married a rich widow, Elizabeth Montagu, daughter of William, 1st Earl of Salisbury and Katherine Grandison.[14] The marriage had probably been awarded him by the king in recognition of his services. It was not the first time Elizabeth had been married for strategic reasons. The ancestors of her two previous husbands, Lord Giles Badlesmere and Lord Hugh Despenser, had been involved in the bloody confusion of Edward II's reign; Elizabeth's marriage to Despenser appears to have been arranged to lessen the enmity between the Montagu and Despenser families. She may not have had any choice in her marriage to Lord Bryan either, but with luck found some happiness and fulfilment in this third union: there were no surviving children by either of Elizabeth's former husbands, but she and Lord Bryan had several, a daughter and at least three sons, the oldest, predictably, called Guy. She died in 1359 after nine years of marriage and bearing at least four children, and was buried next to her second husband in the Despenser chantry at Tewkesbury Abbey. When Lord Bryan died a widower thirty-one years later, he choose to be buried close to Elizabeth just outside the Despenser chantry.

MARRIAGE

One important aspect of medieval marriage was the consolidation of family fortunes to serve joint dynastic ambitions, but there were also other considerations. The marriages of Lord Bryan's two younger sons, Sir William and Sir Philip, demonstrate mixed motives. William's wife was Joan, a niece of Richard, Earl of Arundel. Her mother Eleanor was the daughter and co-heiress of Lord John Mautravers.[15] In that alliance there were important social and political connections as well as the promise of money. In William's marriage Lord Bryan appears to have been guided by entirely orthodox considerations: a potentially wealthy bride with useful social contacts. And if Sir William had served in the Arundel household as a young man, which seems possible, there may have been an element of personal choice as well.[16]

Not so apparently for Lord Bryan's youngest son. Sir Philip's wife, another Joan, was a widow. Joan's father Sir James Chudlegh and her first husband Sir John St Aubyn had both been retainers of Hugh Courtenay, Earl of Devon. Such a connection was obviously useful to the Bryans with regard to their Devonshire estates, and as a widow it was likely that Joan Chudlegh held property in dower. But there were further considerations: on 20 April 1386 Sir Philip Bryan and Joan de Chudlegh sought and were granted the necessary dispensation before their wedding (since they were distantly related and consanguinity was considered an impediment to marriage by the Church) for family reasons, '*ad obviandum guerris et dissencionibus que inter eorum parentes possent exoriri*'.[17] There is no way of knowing what these wars and dissensions were, though we may speculate they were over property. However, Joan and Philip did not have much time to resolve the dispute as Sir Philip died the following year.[18]

Peace-weaving had long been one of the important motives behind marriage and was common in many alliances. Just as Alice's mother-in-law Elizabeth Montagu had been married off to Despenser, so the marriage between Sir Philip Bryan and Joan was arranged to soothe old sores. No such incentive is apparent in Alice's marriage to Sir Guy. Although her interest in the Bures' East Anglian estates must have been a pecuniary attraction, together with the potential useful connections through her stepfather, it is strange that Lord Bryan was not more ambitious and did not try to find a wife for his heir from the ranks of the aristocracy. And while there is little evidence upon which to base an assessment of Sir Guy's personal attractions, he must have represented a good catch, for the Bures' estates were modest compared with the Bryan lands and the Bryans belonged to a higher rank of the nobility.

An increase in rank as well as wealth was a further consideration in medieval matchmaking, though it was generally the woman who paid for her rise up the social ladder. Alice de Bryene's two daughters were married into the ranks of the lesser nobility, but both her granddaughter and great-granddaughter, who were sole heiresses, married earls and became countesses. It should be noted that at this time the peerage was becoming hereditary and a title could descend through the female line.[19] The question then is whether a young man or woman had any say in choosing a future partner. Bearing in mind that the choice of suitable spouses was limited, particularly in the upper echelons of society, only a cynic would argue that most parents were without feeling and so unscrupulous as completely to ignore an unwilling or recalcitrant son or daughter. After all they had had their own experiences of marriage. Nevertheless, it appears that young men and women generally conformed to conventional, collective norms and love may not have been their main criterion either when considering marriage.

Of course there were exceptions, such as the frequently quoted example of Margery Paston who defied her family and their designs and married the family bailiff, a match that was considered well below her station.[20] Sir Philip Bryan's widow also seems to have had her mind set on achieving some marital felicity after two arranged marriages and made her own choice of husband, ten months after Philip's death.[21] Men too might object and make their own decisions: in 1429 John, Earl of Oxford, a ward of the king, married Elizabeth Howard, granddaughter of one of Dame Alice's friends, after refusing a 'competent' marriage said to have been worth £1,000, and had to pay a £2,000 fine for so doing.[22] Canon law did in theory protect those forced against their will into a marriage and it appears that some women like Margery Paston sought help from the ecclesiastical courts to insist on their right to choose for themselves.[23]

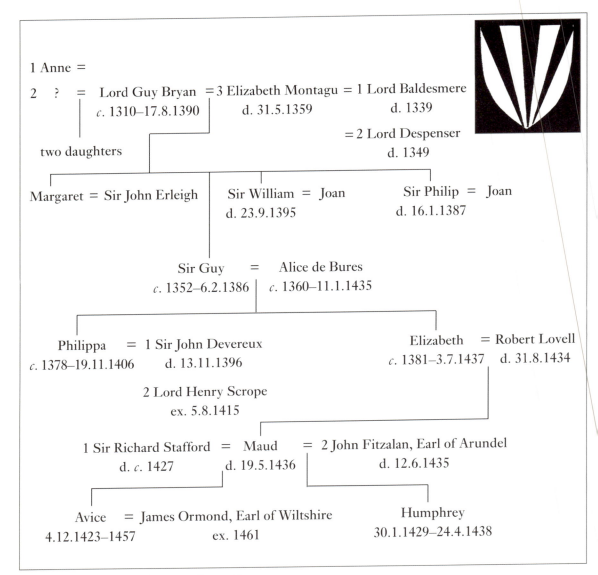

1 Anne =

2 ? = Lord Guy Bryan = 3 Elizabeth Montagu = 1 Lord Baldesmere
            _c._ 1310–17.8.1390   d. 31.5.1359   d. 1339

                                                    = 2 Lord Despenser
                                                        d. 1349

two daughters

Margaret = Sir John Erleigh   Sir William = Joan   Sir Philip = Joan
                                        d. 23.9.1395   d. 16.1.1387

                        Sir Guy   =   Alice de Bures
                    _c._ 1352–6.2.1386 | _c._ 1360–11.1.1435

Philippa   = 1 Sir John Devereux   Elizabeth   = Robert Lovell
_c._ 1378–19.11.1406   d. 13.11.1396   _c._ 1381–3.7.1437   d. 31.8.1434

            2 Lord Henry Scrope
                ex. 5.8.1415

1 Sir Richard Stafford = Maud = 2 John Fitzalan, Earl of Arundel
    d. _c._ 1427   d. 19.5.1436   d. 12.6.1435

Avice   = James Ormond, Earl of Wiltshire   Humphrey
4.12.1423–1457   ex. 1461   30.1.1429–24.4.1438

The Bryan family tree and coat of arms.

Matchmaking was as much the concern of women as it was of men since both
parents had a vested interest in the continuing prosperity of their family. The
general rule of inheritance was primogeniture, whereby the bulk of the property
descended to the eldest son. But this was never certain: as we shall see Lord
Bryan's three sons died without male heirs. Similarly in Alice's family, all the

property accumulated by her great-grandfather was held by six generations of women from Alice's grandmother down to her own great-granddaughter. The irony was that the inheritance was then fought over by four male claimants.[24] 'The gloomy verdict of the chromosomes and the sudden hand of death'[25] could shatter all carefully hatched dynastic plans.

The family are all waiting at the porch of the church, the wedding guests assembled. Alice is now fourteen or fifteen, Sir Guy about ten years older. Presumably the negotiations for the dowry (the property that the bride brought with her) and the jointure (property that was to be held jointly by the couple and would remain with the wife if her husband predeceased her) have been satisfactorily concluded. There have certainly been some financial deals. In June 1375 Lord Bryan gave Sir Richard Waldegrave a recognizance for 500 marks, followed by a further one for £2,000 at Michaelmas 1376, handsome guarantees for securing a wife for his son and heir.[26] Sir Guy had been busy too. In November that year he acquired property in Cockfield and Foxearth in Suffolk and Essex; Alice's name is not mentioned on the deed so possibly it predates her marriage and later became part of her jointure.[27] Two years later Sir Guy acquired Oxenhall manor in Gloucestershire, which his father granted jointly to the couple, apparently after the birth of one of their daughters. A few years afterwards Alice acquired an interest in two more Bryan manors, Sutton Poyntz and Hazelbury, both in Dorset.[28]

The little we know of Sir Guy suggests that to some extent he followed in his father's footsteps, busy on the king's service both civil and military. He and Alice appear to have been based in Dorset, although he may have spent some time in Devonshire and was frequently abroad fighting in France and Ireland.[29] He also sat on various royal commissions in the West Country, acted as feoffee for several of his peers and assisted his father and brother in setting up a collegiate chantry at Slapton in Devon.[30] Two daughters, Philippa and Elizabeth, were born between 1378 and 1381. In 1383 his father and stepfather-in-law concluded an agreement about the settlement of the Bures' estates, providing a greater measure of material security for him and his young family.[31] He was probably overseas in 1384, serving in the king's wars, where it seems he was seriously wounded since he drafted his will in July of that year. In 1386 he was abroad again where he died, not yet thirty-five years old, on 6 February.

It has been claimed that Sir Guy Bryan died in Spain.[32] John of Gaunt's main expedition did not go there until June 1386, so possibly he was one of the advance party. There is no way of knowing how he met his death though it may not have been a heroic end fighting in the chivalric tradition; many of Lancaster's knights died from dysentery on this campaign. This assertion is Froissart's, admittedly not the most accurate of contemporary chroniclers, who explained that the illness was caused by a surfeit of wine and sun and sleeping naked on beaches, an unsuitable pastime for the English who 'live on mild-flavoured food and good heavy ales which keep their bodies humid'.[33]

Sir Guy and Alice had been married for about ten years, for much of which time he was away on military service. During that time Alice had borne him at least two daughters and would have looked after his affairs and managed his estates, moving between the Oxenhall manor in Gloucestershire and Hazelbury and Sutton Poyntz in Dorset. There is nothing to suggest that she did not conform to the current ideal of chastity and obedience, although the vow of obedience was not included as part of the marriage service until 1549 following changes during the Reformation,[34] but otherwise she was probably quite independent. She may also have spent time at her father-in-law's favourite manor at Rampisham in Dorset, for her husband's will was proved there on 30 March 1386.

It was an unusually short will and had been written in French on 7 July 1384. Sir Guy requested burial in the chapel of St Mary at his father's Slapton chantry, appointed Alice as his principal executor and Richard Micheldever jointly and severally. He bequeathed all his property, namely his silver vessels, the clothes in his wardrobe and his 'few poor chattels', to Alice. Since he considered his goods to be of little value, he begged his father to contribute to the maintenance of his children and the payment of his debts to save him from eternal damnation – '*que ma myserye alme ne soyt pery en le fu de purgatoire*'.[35]

The protestations of poverty seem curious, a riddle that cannot be solved. But what should we make of the language used to refer to his wife as his dearly beloved companion – '*mey tres cherement de coer bien ame compaigne*' – at a time when he believed himself to be *in extremis*? It might reflect genuine affection or simply formal courtesy, for it was not an unusual phrase. In a letter written from France in 1396 to Philippa, Dame Alice's elder daughter, Sir John Devereux addressed his teenage wife as '*Treschiere et de trestout mon coer tresbien ame compaigne*' (Most dearest of my heart and best beloved companion) and concluded with a fond '*Trestout le vostre*'[36] – forever hers in sentiment perhaps but not in fact for he died six weeks later. Apart from the formality which unites the two and may be indicative of convention, both use the phrase 'dearly beloved companion', as did many testators in their wills at this time. This raises the question of whether late medieval marriage was companionate and how much the romantic ideal was actually experienced once the wedding had taken place.

Since the principal motive of the marriage alliance in noble and gentry families was to consolidate and further dynastic plans, it is realistic to see marriage as a joint venture in which both parties would usually have been concerned to preserve the family fortune and pass it on to their children. The numerous occurrences of fiercely fought battles between step-parents and stepchildren demonstrate that this interest was paramount. Medieval marriage was a partnership to which each member was expected to contribute according to accepted roles and convention. Similarly the frequency with which husbands appointed their wives as executors of their wills illustrates not only their acceptance of women's managerial skills but also a sense of trust invested in them as capable people with the interests of their family at heart who could be relied upon to carry out this final and important task.

Romantic relationship and fulfilment may have been much less common in medieval marriage but not because the feeling did not exist, as is evident from the *chansons* of the troubadours. Devotion, sentiment and idealization also found a place within the Church and were celebrated by both male and female mystics in the later Middle Ages in the marriage and sexual imagery of their ecstasies. Both Margery Kempe and the anchoress Julian of Norwich, another contemporary of Alice, described with deep emotion their religious experiences, but while Julian writing from the shelter of her recluse's cell reflected calmly and philosophically on the meaning of God's love, Margery wrote at times of her relationship to God with all the passion and enthusiasm of a teenager in love. However, when the husband from whom she had been separated for many years fell ill, she recorded that God advised her to live with him again and nurse him in his old age. This she did, although she found it a very great chore for he had become senile and incontinent. The romantic ideal was certainly contained in poetry, piety and religious devotion, but the reality of marriage as Margery described it was support in difficult times and hard work.[37]

THE FAMILY

Loyalty and emotional support seem also to have been experienced within the household, in the family and the extended family. Women often appointed their mothers as executors, as did Alice's granddaughter Maud when she died in 1436. Maud's second husband had died the previous year and her first husband eight years before that, but she chose his father, that is her ex-father-in-law, as her other executor so they too must have remained in close contact despite Maud's remarriage.[38] The mother and daughter relationship might sometimes have been strained, as was the case with Margery Paston, but there is also evidence of deep affection. In 1402 Lady Elizabeth Zouche, then in her mid-thirties, instructed her agent John Blore to buy her 'a payre bedes of gold fore my lady my moder' with the 'queyntest pater noster', urgently and at whatever cost (and in fact he presented her with a bill for £38) so that she could take them as a gift on her forthcoming visit.[39]

The natal and extended family often played an important part in women's lives. Alice's mother died in 1406 and her stepfather in 1410, though we may guess they often dined at Acton. Her half-brothers, Sir Richard and William, were frequent guests at the manor, occasionally staying the night. Sir Richard was married to Joan, daughter of Sir Thomas Munchensy from nearby Edwardstone, and was knighted sometime before 1391 but there are no significant records of his military prowess. It would appear that he preferred a quiet life as a country gentleman in Suffolk; unlike his father he had no apparent contacts at the royal Court and was not elected to sit in Parliament. However, with other local gentry, he acquired a few valuable wardships, sat on some royal commissions and occasionally acted as feoffee for various neighbours.[40]

In the period for which we have records, Sir Richard visited Alice eleven times, sometimes *en famille* but more often with just a squire. His brother William also came frequently. On 10 January 1413 Richard sent his minstrel to Acton and came to dine there the following day. The guest list gives no indication that a particular event was being celebrated, whether religious, social or agricultural, so the gift of music may have marked some personal feast day, possibly Alice's birth or baptismal day, which he was unable to attend in person. Curiously Dame Alice died twenty-two years later on 11 January. If 10 January *was* a day of personal significance, then it suggests she may have been a tough determined lady intent on celebrating a special anniversary, her seventy-fifth birthday perhaps, before her death.

Other relatives, like her cousin Margaret Sampson and a more distant cousin Agnes Rokewode, were often made welcome at Acton. Though Margaret was a close neighbour, she also sometimes spent the night at the manor. Their children were invited to dinner occasionally as well. Alice's uncle Andrew Bures, father of Margaret Sampson, had died in 1397 and the line continued through his son Andrew. Though he did not live far away, having property in Colne Engaine,

5 miles south-west of Bures, in Hemel Hempstead and Cambridgeshire, he was not a guest at Acton in 1412–13. Visits from relatives, however, must have reinforced family traditions and as we shall see family feast days were frequently observed at Alice's manor.

Although relationships with the family could be affectionate, or at least were normally cordial especially when there were shared interests, they could also be exceedingly acrimonious. The dispute between Alice's father-in-law and brother-in-law illustrates how family loyalties could be divided and to what extent blood relatives were prepared to go especially when property was involved. Eleven months after Sir Guy's death in 1386, his youngest brother Sir Philip also died. After this Sir William, the sole surviving brother, attempted to defraud Alice and her daughters of their inheritance and relations quickly deteriorated between him and his father, with both presenting letters patent and statements at Westminster. In the summer of 1388 Lord Bryan claimed that William had induced certain strangers to change one of his trusts, so that if he had no sons but only daughters they would inherit before Alice's children.[41]

The lords Lovell and Devereux, as prospective fathers-in-law of Alice's daughters, showed a keen interest in the events that they demonstrated with physical violence and were bound over to keep the peace, as was Sir William.[42] Lord Bryan then broke into William's inn in London and recovered a deed relating to the Hazelbury manor, which in fact now belonged to Alice as part of her jointure.[43] William had been planning to go to Brittany but changed his mind and stayed in England. Relinquishing the opportunity of collecting some war booty, he had other plunder in mind: sometime that autumn he retaliated by climbing up the walls of his father's Tallagharn castle in Wales and stealing silver and gold worth £25.[44]

Finally he sought help from the Pope and the Bishop of Exeter, claiming that his patrimony had been stolen and subsequently the Papal Court threatened to excommunicate the perpetrators.[45] Their mandate was issued a couple of months after Lord Bryan's death in 1390 but William had already lost any chance of a settlement in his favour: Lord Bryan appointed Alice de Bryene as one of his six executors, together with Sir Robert Fitzpayne and Sir John Chandos (who were married to two of Lord Bryan's daughters by a previous marriage), Lord John Devereux, Walter Trote (rector of his Slapton chantry) and Richard Micheldever, and excluded his only remaining son.[46] Sir William died on 23 September 1395, without heirs, and was buried not at the Bryan chantry at Slapton, but in the parish church at Seal in Kent, where he is commemorated by a monumental brass.[47]

At the height of the quarrel Sir William offered to defend his position in the court of chivalry and claimed that his father had committed errors in favouring Alice's daughters because of 'ignorance, his . . . great age, evil counsel and untrue information of others'.[48] Ignorance? His father's great age? It would be difficult to concur with the first. His father *was* old, but not too old to be summoned to sit on various royal commissions and young enough, as we have seen, to do some burglary. It is true that he may not have been well, for a few years earlier the valuable custody of St Briavel's castle and the Forest of Dean that he held had been promised to the Earl of Essex after his death.[49] Perhaps he had been shaken by grief at the deaths of two of his sons within one year. Or might the malady that had inflicted *his* father have begun to manifest in him? As for evil counsel, Dame Alice and her daughters certainly appear to have had some champions, though one wonders what they thought of the threat of excommunication, that dreaded spectre of bell, book and candle.

Greed and jealousy are common human characteristics. Without doubt Alice de Bryene did her best to protect her daughters' interests and sought support when necessary. On the death of her grandmother in 1392 it appears she turned to Lord Devereux for help when there may have been a problem about her own inheritance; details of this are discussed in Chapter 7. But while contemporaries might be called upon for support, the younger generation could express their loyalty and affection. Alice's elder daughter had married the eldest son of the Devereux family, Sir John, in about 1390. When Sir John wrote to his wife Philippa in September 1396 from France, where he had gone to assist with the arrangements of the wedding celebrations of the French Princess Isabel to Richard II, he also sent his mother-in-law a brief letter. It may have been something of a chore since, apart from the introductory salutations and concluding sentence of each, they were almost identical.[50] If mother and daughter shared their correspondence they must have been disappointed. We should however credit Devereux with dutiful behaviour.

The letter written to Alice a few months earlier from Ireland by her other son-in-law, Robert Lovell, was much more effusive.[51] In essence it was little more than a charming 'bread-and-butter' letter. Addressing Dame Alice affectionately as '*bien amee dame et miere*' (dearly beloved lady and mother), he showed considerable concern about her welfare, '*qar certes ma ioie est renouelle quant ieo en ay bonnes nouelles de Vous*' (because certainly my joy is renewed whenever I have good news of you), reiterated the great gratitude he felt he owed her '. . . *esmerciant et remerciant en quantqe ieo puisse de lez tres grandes tendresche et chierte qe vous auetz de ma personne et des aultres ennumerables bontez queux vous ad pluz de vostre treshaulte gentillesse'* (thanking you and rethanking you as much as I can for the great tenderness and love you have shown me and all the other kindness you have for me from your great gentility), and concluded '*Vostre humble filtz si vous plaist*'. Robert had married Elizabeth, Alice's younger daughter, a few years earlier.

Both letters, while exhibiting different degrees of affection, demonstrate a display of good manners and courtesy in familial relationship. Despite the prevalence of competition and the struggle for survival during this period, loyalty to one's kin was a significant impulse because identity lay as much with the group as the individual. Robert Lovell's sentiments, which might in part be a reflection of the exuberance of youth and delight in fine phrases, may also stem from a very genuine and deep mutual affection. Many young men at this time were separated from their mothers at an early age and may have sought maternal affection in the households to which they were sent from women deprived of their own young sons. Maternal affection would then have been transferred to a mother–in–law, and likewise by women to their surrogate sons.

Shortly after the death of Sir John Devereux in November 1396, Philippa married again. Her new husband was Lord Henry Scrope of Masham. Together they acquired the manor of Naylondhall in Suffolk not far from Acton.[52] Though Philippa was wealthy, her Bryan properties were far away and Scrope's estates were mostly in the north of England. Possibly the Suffolk manor was part of her jointure, a wedding gift from her new husband, so that she might occasionally be close to her mother. Scrope, as we shall see, was also devoted to his mother–in–law. Alice may have had more opportunity of seeing her elder daughter now than she had before. Some time later in 1398 Philippa and Henry Scrope obtained a papal mandate granting them dispensation for having married despite being distantly related. This post *de facto* indemnity may have been sought because Philippa was pregnant and wanted to ensure the legitimacy of her offspring. But little babies, dead or alive, rarely appear in records and when Philippa died eight years later in 1406, not yet in her thirties, she left no heirs.[53]

Scrope's second wife was Joan Holland, Duchess of York and stepmother of Richard, Earl of Cambridge. This new alliance revived his political affiliations with the Yorks; he and his father had both been ardent supporters of Richard II, although on his downfall they swiftly changed their allegiance to the Lancastrian kings. Politics at this time was a dangerous game and his change of heart was regarded with suspicion and may have invoked envy. Walsingham thought Scrope much too close to the king: 'he made such a pretence of gravity in demeanour, of modesty in bearing and of piety in speech, that the King took everything he said as an oracle from Heaven'. In 1415 he was implicated in that obscure conspiracy known as the Southampton Plot, masterminded it would seem by Cambridge, was tried on the eve of Henry V's departure for glory at Agincourt, suffered the indignity of a public execution, that is he was laid on a hurdle and dragged to the place of execution, and his head was dispatched to York for impalement on the Micklegate Bar.[54]

Nothing remains to indicate what Alice thought of this tragedy but Scrope had not forgotten her, though ten years had passed since Philippa's death. In his will written two months before the accusation of treason, he specifically named her as one of those few for whom prayers were to be said at his funeral masses. He also left her a quantity of valuable items, including a silver mazer, a golden tablet engraved with the image of the Virgin Mary, a crystal bearing the image of St Christopher, a mantel, some tapestry and several fine devotional books in Latin and French, one of which was illuminated. His former sister-in-law, Elizabeth Lovell, was remembered too with the gift of a silver *tracleere* (a reliquary?) gilded with crystal sides.[55] Scrope was not the only one of Alice's close relatives who lost his head as a result of miscalculated political loyalties: the murder of John Montagu, 3rd Earl of Salisbury, will be discussed in Chapter 7.

Alice's other son-in-law, Robert Lovell, was another whose political affiliations may have constituted something of an obstacle to his advancement. Like many of his class, his father Lord Lovell ran with the hare (perhaps hart would be more appropriate in this instance since it was Richard II's personal emblem) and hunted with the hounds. A renowned Ricardian courtier, Lord Lovell was one of the first to change sides during the crisis of 1399 and join Henry Bolingbroke, later serving him when he became king. The Lovells, like the Devereux family, appear to have profited from Richard II's largess during the last two decades of the fourteenth century. But fortunes cannot always be made by prowess in war and sycophancy to royalty. Robert Lovell was to suffer from the vicissitudes and parsimony of royal gratitude and patronage and over the next three decades might have slid down to join the *nouveaux pauvres* had he not been able to use some of his wife's substantial property to save himself.[56]

At Michaelmas 1412 Robert Lovell and/or one of his household (the record is not clear) came to dine at Acton. For the rest of the year neither he nor Elizabeth visited Alice. However, it seems relationships between them remained cordial: Lovell occasionally collected money for his mother-in-law from her Oxenhall

Woodsford Castle, Dorset, home of Lord Guy Bryan and birthplace of Dame Alice's great-granddaughter Avice. It can be rented from the Landmark Trust.

estate,[57] and it appears that in 1410 she let him use her London inn to host a meeting of the Royal Council, which included his brother-in-law Scrope and Prince Henry.[58] Lovell died on 31 August 1434; his wife Elizabeth survived until 3 July 1437. Their only child, a daughter Maud, had married Sir Richard Stafford by whom she had a daughter Avice, born at Woodsford castle in Dorset on 4 December 1423. On Stafford's death in 1427 Maud married John Fitzalan, Earl of Arundel, by whom she had a son Humphrey. She died in 1436, a year after Arundel. Their son died in 1438, leaving Maud's daughter Avice as the sole heiress of the Bryan and Bures' estates.[59] Avice married James Ormond, Earl of Wiltshire, and died in 1457 with no living issue.[60]

WIDOWHOOD

Elizabeth and Robert Lovell's marriage was unusual in that it lasted for over forty years and neither married more than once. Alice de Bryene had been married for just over a decade when Sir Guy died. We cannot tell how she greeted the news of his death, with anguish or stoicism, or whether she reflected

Wheel of Fortune, from a French manuscript of c. *1400.*

that it was a turn of fortune's wheel, wept, then lit a candle and said her prayers. But why, since she was still a young woman, only in her mid-twenties, did she not marry again like her grandmother, mother, eldest daughter and granddaughter? It cannot have been because she lacked suitors. However ill-favoured or bad-tempered she may have been, her inheritance would have ensured her plenty of offers. Though we may speculate about her personal attributes, we shall not find the answer there. From a practical point of view, Alice had fulfilled one of the canons of medieval marriage practice: though widowed early she had borne two daughters, both of whom were well married soon after her husband's death.

A modestly wealthy woman, able to make her own decision about remarriage, she chose to stay celibate, in the original sense of the word: staying single. While we shall find a suggestion later on of a knight seeking her favours, we can only speculate whether it was just marriage she rejected: her sexual life is hidden from us. In her particular circumstances it is possible that the importance of being 'lord' of the manor and head of her household, with all the interrelated responsibilities and obligations, may have been one reason for her decision to remain a widow: she may have relished the opportunity of being entirely independent and autonomous. Some might have thought the path she chose condemned her to a life that was tough, demanding and lonely, though she did not lack companionship judging by the numbers of men and women who came to dine with her. If she wanted for anything it may have been an intimate relationship: and we might then wonder whether she had loved Sir Guy too much or not at all. Yet however clear-sighted we may wish to be, we do not have the appropriate vision to peer into the mysteries of the human heart.

Widowhood was not an uncommon state in the later Middle Ages, which may have facilitated Dame Alice's decision. An analysis of remarriage within the peerage from 1350 to 1500 demonstrates that an average of 30 per cent of men did not remarry after the death of their first spouse.[61] The number was probably higher for women, for a further analysis of title holders in the fifteenth century indicates that there were almost three times as many widows dying as widowers or unmarried men.[62] Many who had experienced marriage and widowhood chose to remain unmarried. Widows who had had managerial experience as married women must often have felt that running their own estates did not present an impossible challenge and perhaps they welcomed the opportunity of complete independence. Widowhood permitted them to have absolute control over their temporal resources. Besides there might not have been any satisfactory or eligible men with whom they wanted to share their lives.

The condition of chastity had not been imposed on Alice under her husband's will, though this did happen occasionally. In 1442 Sir Gilbert Denys bequeathed all his movable goods to his wife Margaret 'if after my death [she] vow a vow of Chastity', otherwise she was only to receive the customary third.[63] This may not have been a jealous hand from the grave attempting to control his wife's sexuality, but a device to safeguard their children's inheritance from a new husband. There is no evidence from the episcopal registers, however, that Alice opted to make such a vow. Vowesses are sometimes visible from their monumental brasses, where they are depicted wearing a veil or a ring, but Alice's image displays neither though she does wear a wimple. It could be that she had no need to protect herself by making a public statement since she was assertive enough to protect her right to live as she chose. Even if she had made such a vow it need not necessarily have restricted her freedom of action in any way: a vow of chastity was neither a promise of obedience or poverty. It was often not even perpetual.[64]

Advice on remarriage was not uncommon in the Middle Ages demonstrating that not everyone believed marriage was the only way of achieving self-fulfilment. In 1405 Christine de Pisan counselled against tragic representations of emotion and continual grieving and recommended that the widow take full responsibility for her future. Furthermore she wrote: 'If in married life all was repose and peace, truly it would be sensible to enter it again; but because one sees quite the contrary, any woman ought to be wary of remarriage, although for a young woman if may be a necessity or anyway convenient. But for those who are already passed their youth and who are well off enough and are not constrained by poverty, it is sheer folly, although some women who wish to remarry say that it is no life at all for a woman on her own.'[65]

A few decades earlier William Langland also had something to say about the marriage of young women and widows but in a less pragmatic and more critical vein:

> It is an uncomly couple, by Crist, as me thynketh –
> To yeven a yong wenche to an[y] olde feble,
> Or wedden any wodewe for welthe of hir goodes
> That nevere shall barn bere but if it be in armes.
> In jelousie yoyeless and janglynge on bedde,
> Many a piere sithen the pestilence han plight hem togideres.
> The fruyt that thei brynge forth arn [manye] foule wordes,
> Have thei no children but cheetse and chopp[es] hem bitwene.[66]

The choice of place of burial can tell us much about where affection and attachment really lay. Men and women who had married several times did not always request burial with their most recent spouse.[67] As noted Lord Bryan was buried close to his last wife and not in his Slapton chantry, though she lay together with her previous husband in the Despenser chantry. On occasion women, and especially widows, chose entombment with their ancestors or even with siblings.[68] Widows might also ask to be buried in the grounds of a religious

Peace and concord among all people, mid-fourteenth century, English.

house where they had spent their last years.[69] Elizabeth Lovell directed in her will that she be buried in the Bryan chantry at Slapton. There is no indication where her husband had chosen burial but Elizabeth's decision can be seen as a statement first and foremost of her position as the Bryan heiress and custodian of the estates. Similarly, Alice de Bryene chose the Acton parish church as her final resting place. It could be argued that this was not only confirmation of her status as head of those estates that she had inherited from her father, but emphasized that which was ultimately her home, the place where she was born, had lived and worked, and was more important to her than marital relationship. The relationship with the wider community was apparently another source of satisfaction, stimulation and fulfilment.

CHAPTER 3

Estate Management

It is dawn on Thursday 23 March 1413. John Lytleton, bailiff of Alice de Bryene's Oxenhall manor in Gloucestershire, is waiting outside in the cold courtyard. Stamping his numb feet and rubbing his hands together, he blows on to his frozen fingers and watches his warm breath condense into small clouds of steam. Perhaps the rising vapours remind him of the painting of hell fire at the Last Judgement above the chancel arch of St Ann's. Over the treetops echoes the peal of bells calling the hours of Prime. But he has a long journey ahead of him to Acton in Suffolk and there will be time to say some prayers along the way. As he crosses himself the barn door bangs and his companion comes walking towards him leading two horses and a cart.[1]

They climb up and set off quickly talking about the route. Gloucester and Tewkesbury are equidistant, over 200 miles from Acton, though the road to London via Tewkesbury, Woodstock and Brill is more direct than the Gloucester road. Both are pilgrimage routes so there will be company along the way and vagabonds too perhaps. Twelve years previously Lytleton had made two journeys to Dorset to deliver cash to Richard Micheldever, Alice's receiver, once claiming 3s extra for bringing along another man to frighten away thieves.[2] The journey ought to be easier this year than last, however, when they travelled in February: the days are lengthening and it should be getting warmer. But whichever route they choose it will be fairly slow going with the cart averaging about 12 miles a day. They plan to reach London on 7 or 8 April. From there it will be an easy journey to Acton via Colchester on a busy well-maintained road.

They reach the top of the hill where the road divides. Looking back over the expanse of 300-odd acres, largely wooded but some strips newly ploughed for seeding, Lytleton feels a tug of pride. Oxenhall is not as large and productive as the Lady de Bryene's Dorsetshire or East Anglian estates yet in his ten years as bailiff there he has rarely accounted for less than an annual £18 profit. The rents continue to come in and the sale of coal is steady. Patting the coins in his purse he takes up the reins and they set off at a fast trot.

If John Lytleton's journey actually took him through London, and it would be surprising if it had not, then he may have been there at about 9 April, which was Passion Sunday and the day of Henry V's coronation. And whatever association we have with spring days and April weather, this one was different. Adam de Usk reported at the time: 'On the same day an exceeding fierce wind and unwonted storm fell on the hill-country of the realm and smothered men and beasts and homesteads and drowned out the valleys and the marshes in marvellous wise, with losses and perils to men beyond measure.'[3] Another chronicler, Thomas Walsingham, thought the unseasonable weather a harbinger of good fortune reflecting contemporary optimism at the start of a new reign.[4] Such portents however were hardly likely to be greeted with much enthusiasm by Dame Alice and her bailiffs, for whom freak weather presaged poor harvests and general shortages. In any event it was probably a tired and bedraggled John Lytleton who turned up at the Acton manor on Monday 10 April in time for supper.

Personnel such as bailiffs, officials, farm-workers and tenant farmers employed on Dame Alice's estates comprised by far the largest percentage of all her dinner guests in 1412–13, a phenomenon which must be true of many other medieval

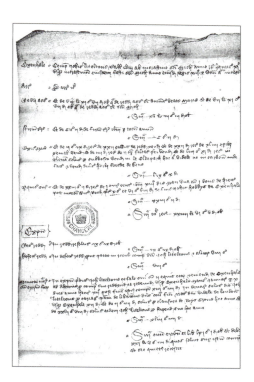

John Lytleton's account for Oxenhall, 1410–11. He probably brought a shortened version like this with him to Acton in 1413.

households. Farm-workers from the Acton area would often have met in the vicinity of the meadows and fields of the manor, but when Alice invited them to dinner she could take the opportunity of discussing strategy and the agricultural timetable with them in person. Other guests like Lytleton came from much further afield to account themselves, though they sent annual reports as well. The fact that these business meetings over dinner continued throughout the year on weekdays, Sundays, high days and holy days emphasizes the central position of the estates in the household and suggests management was kept under constant supervision. Agriculture and husbandry would have been two of the chief topics of conversation at Alice's table, indicating that farming was not only a matter of subsistence but also a major occupation in medieval society, and even if the business of woolfells, wheat and landrents brought riches and prestige it was also a matter of social obligation and constant hard work.

Altogether Alice de Bryene had possession of estates totalling about 6,000 acres. The three properties in the West Country that had come to her through her marriage to Sir Guy accounted for slightly less than half this amount. Hazelbury and Sutton Poyntz in Dorsetshire were both substantial farms, while Oxenhall in Gloucestershire was much smaller. The property in East Anglia was her patrimony. It consisted of six viable farms, each between 200 and 900 acres at Acton, Bures, Raydon, Wherstead and Layham in Suffolk and Foxearth on the Suffolk–Essex border, property and a small farm in Great Waldingfield and a small commercial property in Polstead. She also had an interest in two other properties, Thorp Morieux and Cramaville in Melford, as well as a house in London.

GENERAL ESTATE MANAGEMENT

A variety of officials was needed to help run these estates. In common with other estate owners, Alice employed a receiver who was responsible for the financial aspects of a group of manors in general, especially when they were leased for cash. Richard Micheldever acted for her in this capacity until his death in 1400, supervising the auditing of accounts and collection of moneys from the West Country farms. He had been joint executor with Alice of both her husband and father-in-law's wills. His own lengthy will drafted in 1397 suggests he was a close friend as well as a business associate and gives us an idea of the sort of people Alice employed. Long service and unfulfilled obligations may in part explain his numerous bequests to the Bryan chantry in Devon, which included a golden image of Our Lady, vestments, a chalice, Latin Bible and *The Golden Legend*, together with large sums of money for numerous services to be sung for himself, Lord Bryan and Sir Guy Bryan. He also left gifts and grants to other religious foundations and individuals, as well as £6 13s 4d to *Sir* Richard Dynham, Alice's chaplain, to sing St Gregory's Trental for him the year after his death – a bequest worth 4d a day – and money for masses to be sung for Sir William Bryan whom he may have believed would benefit from extra intercessions.

Faced with the prospect of death it is apparent that apart from religious solicitude Micheldever intended to leave no debts unpaid. But what perhaps characterizes his will as much as his piety is his involvement with agriculture and the land. To his brother-in-law Walter Chauntermerle and his wife he left firstly draught animals, cows and 600 sheep and then the ubiquitous mazers, silver vessels and spoons, and beds. A nephew was left sheep and Slye the shepherd awarded 13s 4d and given a hood and a jacket. In employing Micheldever as her receiver Dame Alice would have been assured of his integrity, experience, knowledge and commitment to farming.[5]

Micheldever was not the only former member of the Bryan affinity whom Alice retained. In fact it has been argued that inheritance was as much a unit of social life as land ownership.[6] The ongoing patronage of family retainers guaranteed a mutual trust and continuity and ensured that local tradition was recognized, understood and upheld. Another visitor to Acton in 1412–13 who came a great distance was Morgan Gough. He had been a trustee of Sir Guy's lands and sat on various royal commissions in Dorset in the 1400s. The Goughs had been in service with the Bryan family for many years, very many perhaps for the name has a Welsh pitch. Since Morgan Gough came from the West Country it seems likely that on Micheldever's death Alice appointed him as her new receiver for her estates there.[7]

Engaging local officials to work on distant estates was good policy for they could wield their influence in their home counties and were knowledgeable about the immediate environment. In the 1390s Alice employed Robert Whittington, the elder brother of Richard Whittington Lord Mayor of London, to advise her about her Gloucestershire property. As a Member of Parliament for that county six times and a commissioner with numerous local official duties, he was ideally placed to do so.[8] It was he who appears to have recommended the marketing of coal at Oxenhall. His eldest son was called Guy, possibly a godson of Lord Bryan or Sir Guy, an indication that his family had benefited from previous Bryan patronage.

Stewards had to be engaged as well to supervise the running of courts, make local appointments, negotiate tenancy agreements and accompany the auditors when the annual accounts were checked. As we have seen most of Alice's household stewards came from the ranks of the clergy, in which case one would presume that she appointed those who also had some knowledge of law and husbandry. It is not clear, since the term is generic, whether in a comparatively small household such as hers the household steward was also involved in the management of the estates and manorial courts. It does appear, however, that there was a certain flexibility of roles in the estate management at Acton and a man like John Pellican, custodian and receiver of Alice de Bryene's East Anglian estates, accompanied the stewards when they held courts where she had jurisdiction.

In one of her stewards' household accounts Alice's bill for liveries is specified as being for 'diverse ministers as well as household servants and various others of her council, bailiffs, farmers and other officers retained by the lady'. Apart from her retainers the members of her council were people she could turn to for specific advice and management, her well-connected dinner guests and other local dignitaries. Essentially the composition of her council, like those of her contemporaries, was pragmatic and use was made of hiring local professionals as well as relying on in-house staff;[9] for example, Alice occasionally used the services of Micheldever's chaplain John Lodewell, and she once paid a 10s reward to the Earl of March's rector who seems to have helped her negotiate a deal concerning the Hazelbury manor.[10] Recourse to help and advice from men who were not on the regular payroll but had useful connections was another way of greasing the wheels of estate management. From time to time the service of lawyers was also needed. No specific names are mentioned in Alice's accounts but there is evidence that there were legal problems at Hazelbury, Sutton Poyntz and Cramaville and that Alice occasionally had to litigate.[11]

Drawing up the annual account was the responsibility of the bailiff whose job it was to manage the day-to-day business of the farms, together with the rent collector. None of Alice's bailiffs' accounts appears to have cipher marks to demonstrate that they were checked, except those for Bures which are heavily marked with allowances crossed out and supplementary material added. Alice had bailiffs at all her manors although where a manor was farmed mainly for cash, the bailiff was less involved with husbandry than overseeing the tenant and maintaining a presence there to safeguard the landlord's interest. It has been shown that by the end of the thirteenth century the position of the bailiff was subject to many legal checks. His previous policing powers as law enforcer so far as labour was concerned, his right to lease land and sue in the manorial courts, had largely diminished. Although still in a powerful position since he traded with his lord's goods and received his lord's monies, his accounts were carefully

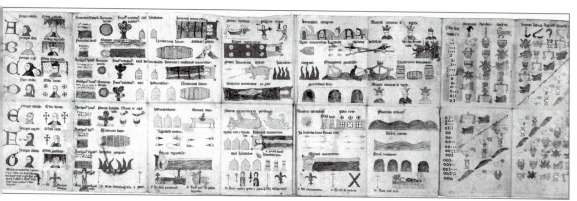

Fortune telling and prognosis for seven years from an English almanac, second half of the fourteenth century.

scrutinized by auditors and he was ultimately accountable for any deficiencies.[12] Nevertheless a widow like Alice needed to be cautious in appointing her bailiffs. On some estates the harvest-reeve might still be responsible for collecting rents or enforcing the obligation of boon work. A rent collector or harvest-reeve often figures in Alice's accounts. Though there were few bondmen left in Suffolk by 1400, most tenants were liable for some boon work especially during the harvest, while the rest of their labour service was commuted to cash or commodity rents.

Finally there were the permanent agricultural workers, grangers, carters, members of the plough team, reapers, mowers, shepherds, herdsmen and a maidservant in each manor to complete the estate staff team. Extra work was often contracted to casual labourers or tenant farmers who were employed part-time to shoe traction animals, dig ditches, herd animals, cart hay and produce, mend farm buildings and implements and help with the various aspects of arable cultivation.

Each year the bailiff presented an account with detailed sums of rents for cottages and land, income and expenses and the quantities of livestock and grain at each manor. Though they appear on the surface less interesting than a weekly shopping list, reiterating as they do year in and year out the exact measure of grain in the barns, sheep dead from murrain, precise number of nails bought to mend the carthouse roof and the uncollected rents, they should not be considered dry and tedious. For through them we can gather a harvest of information, learn how Alice's farms were managed and by whom, begin to appreciate the interdependency of estate owner and tenant or employee and become better acquainted with the cycle of the agricultural calendar.

Just as the actual supervision of the household was often a married woman's task while her husband was away fighting, attending to business or extending his patronage, so too she would have busied herself with the management of the estates. For a widow like Alice de Bryene with substantial property the main difference may have been a larger degree of centralization, a tendency to rent out a higher proportion of estates and a greater ability to reinvest such monetary profits that might have accrued in the land, rather than milk the estates to pay for business ventures, whether they were military or political enterprises or the accumulation of more property. Furthermore if her children were already provided for, she would not have had to concern herself with increasing her capital assets.

While Alice's estates were split between the West Country and East Anglia, there is no evidence that she travelled or divided her residence between them in her later years. The tendency of widows to remain relatively stationary could have had a profound effect on their estates and the local community in which they lived. Continuous supervision throughout the year would have increased the efficiency and profitability of their farms, as seasonal changes could be noted and new strategies implemented if necessary: authority did not have to be delegated and personal decisions could be made. By remaining in one place for a long period of time, a widow would also have been more personally involved with her workers and employees in general. The widow's power of dispensing patronage is likely to have been a more effective tool and bonds of loyalty and affection could be strengthened.

However, although there is evidence that Dame Alice treated her staff and tenants with consideration and occasional generosity, settling her cottagers and crofters' tax bills in Gloucestershire, for example, and returning the 'old beast' worth 4s, which was the obligatory payment or 'heriot' levied on the death of a tenant, to a widow at Bures (interestingly enough at the supplication of her half-brother),[13] it would be inappropriate to evaluate these practices as gender specific or an illustration of the charitable nature of women. Rather good labour relations stemmed from hard-headed business considerations and local custom, as did the granting of free accommodation to some of her permanent workers, such as the shepherds.

Variations in Alice's agricultural and managerial policy reflect the differing demands of individual estates. Diversification and flexibility were important strategies if the farms were to remain profitable or at least be self-supporting. Moreover innovation was limited by established practice, local tradition and existing circumstance. Let us take a quick walk around Alice de Bryene's properties and look at the different ways that they were managed, which must have been common to many estates at this time.

THE ESTATES IN THE WEST COUNTRY

Oxenhall, which means 'a nook of land where oxen are kept', is today hardly even a hamlet. A couple of signposts direct you off the busy M50 motorway to a sprinkling of small farms and holiday cottages. The lanes are overgrown, the terrain hilly and wooded. No evidence remains of a medieval manor house today, though one or two of the houses have working dovecots. In 1386 it was noted that, apart from the main house with its dovecot, there was a carucate of land (that is the area that could be worked annually by one plough and eight oxen and was usually taken to be 120 acres), 6 acres of meadow, a park and a large area of woodland. Annual income came mainly from fixed rents of over £15, supplemented by payments from the manorial courts. Although this represented a steady dividend, opportunities for an increment were not overlooked. In 1401 Alice's council investigated the possibility of selling coal, a policy that was soon implemented. Sales continued steadily, reaching a peak eight years later when various men from the established mining area of the Forest of Dean paid £10 for the right to make charcoal. No doubt this operation was both economically and ecologically sound, cash–cropping from the woodland while leaving the pastures and meadowlands free for rent.[14]

Alice's Hazelbury and Sutton Poyntz estates were not at all like Oxenhall. In gentler rolling countryside, they were larger and managed in a completely different way. Like Oxenhall, both were part of her jointure. They had been acquired by Lord Bryan in the early 1360s, taking advantage of cheap prices occasioned by the second epidemic of the Black Death. Hazelbury in north Dorset, some 15 miles north of Dorchester, is in undulating terrain, well–watered by numerous streams and brooks. The manor at Alice's death consisted of over 1,000 acres, mainly pasture land with some meadows, woodlands and two large orchards. Apart from the manor house, with all its various barns, outbuildings and stables, there were 47 messuages, 7 cottages and 2 water mills as well as 3 carucates of land at Crockernestoke and Tubervylestoke.[15]

Alice also inherited the advowson of the church, which must have been something of a financial liability since a large part of it was rebuilt while under her patronage. It has probably not changed much since then. An old tithe barn next to the graveyard, some strangely shaped hillocks that may conceal building rubble, various ponds that might once have been stew ponds or the remnants of a moat and a renovated farm house close by suggest this was the site of the original manor, especially since no other localities in the village present themselves as possibilities.

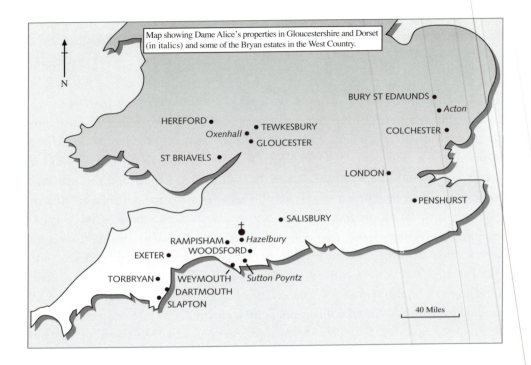

Map showing Dame Alice's properties in Gloucestershire and Dorset (in italics) and some of the Bryan estates in the West Country.

A notice on the left side of the porch in the church entrance, installed after the Second World War, records that the name *Hazelbury Bryan* was obliterated from the board in 1940 in order to obstruct the enemy should he succeed in landing, and concludes with the statement that the name will never be replaced 'in order to serve as a memorial to his defeat and the deliverance of our country'. Alice and her entourage would have been mystified. Hazelbury did not acquire its patronymic until some thirty years after her death when Henry Percy, 3rd Earl of Northumberland, was summoned to Parliament as Baron Poynings, Fitzpayne and Bryan by the right of his wife. If it was a ploy intended to secure Northumberland the entire Bryan estate it was unsuccessful; though he was acknowledged to be the heir general of Guy Lord Bryan, the Hazelbury manor was awarded to Thomas, Earl of Ormond and the Bryan barony went into abeyance. But it indicates that Hazelbury was considered a very valuable property by those litigating over the Bryan estates.[16]

The farm at Hazelbury was probably similar to those there today. We know from the inquisition held at Alice de Bryene's death that the majority of land was pasture. Today herds of cattle predominate, though there may have been more sheep in the fourteenth century. Two water mills are mentioned which suggests some grain was grown. But pastoral farming is less labour intensive than arable, an advantage at a time of labour shortages particularly in an area hard hit by high mortality. Weymouth, the port of entry of the Black Death in 1348, is only a day's ride away. There were also a couple of orchards at Hazelbury but we do not know if they were large enough to make cider or perry a viable commercial activity.

Hazelbury may have been farmed directly while Sir Guy was still alive and based in Dorset. Lord Bryan also apparently kept stock there.[17] After her grandmother's death in 1392, Alice inherited the bulk of her patrimony and it seems the time had come for some modification. In 1394 William Carpenter and Robert Turner were chosen as tenants to take over from the bailiff Roger Kayn and farm the entire Hazelbury estate between them. The annual rental income was approximately £46. Though we hear nothing of them after 1400, the arrangement appears to have been satisfactory: in an extant account dated three years after Alice's death relating to some of the properties belonging to James Ormond, husband of Alice's great-granddaughter, Hazelbury was still being farmed for cash and the tenant was one John Carpenter.[18]

Sutton Poyntz is 15 miles due south of Hazelbury. At the edge of the chalk downs nestling under the brow of a hill, it is approached either by the coast road from the east or the main Dorchester–Weymouth highway. Narrow winding lanes ensure that despite its rural charm it is hardly overrun by tourists. And it *is* charming. A typical Wessex village with thatched cottages and country gardens, old brick mill and mill pond awash with water fowl, its scenic appeal so enchanted Thomas Hardy that he changed its name to Overcombe and used it as the setting for his novel *The Trumpet Major*. There is no church at Sutton Poyntz; St Ann's at Preston is about a mile away. Less than a mile beyond that is the sea.

Like Hazelbury, Sutton Poyntz was a fairly substantial estate of over 1,000 acres, with a manor house, stables, 29 messuages, 11 cottages, 6 closes, 8 tofts, a water mill, grain mill and a decayed fulling mill. Sheep and chalk downs are usually synonymous and the sloping hill with its grazing sheep behind the village is no exception. Five centuries ago much of the land was pastoral and sheep folds are mentioned in the inquisition held at Alice's death. There was also land valued at 12*d* and 2*s* an acre, which must have been the fields of the coastal plain. In *The Trumpet Major* the good-natured and hard-working Miller Loveday was a man noted for his wealth. If the area was able to produce abundant grain in the nineteenth century then it could have done so 400 years earlier. Sutton Poyntz seems to have been a well-balanced estate, suitable for both arable and pastoral farming and capable therefore of providing most of the basic needs of a medieval household.

Can we deduce from this that Dame Alice lived at Sutton Poyntz? A modern house called St Briavels close to the mill, named perhaps after the field in which it was built, may be evidence of the Bryan ownership, for Lord Bryan owned St Briavels castle in Wales. This saint, reputedly a hermit from the Forest of Dean, did not enjoy much popularity beyond a local cult. But this does not tell us anything about Alice. However, in 1395 only a small proportion of the average £60 annual income from rents was recorded by Micheldever as having been paid in silver and gold. Other amounts are mentioned as if they were rents in kind, such as 4s 4d 'as of the price of 2,000 oysters', 106s 8d 'in place of two pipes of wine' and 20d worth of white salt. These items together with values rated as pigs, stockfish, herrings and eels imply that Alice was resident there for some time that year and had instructed her receiver to buy victuals with the cash he collected from the rents.

No manor house remains at Sutton Poyntz. Hardy wrote of 'an ancient building formerly a manor-house but now a mill', though whether this was based on oral tradition or an example of poetic licence is impossible to tell. The present old brick mill does not look as if it could ever have been anything else, but the manor house must have been close by. Opposite the mill were old barns and farm buildings, now converted into houses and flats. The rest of the village is clustered around the mill race and the small lane that descends across the side of the Downs. But wherever and whenever Alice lived at Sutton Poyntz it must have presented a complete contrast to her other manors with its sheltered position and open vistas down to the sea. We do not know with what sadness she left it nor the nostalgia for Dorset that chill East Anglian days may have induced, but Hardy paints an idyllic picture:

Immediately before her was the large smooth mill-pond, overfull, and intruding into the hedge and into the road. The water, with its flowing leaves and spots of froth, was stealing away, like Time, under the dark arch, to tumble over the slimy wheel within. On the other side of the mill-pond was an open place called the Cross, because it was three-quarters of one, two lanes and a cattle-drive meeting there. It was the general rendez-vous and arena of the surrounding village. Behind this a steep slope rose high into the sky, merging into a wide and open down, now littered with sheep newly shorn. The upland by its height completely sheltered the mill and village from north winds, making summers of spring, reducing winters to autumn temperatures, and permitting myrtle to flourish in the open air.[19]

DAME ALICE'S EAST ANGLIAN ESTATES

When Alice was first married she must have considered the possibility of making her home in Dorset and renting out the Suffolk farms. Sir Guy's early death in 1386 need not have freed her from a sense of attachment to the West Country and anyhow she would have been bound by the ties of her husband's affinities. Once widowed, however, with both daughters married, an inheritance waiting for her, her mother and half-siblings settled in Suffolk, it is not surprising that she decided to return to Acton. Moreover the proximity of most of her East Anglian properties meant that she could manage these estates personally, support her household largely with the produce of the land and be more or less self-sufficient.

East Anglia was an expanding area in the later Middle Ages and enjoyed a dynamic economy. Recovery from the ravages of the plague epidemics seems to have been swifter here than in many other areas. Farmers prospered from the fertile soil, a productive fine loam over clay and medium to heavy clay loam, which was ideal for arable cultivation. Conditions were also suitable for pastoral farming and a buoyant cloth trade flourished in the numerous small villages of the Babergh Hundred where most of Alice's farms were. Many East Anglian families rose to prominence in the fifteenth century from the rich rewards of successful farming.

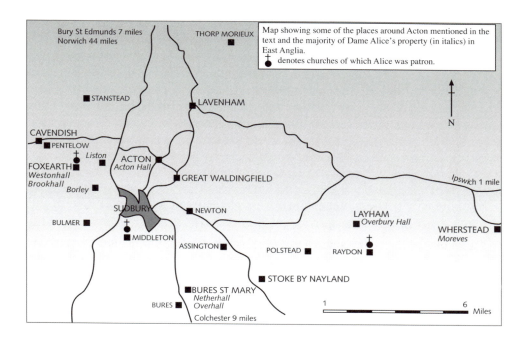

Map showing some of the places around Acton mentioned in the text and the majority of Dame Alice's property (in italics) in East Anglia.

✝ denotes churches of which Alice was patron.

The Acton manor that Dame Alice made her home was a very profitable farm even when her great-grandfather Sir Robert de Bures had acquired it from his wife, Hilary de Hodebovile in 1310. It was still being well maintained with a complete estate staff on the death of Alice's grandmother in 1392, although she had lived at Wivenhoe and had produce sent to her there. A few years before this it was estimated to be worth over £90 gross in terms of income and produce and the figures show there was an even distribution between money-producing income, such as rents, and goods-producing like wool and stock.[20] With nearly 900 acres of meadow, pasture and woodland it could have been entirely self-sufficient for a small household, but it was managed in such a way that the potential of the other estates could also be exploited.

The hallmark of Alice's managerial policy in East Anglia rested on the interdependency of those of her manors and lands that were within reasonable reach of Acton. There was considerable movement of stock between the manors, and the outlying farms contributed to the quantities of stock and grain that were needed to maintain the Acton household, feed the guests and provide liveries, with some surplus for sale. Apart from this direct farming, parcels of land and cottages on the other estates were also rented for cash. Those properties that were further afield were largely let with small areas kept to support the main farm.

On the death of her mother in 1406 Alice inherited Brookhall and Westonhall at Foxearth, 5 miles to the west of Acton, totalling nearly 700 acres. The land was particularly suitable for cattle farming and manure from the herds helped to increase the arable yield. Generally at least double the quantity of cattle that grazed at Acton were at pasture on the Foxearth estates and the production of corn was sometimes high. In 1409, for example, the bailiff there accounted for some 67 cows and 30 calves as well as over 180 quarters of newly harvested corn. Even after a large proportion of this produce had been issued to the Acton household, wheat for the daily bread, barley for making ale, mixed grain for the workers' quarterly liveries and the stock that provided roasts of beef, veal, mutton, lamb, pork and suckling pig, there was sufficient surplus to raise over £20 in sales.

Stock, especially sheep, was frequently driven between Acton and Foxearth and also to another of Alice's properties at Bures St Mary, 6 miles to the south. This was a smaller estate of 300 acres, some of which was alder, broom and thorn trees, with two farms called Overhall and Netherhall. Cash income came from land rents and property in Bures St Mary, together with the rent of a dairy herd and sale of timber. Alice and her household also enjoyed a variety of more exotic produce from Bures, including sticks of freshwater eels, conies and pigeons.

Raydon, 10 miles to the east with also about 300 acres, had been part of Alice's grandmother's dowry. It was another estate that had been farmed directly by the de Suttons who had frequently had produce sent back to their main residence at Wivenhoe. Alice appears to have continued this practice of direct farming for some time. However, maintaining staff there, together with the costs of repairs for farm implements, buildings and houses, became a mounting expense and there was also an annual £12 charge on this small estate for the manor of Merkys which Alice rented from her half-brother.[21] When Alice first settled at Acton, cattle and sheep were driven to pasture in the Raydon fields and beef and pork occasionally sent to stock the Acton larder. By 1428, however, the management of this small estate had been rationalized: the manor house was rented out, although some of the demesne lands were still retained for Alice's use and smaller quantities of stock and produce issued to the Acton household.

Closer to Acton, a mile to the east, is the small hamlet of Great Waldingfield. Alice's holding here was something over 100 acres. No manor house was specified in her Inquisition Post Mortem, but in an undated account the Waldingfield bailiff accounted for the rent of one together with a garden, dovecot and pightle (a local Middle English word for a piece of land). Evidence from extant accounts of 1428 and 1431 indicates that a large proportion of this property was let to Thomas Reigham for over £15 and on one occasion Dame Alice employed Reigham's reapers to help with the Acton harvest. She also collected an annual £5 rent for a barn there, but continued to retain some of the land for her own use, for grazing sheep and making hay. Once a tenant had been found who was prepared to rent the Waldingfield estate, it made better sense than renting out several small plots or attempting to farm it directly. However, the proximity of Waldingfield to Acton made flexibility in terms of the lease, or attitude of the tenant farmer, desirable.

Wherstead, with its manor called Moreves and 250 acres, was some 15 miles east of Acton and rented for cash. Maintaining a farm staff at that distance to cultivate land and graze animals for the household's use would have involved high transport costs, a major consideration in agricultural policy. Revenue here was very low compared with the similar property at Great Waldingfield which suggests a copyhold or long lease, negotiated at a time of low rents. In 1428 the tenant John Payn claimed several allowances for repairs to the house and dovecot; further expenses included the costs of various members of Alice's council going there to hold courts. In 1413 the wife of Thomas Payn was invited to dinner. Since Ralph Chamberlain, a member of Alice's council, was also a guest that day, it seems likely that her husband held the Moreves' lease at that time and there was business to discuss.

Alice's tenant in 1428 at Thorp Morieux was John Pypere. Like Moreves the farm at Thorp Morieux was not farmed directly and it is not easy to locate significant evidence of how it was managed. It does not appear to have been part of the original Bures' estate since it was not mentioned in the inquisitions held on the deaths of Alice, her mother or great-grandmother, but it passed to Alice's daughter in 1435.[22] It had originally belonged to the Morieux family and passed to John Strange, MP for Norfolk between 1388 and 1406, when he married the Morieux heiress. Subsequently Strange was crippled by debt and it appears Alice's stepfather had an interest in it.[23] It has not been possible to ascertain whether Alice acquired tenure of this estate by purchase, mortgage or inheritance.

Although Alice's receiver accounted for rent and allowances from Thorp Morieux in 1428, two years later there was a modification in the accounting system and along with figures for Acton and Wherstead it was noted that it was dealt with elsewhere, as was the revenue from a further property at Polstead. This was a small tenement called Bakespyes, rented by the appropriately named John Bakyswell. Possibly he did not live up to his name for in 1431 there were outstanding arrears of over 40s though the annual rent was less than half that sum.

Gradually over the forty-odd years that Alice de Bryene had been farming her East Anglian estates there is evidence of some change. Acton, Foxearth and possibly Bures were still being farmed directly with some demesne lands being rented out as they had always been when not needed by the home farm. At Waldingfield and Layham, like Raydon, there was a retreat from direct farming towards greater leasing, a cheaper and administratively more effective method of capitalizing on assets. It is impossible to tell whether this was a deliberate policy in response to changing circumstances, economic or otherwise, but it parallels developments on other estates at this time. Alice's basic needs had not changed: she still had the primary task of providing for her household and estate workers and getting the farms to pay for themselves.

What then was Alice worth? In attempting to assess her income it is impossible to exclude a proportion of the value of her crops since to reach an estimate the most practical method is to use the *valors* (the estimated sum of the cash value of the estate) quoted at the end of the bailiffs' reports. Taking an average from all her estates and estimating totals where it is not always clear, we come to an approximate sum of £425 or 637 marks. In 1388 at the height of the quarrel between Lord Bryan and Sir William Bryan, the latter disclosed that Alice's daughters stood to inherit an income of 700 marks (£466) from their mother on her death. Let us then award Alice an annual income of about £400, the kind of wealth that has been described as impressive but hardly fabulous.[24] Insofar as it is possible to have confidence in any medieval figure, this sum is almost confirmed by figures from Alice's receiver's account of 1428–9; excluding income from Acton, and after various expenses, the receiver calculated he owed nearly £150. The estates in Dorset and Gloucestershire brought in about the same amount and Acton was worth at least £50.

Farmers are generally a conservative people and farming methods governed by tradition. Much of Alice de Bryene's policy was dictated by the fact that she chose Acton as her sole residence. Her needs were tailored, as were many landlords' at this time, by the demands of her household, and once she had established a routine that worked, there was little need to change it. She may also have been inhibited by previous *modi operandi*, such as long leases, though the decision to lease out Wherstead and reduce the staff at Raydon made good economic sense. We can, however, detect a few signs of innovation in an attempt to diversify and secure extra income, such as the marketing of coal at Oxenhall. In 1423, when Dame Alice was in her sixties, a new heading appeared on the back of the Acton bailiff's report between 'Garden' and 'Pigeons'. It read '*Cisera*: 3 pipes, 1 barell and part of a barell'. She made 16*s* 5*d* on the sale of this cider that year to various employees, but brewing it may not have been economically viable or perhaps it did not please the East Anglian palate, for the item did not appear again.[25]

SHEEP FARMING

Dorset and Suffolk were both areas where the growth of the economy in the 1500s related partly to the expansion of sheep farming: the fine medieval buildings in those counties and the surrounding areas bear witness to the rich returns earned by a flourishing wool trade. Sheep were a significant feature on Alice's estates and run on an intermanorial basis. She maintained shepherds and flocks at Acton, Foxearth, Waldingfield and Raydon, although the size of the flocks and income from wool sales varied greatly. In 1412–13, for example, there was a dearth of mutton and lamb for the larder during the winter and spring months and sometimes, as at Foxearth in 1405, there were no wool sales at all and only fourteen fleeces were released to the Acton household. Fleeces and wool

Shepherds with their flocks, from Queen Mary's Psalter, c. 1320.

flock were, however, often issued in other years to the steward to distribute to the household members. Ewes' milk was highly prized and used to make cheese once the lambs had been weaned. Outside sales of live animals were high. Sheep were often the means by which Alice's tenants and workers enriched themselves. In 1422–3, for example, she sold ninety-seven lambs to various tenants: once they could afford the initial investment, they built up their own flocks and after a few years were selling sheep back to Alice.

The expense of maintaining sheep proportionate to their value was minimal. The normal annual cost at Acton was £2, that is 10s for each shepherd's wage and less than a £1 for essentials, such as hurdles to secure the flocks at night, grease and tar for treating wounds and infections and pitch and ruddle for branding. Washing and shearing the sheep was not generally an expense: it may still have been a customary obligation of Alice's tenants in which case the women usually did it. However, a supervisor had to be paid when the shearing was done and bread and cheese provided. Oil was bought for the lamps used during the lambing season, and there were other incidentals like the occasional rent of extra pasture, supplying oats to fatten the lambs, winter fodder, repairs to the sheep house, purchase of new stock and the payment of tithes.

To be a shepherd is possibly a lowly job and certainly a lonely one, but its affinity to the Christian ideology may have raised its status. Didactic literature from an earlier century, such as Bishop Grosseteste's *Rules* (written in 1240) and the anonymous *Walter of Henley* (written in about 1270), which were both still in circulation in 1400, was full of advice to estate owners about the appointment of shepherds and their necessary qualities.[26] First it was important that each shepherd find good sureties 'delt trover bon plegges' to answer for his behaviour, since a flock was a valuable asset and owners needed to be wary of the employee who left his flocks to go, for example, to wrestling matches or the tavern. The shepherd's duties were manifold: he had to repair fences and hurdles, make folds, be especially vigilant during the lambing season, wean the lambs, check for disease and worms, help shear and brand the flocks and know which creatures to cull or sell and which to fatten for the table.

A gentle nature was essential: 'Looke that your sheapherd be not too testye [angrie] for thorow anger some of the shepe may be harassed', and the employer was advised to see 'wheather your sheepe goe feeding with the shepheard going amongst them, for if the sheepe goe shunning him it is no signe that he is gentle with them'. It was expected that a good shepherd would sleep with his sheep, as indeed should carters with their horses and cowherds with their cattle, though swineherds were not required to spend the night with their pigs. Particular care had to be taken as winter approached in case any animal ate 'the film of an autumn fog and small white snails'. This 'white dew' was especially pernicious between late summer and early autumn, and it was recommended that a herb called amerock or 'mayden's wede' be gathered, dried and put in the sheepcots at Martinmas to drive out 'the evil humour'.[27]

WAGES OF FARM STAFF

Such labour and dedication obviously cost money. But where the wages of most of Alice's estate staff were gradually increased, those of the shepherds remained the same over the years. The wages she paid her estate workers in the 1390s were already in excess of those laid down by law a few years earlier. In 1388 Parliament reaffirmed the wages recommended by the Ordinance of Labourers 1349, when a shortage of labour after the first epidemic of the plague had caused a crisis. The Ordinance had stipulated an annual wage of 10*s* for a carter, 6*s* 8*d* for an oxherd and cowherd, 7*s* for plough drivers and 6*s* for swineherds and women labourers.[28] In 1396–7 Alice's bailiff received 20*s*, the harvest-reeve got 15s, carters were paid 13s 4d and members of the plough team and the herdsmen were given 10s each. Twenty-two years later, the bailiff and harvest-reeve received bonuses worth 6s 8d and 5s respectively in the form of a clothes allowance, the carters' pay had increased to 18s with both receiving clothes allowances and bundles of faggots as well. The chief members of the plough team had also received increases, now earning 13s 4d, while the shepherds still had 10s each, the swineherd 2s less and the cowherd was only paid 5s: this may reflect the decreasing size of the manor herds since more cattle were rented out. Throughout this period the salary of the manor maidservants remained the same at 8s per annum.

By 1431 the wages of one of the carters had equalled that of the bailiff and the plough team were being paid more, but herdsmen were paid less and there was only one shepherd at Acton. This could be because the Acton flocks were smaller than previously, although we cannot tell whether this reduction was a deliberate policy or a seasonal shortage. The decrease of the other herdsmen's salaries in comparison with the wages of the rest of the workers demonstrates that the cost of arable in contrast to pastoral farming was increasing quite rapidly and the cost of transport had become a major item. The fact that Alice de Bryene's permanent farm staff were being paid above the recommended national wage may be an indication that current market rates in East Anglia were higher than elsewhere, a reflection of local prosperity.

CATTLE

Cowherds were traditionally paid less than shepherds. Alice's received an average annual stipend of 5s but compared with the shepherd's it was a less demanding job. Advice to estate owners on the management of cattle was as rigorous and detailed as that given about shepherds. Among other suggestions, Walter of Henley advised, 'if theare bee any beaste that begynneth to falle in fleshe bestowe the coste to helpe him up againe, for it is commonly sayed in reproofe, "Blessed be that peny which saveth meny"'.[29] The Acton herds were insufficient for the table, and beef and veal supplies were often bought in. In fact there is evidence that there were occasional problems with Alice's cattle: in 1419 all the cows were barren despite the fact that at the beginning of the year two bulls were at pasture in the Acton fields, and calves frequently died of murrain.

Cattle were also kept for lactage and manure and renting out the dairy herds increasingly became a useful source of income. But overall the profit margins on

Cowherds with their cows, from Queen Mary's Psalter, c. 1320.

cattle were less than sheep. New stock was much more expensive – the average price of a cow was over 10*s* compared with a shilling for a sheep and a penny for a lamb. In the winter months large quantities of hay and fodder had to be expended to keep the herds alive. Nevertheless, like Alice's sheep, cattle were an essential part of the farm. And nothing was wasted: hides were tanned and sold and leather used to make tackle for horses and to repair carts.

ARABLE FARMING

On 15 June 1413 the harvest-reeve dined at the manor with nine manor workers and four carters. This was the beginning of the hay-making season and dry weather was essential to ensure the necessary supply of winter fodder for stock. For the next two weeks the carters were often guests at Acton, a welcome respite no doubt from their labours. However, it seems they did not work over the midsummer weekend (24–5 June), a time of traditional rural festivity and revelry,[30] and we know the weather was sultry and hot that year, at least in the north of England. Margery Kempe was returning from a pilgrimage with her husband and recounts, '. . . one Friday, Midsummer Eve, in very hot weather – as this creature was coming from York carrying a bottle of beer in her hand, and her husband a cake tucked inside his clothes against his chest . . .'.[31]

Although the cost of labour was rising there was no obvious increase in yields of corn, but then the success of arable farming depends as much on the weather as farming practices. The measures required to grow corn and pulses dominated the medieval calendar and cash had to be paid for numerous expenses such as ploughing, sowing, reaping and carting, and the capital investment in a stock of plough beasts and their maintenance could be very high. Then there were repairs to the ploughs, purchase of seed where necessary, the wages of the workers engaged in all aspects of the harvest, and the expense of the harvest feast itself.

The arable cycle started soon after Michaelmas when the fields that were to be sown with the winter crops of wheat and rye had to be ploughed. On 2 November 1412 the harvest-reeve dined with nine workers, either in preparation for or as a celebration of the event. Even as these bread grains were being sown, the previous summer's crop had to be threshed and winnowed. Members of the household were paid extra for this task. During the autumn and winter months, the plough beasts were kept in to be fattened and the ploughs and carts repaired. Various carpenters, who came to overhaul the farm machinery, ate at Acton in November and February 1412–13. The spring ploughing began a little late that year, perhaps because of the inclement weather, and the bailiff, harvest-reeve, various household members and twelve 'strange' ploughmen came to dine on 27, 28 and 29 April. This may have marked the completion of their labours since a minstrel joined the company on the last day and special food such as garfish, sole and plaice was included on the menu.

Before the spring sowing of barley, oats, legumes and vetches, stable dung, soil from the dovecots and marl were spread over the fields. But members of the plough team were not yet entirely free to attend to their own plots because the fallow fields had to be ploughed as well. Once more the ploughs needed attention: on 2 June two carpenters were invited to the manor again. As the days lengthened and once the seed had sprouted, presuming the human scarecrows had done their job properly, the corn fields needed to be weeded. By August the harvest was ready, and in 1413, at the beginning of that month, the harvest-reeve and sixteen boon workers assembled at the manor. This was Lammas, a feast associated with both husbandry and the spiritual harvest, for traditionally it was not only the day when the harvest was actually supposed to begin but also when the first newly harvested grain was consecrated as a Eucharist offering. Boon workers coming to work in Alice's fields that year accounted for the equivalent of over 590 days' work, the household 225 days. The bulk of the harvest was completed 28 days later on 29 August, just a month before Michaelmas.

The harvest was a significant charge on the manorial income. Tenants, neighbours and local farmers were paid to help but most of the work was done by the boon workers for whom the customary obligation may have been something of a chore. Throughout August the Acton household was busy baking and brewing. Instead of the usual five- to six-day interval, these tasks were undertaken every two or three days for the harvest was a wet boon with workers receiving ale with their wheaten loaves at the midday break. More meat and fish than usual were delivered from the store house to the kitchens, and eggs and dairy produce purchased in abundance. Gloves were provided for the chief reapers and dishes, jugs, spoons and cloths purchased for the feast. In 1421 over £9 was spent on victuals for the harvesters, £2 more than the cost of the harvest work itself. Money for the feast held at the completion of the harvest was paid by Dame Alice rather than her bailiff and we can be fairly certain that she attended it herself. Until the end of the nineteenth century the harvest in Suffolk was celebrated with the 'Horkey Feast', which comprised all kinds of rituals, noisy pantomimes and a great deal of quaffing of ale; 'hallooing largesse', when reapers demanded a tip from visitors to the fields (usually the landlord or farmer), was a traditional pastime.[32]

We have walked enough around Alice de Bryene's estates to appreciate that she must have been very much involved in administration and forward planning, as any estate owner would have been. Many women of her class would have participated in this type of management in a similar way if they wished to reap the maximum benefit from their farms. Although much of the day-to-day organization was delegated to employees, the supervision would have been considerable, with decisions to make and new strategies to implement. There were changes over the forty-year period during which Dame Alice was in possession of these estates, but nothing of a radical nature. The bailiffs' reports begin to have a different physical appearance, but this may be due as much to the rise of lay literacy and the improved training of officials as to a growing ambition on the part of landowners to have as much information as possible about their estates. The annual reports become longer and more detailed over the years and in the last two there are even separate receipts

The day's end: calendar page for February, c. 1380.

attached. In the decade after Alice's death some of the rents and the income from her manors appear to have fallen as is demonstrated by the accounts of James Ormond, due in part perhaps to the absence of a landlord at the manor and the lack of a continual personal involvement with the daily activities of the farms. The next century was to bring even more dramatic changes.[33] But for the most part during Dame Alice's tenure, despite the turmoil in the wider world of politics and religion, day must have followed day on her estates in as predictable a fashion as life on a farm can be.

CHAPTER 4
The Gentle Lifestyle

When Richard II chose the white hart as his emblem and had badges made in its image for his retainers to wear, it was as if he had appointed himself the head of a primitive totem and his followers could expect to benefit from the inherent symbolic qualities of the hart – its potency, regal stance and connection with the Christ image, resurrection and rebirth. Livery badges were just one way of displaying affinity to a particular magnate or family. Display and appearances mattered in the Middle Ages and were essential features of any household. This display was part of a person's 'worship' or 'honour', relating to his reputation and

Badge of the White Hart, c. 1377–99, which may have belonged to one of Richard II's followers.

the esteem in which he expected to be held. To be associated with such an honour was an important status symbol and the means by which people prospered and humbler folk might improve their situations. When Richard Micheldever wrote to Alice de Bryene in about 1397 concerning the governance of her household, he expressed the wish that her honour would increase and added that it would bring joy and comfort to all her friends and servants – '. . . tiele en[cress]e de vostre honour qe a tous vos amys & seruantz del oier soit ioie et confort'.[1]

Alice's marriage to Sir Guy Bryan had brought the promise of greater wealth and status – had he lived he would have inherited not only his father's estates but also possibly his title. This potential pecuniary and social advancement faded with his early death. While her decision not to remarry removed another opportunity to join the ranks of the nobility, it did not deprive Alice of an honourable status. As a widow she was 'lord' of the manor and head of her own household. It has been said that even in widowhood women were ensconced within 'a male-dominated, male-orientated patriarchal superstructure';[2] this may have been the reality, but that does not necessarily mean they acted exactly like men. It has also been argued that honour stemmed not only from masculine concepts of chivalric virtue, such as being bound to one's word and prowess in the field, but also and especially for women from acting with integrity and giving help and protection to friends, family and servants.[3] Women contributed different concerns to the communities in which they lived, attitudes that may have been more personal. Many married women headed households in the absence of their husbands, but widows had the advantage of complete autonomy and ultimate accountability to no one but themselves. Within the structured hierarchy of medieval society, which admittedly was fluid as fortunes rose and fell, widows like Alice can be said to have belonged to a class of their own.

A widow from the land-owning class was able to enjoy running her own household because she was financially independent, unlike peasant widows who often had a hard struggle to eke out an existence. However, as we have seen in the quarrel between Lord Bryan and Sir William, they needed to be constantly vigilant to protect their inheritance or that of their children. Wealthy married women could not always be assured of an easy time either: Elizabeth Berkeley became involved in a property dispute with her cousin James on the death of her father in 1417, a lawsuit that was not finally settled until 1609. Her household accounts of 1420–1 give details of a very hasty journey that appears to have been related to an attack on one of her properties by James Berkeley. That year she also made journeys to conduct business in London and join her husband for two

Encaustic tile with the Bryan arms, formerly at Shaftesbury Abbey.

months in Walthamstow while he was on leave from the French wars. But otherwise her accounts record the usual domestic details of the management of a great household.[4] The focus in Alice's accounts is similar but should also be seen in the context of her individual circumstances in the 1400s. Essentially she was a farmer and life in her sedentary household reflects that of an estate owner based in a rural landscape. Moreover as a widow the quality of her lifestyle may have related more to the maintenance of her status than a desire for social advancement.

Status was related to wealth with which the display was commensurate. A show of wealth, courtesy, largess and hospitality helped to remind visitors of the power and influence of their hostess and her household and the benefits that might accrue from an association with her. In a recent study of medieval noblewomen, households are described of those whose annual income ranged from the fabulous £3,000 of Margaret de Brotherton, Duchess of Norfolk, to the more modest £400 enjoyed by Alice de Byrene.[5] The main difference was one of degree. All aspects of life in the household were expected to reflect the honour of the householder, the quality and quantity of plate, jewels, livery, gowns, furs, furniture, gifts, retinue, mode of travel, type of food served, entertainment provided, books owned – consumption had to be conspicuous. Association with social and influential peers and the dispensation of patronage were also important factors. Nor was piety neglected, with alms given, masses said, feast days and rituals observed, and fine vestments, vessels and tapestries on display in the chapel.

Alice's annual income was sufficient to guarantee a modestly lavish display and ensured that these trappings reflected her position in the local community. Visually, in the absence of a complete wardrobe account, this requires some imagination. First it was essential that retainers were appropriately dressed so that the householder's social status was immediately visible. The granting of livery was an expensive charge on the household. It was not only a way of ensuring a display of rank but also of providing remuneration in kind, above the annual cash wage and sustenance in the household. One summer at Acton, when livery had to be provided for twenty-four household members, Alice's chamberlain and her nine valets were dressed in green coloured cloth; since it appears that each was awarded nearly 8 yards, at just under a shilling a yard, their apparel may have included capes and hoods as well as tunics and surcoats. The six boys, being smaller perhaps, and certainly less important, were clothed more cheaply: their liveries at 5s each consisted of only 6 yards of material, valued at 10d a yard. The two maids, squires and chaplains were granted a sum of 8s each rather than specific cloth, so there may have been a variety of colours amid the green if this implies they were given freedom of choice. Alice paid over £8 for this summer livery; no details were given that year for winter cloths.[6]

Sometime before this, however, we know she paid £36 for the annual liveries and £26 for the winter clothes, which included furs for her ministers and the various members of her council. In another account the number of furs is specified as twenty. Earlier her receiver in the West Country had accounted for an annual charge of £11 for livery for her retinue there. That cloth, which was purchased locally in Salisbury, was striped. Whether the particular colour or design reflects an idiosyncratic impulse or a limited choice on the market cannot easily be determined, but no doubt Alice's retainers looked elegant in their summer and winter attire and their uniform appearance reflected the honour, unity and authority of her household. Even Alice's bailiff at Oxenhall was expected to wear her colours there, although she may have visited the estate very infrequently, if at all, in later years.

The warm winter clothes also served a practical purpose as insulation against the cold and draughts. Enormous quantities of firewood were expended annually at the Acton manor, though much must have been consumed in the kitchen, bakehouse, for brewing ale and heating water for laundry and washing. But we can also be certain that there was a large open hearth in Alice's hall even if parts of the rest of the house sometimes suffered from a winter chill. Timber and logs were culled from the estate and faggots provided for the chamber, which indicates that Dame Alice had a fire in her private quarters as well. Damp walls and rough floors need not necessarily have been an eyesore since floors were often tiled and walls decorated with painted designs. The carpets and tapestries that Henry Scrope left her in his will[7] are unlikely to have been the only ones owned by Alice and may well have graced her chamber, while the floor of the hall, the communal living and eating area, even if tiled, would have been strewn with rushes, herbs and sweet-smelling grasses.

Though we have to imagine her retinue in their splendid green or striped costumes, we can find visual images of the kind of dress Dame Alice may have worn on the monumental brasses in many parish churches. She would probably have had a head covering of some sort, for usually only young girls were bareheaded,[8] and worn a long gown or tunic. We know she favoured dark colours, as was considered appropriate for widows, for in 1429 her receiver claimed for the cost of a dozen yards each of both blue and black linen at 3s 4d and 2s 8d a yard. He also bought half a yard of black velvet, useful for an elegant but subtle trim, and 5 yards of blue lierre which at 5s a yard was very good quality woollen cloth. Lierre came from a town of that name 10 miles south-east of Antwerp. In 1441 Margaret Paston complained to her husband that she only had one winter gown made of lierre and it was 'so comerous that I ham wery to wer yt';[9] she was also carrying his child. But if Alice did not generally embrace ostentation, she did not deny herself some luxury: over 100 small rabbit skins were delivered to her chamber in 1419, sufficient to make caps, muffs, mittens and line the collars and sleeves of several gowns. Further elegance could be provided by a valuable brooch used to fasten the tunic, silver, gold or jewelled buttons on the sleeves and a finely woven silk girdle tied at the waist.[10] Women often carried their personal seals with them tied at the end of their girdles.

Clothes have always been items of display. Once an immediate way of recognizing social status, the Sumptuary Laws of 1363 attempted to regulate the lifestyle of the different social orders to reaffirm social distinctions, since the lower ranks had begun to ape the fashions of the nobility. This was particularly so in styles of dress as many retainers were left clothes by their employers. Testators often described their gowns and furs in meticulous detail while others were more modest. Alice's daughter Elizabeth left garments to various women friends and servants, which she recorded with the minimum of fuss thus '*unam togam negram*' (a black gown), '*unam tunicam*' (a tunic), though we may presume they were of good quality and reflected her rank.[11] Furs could also be expensive and were often imported. Lady Peryne Clanbowe left four gowns in 1422 to women friends, all lined with different kinds of Baltic squirrel.[12] The furs that Alice de Bryene granted twenty of her retainers at Christmas 1419 were not described but said to have been worth 1*s* 3*d* each so are likely to have been tippets for collars, sleeves or hoods. This appears to have been a standard grant for almost exactly the same sum figures in an earlier account.

Apart from liveries and clothes, a further opportunity for display was the collection of silver plate traditionally exhibited on a sideboard in the hall and set on the table for dinner. Silver was frequently bequeathed in wills: Sir Guy left all

The Rokewode mazer, or drinking cup, made of maplewood, c. 1400. The inscription reads (in modern English), Hold your tongue and say the best, and let your neighbour sit in rest; Whoso lusteth God to please, let his neighbour live in ease.

his silver vessels to Alice, and by her son-in-law Henry Scrope she was promised a covered gilded mazer. Mazers were traditionally made of maplewood and often bound in silver. Other drinking vessels might be made of silver, glass or even more exotically of coconut.[13] Silver bowls were often custom-made, such as the one Lady Alice West left her daughter Alianore on which were engraved her arms and those of her late husband.[14] Spoons and cups might be engraved as well, for example, those bearing the Bryan arms that Walter Trote, rector of the Slapton chantry, bequeathed to the college in his will.[15] Alice would have had similar items to impress her guests. On Lord Bryan's death she appears to have exercised a concession sometimes given to executors to purchase chattels at a reasonable price before they were offered on the open market, and spent over £80 on a variety of goods, most of which were clearly luxury items. These included a dozen salt cellars and dishes, 4 basins, 3 candlesticks, 2 wine decanters and 2 ewers, all in silver. The salt cellars and dishes alone cost £22, which suggests they were rather decorative and ornate items.

Alice's other purchases from Lord Bryan's estate were quite curious. The half-tester she bought for 3s 4d, which would have graced one of her beds, may have had some sentimental value, and the hoods or caps embellished with the Bryan coat of arms, for which she paid an impressive 5s a piece, must have enhanced her prestige when worn by her household officials. But what are we to make of the purchase of two coats of armour, one of which was engraved and came with a set of arms and the other, which cost 30s, less than half the price of the first and described as 'old'? She may have thought of giving them to her sons-in-law or perhaps she bought them for their scrap metal or sentimental value. Whatever her motives we might reflect on her commercial sense and ask whether she had an eye for a bargain. But perhaps we should not be too certain that Dame Alice was interested in economy or wanted to have mementos of her loved ones, because four years later she paid fairly substantial sums to have new silver articles made from old: £6 was spent on refashioning twelve new silver dishes from sauce boats, a dozen specially designed spoons and a couple of new chargers. Refashioning old silver was not unusual and suggests that like many of her contemporaries Alice was keen to keep up with the latest fashion, another way to impress acquaintances.

Silver was an investment as were jewels, which could be fashioned into valuable items. Scrope left Alice a little gold tablet containing an image of the Virgin Mary with glass in front and carved behind, and a crystal with an image of St Christopher at the back. While these might have been on show in her chamber

Heron, an epicurean delight, served by Alice de Bryene to her favoured guests and occasionally given as a present.

or chapel, they could also have been worn like the diamonds and sapphires left by John Filliol to his daughters, who lived with Alice in the 1390s.[16] We have no evidence of any of Alice's personal jewellery but if Richard Goldsmith, an Acton guest in July and August 1413, lived up to his name, then she may have been investing in gold. In 1429 when she was nearly seventy her receiver John Pellican was instructed to buy a gold brooch or badge worth 13*s*, two gold rings at 7*s* 6*d* each and another for 5*s*. These may have been New Year gifts for at the same time he purchased a dozen pairs of gloves at 7*d* a pair. Giving presents was another way of enhancing one's prestige. Rings might be given or lent to friends or loved ones as a memento, such as the one bearing the image of St Margaret that Margaret Paston sent to her husband in 1441 'for a rememrav[n]se tyl ye come home'. It was a token of affectionate irony since St Margaret was not only her namesake but the patroness of childbirth and she was pregnant at the time.[17]

Gifts could be more ephemeral in the form of delicacies like the herons, swans and conies Alice occasionally gave her favoured estate workers. The provision of exotic food and a sumptuous spread were an essential feature of any large medieval household. At Acton a special effort was made to impress important guests: swan, goose, heron, cony, pheasant, partridge, pigeon and shellfish were frequently served when Alice's peers came to dine. However, while it is often believed that medieval households were open to all who wanted a meal, a scrutiny of Alice's guest list challenges this assumption. It was customary to offer food to diners in pairs, but on only fifteen occasions in 1413 were there an odd number of visitors for dinner, suggesting that guest lists were actually carefully planned.

The winter season is generally considered to have been the period for hospitality since the demands of husbandry and routine farm administration made summer a less popular time for entertaining. But when exceptions are made for the increase in numbers in January due to the New Year celebrations that Alice hosted and the extra meals for the harvesters in August, then the monthly total of guests at Acton was fairly consistent with a noticeable drop in numbers between January and the end of March. This may reflect the fact that the majority of guests at Acton were agricultural workers and winter a fallow season, rather than the scarcity of fresh food and austere diet that the Lenten ritual imposed.

The most popular days for guests were the flesh days, with most visitors calling on Sundays, then Thursdays, followed closely by Mondays and Tuesdays. Of the fish days Saturdays were the least popular. Visits from ecclesiastics were evenly balanced and appear to reflect the liturgical calendar. Some, like the Colchester friars, may have taken a vow not to eat meat, since they usually came on a fish day. Social peers might call on any day of the week. Though the number of visitors was higher on Sundays, the guest lists for those days were in no way remarkable, consisting of the usual mix of estate officials, workers, clergy and social peers, except that proportionally more women were invited. Catering reflected seasonal supply, but generally Alice was able to organize balanced and varied meals throughout the year.

There is no real evidence of a paucity of fresh meat at the dinner table in the winter months after the mid-November Martinmas kill because when her home-farmed supplies were low she increased her purchases of beef, pork and lamb. Excluding the Lenten season, beef and pork were served every month of the year in 1412–13 in consistent quantities, veal from December to August and suckling pig from December to July. Lamb and mutton were plentiful in the summer months but less evident during the rest of the year and neither was served between mid-February and the end of May. Taking Lent and fast days into account, meat was actually only eaten for about 50 per cent of the year, providing an average daily helping of over 1 lb per diner.[18] However, helpings were probably considerably less than this once bone and inedible parts were excluded and some used for making stock and patties.

As well as the provision of high status food like swan and heron to impress special guests, delicacies such as veal and capon were served in most months and, as in other contemporary households, pigeons were not eaten in the winter.[19] Game such as venison and wild boar was not served in 1413 perhaps because a large proportion of the land around Acton was cultivated, although partridges for the table were reared in the manor grounds. Alice's great-grandfather had been granted free-warren at the Wherstead manor and her stepfather had a similar right on his Smallbridge estate. The last hunting party to be mentioned in the accounts was at Raydon in the late 1380s. If the huntsman who stayed the night at Acton on 1 July 1413 had been employed by Alice to procure game, he was unsuccessful that year. But, nevertheless, the steward did account for boars purchased and presented to Alice for the table in other years, so they must have occasionally been enjoyed by her guests.

Fish was plentiful. The staple fish diet consisted of herrings, with more of the cheaper smoked red herrings bought than the pickled white. They were normally purchased in bulk, though sometimes on a daily basis. Salt fish and stockfish were served regularly, continuously throughout Lent with other fish and on most Fridays and Saturdays. Barrels of salmon and sturgeon were occasionally bought especially when there was a shortage of herrings. The proximity of Alice's manor to the coast meant that she was able to offer her guests an impressive variety of seafood: in 1412–13 she bought sole, haddock, plaice, mackerel, merling, turbot, brill, butts (a flat fish), cod, garfish, sparling, flathe, skate and sea-pike, as well as oysters, crabs, crayfish, mussels, shrimps and whelks. Oysters were plentiful and cost 2*d* for 120, though on 28 December, when there was probably a heavy local demand for the Christmas festivities, the price went up by a ½*d*. None was eaten between May and the end of August, a restriction still observed today, at least for home-reared produce – 'never eat an oyster unless there's an R in the month'. Eels were sent regularly by the miller from the stew pond at Alice's Bures estate, but occasionally there was a short supply when the pool had been poached.[20]

Contemporary cookbooks, such as *Curye on Inglysch*, compiled at the time of Richard II, contained a variety of recipes for many of which Alice had the ingredients in her store cupboard. Something for example like 'Connynges in Cyrip' may well have been served at Acton on 2 February 1413, the day dedicated to the Purification of the Blessed Virgin Mary when rabbit was on the menu:

Take connynges and seeth hem wel in good broth. Take wyne greke and do therto with a porcioun vyneger and flour of canel [cinnamon], hoole clowes, quybibles hoole [pepper] and oother good spices with raisouns, coraunce [currants] and gynguer ypared and yminced. Take vp the connynges and smyte hem on pecys and cast hem in to the siryppe and seeth hem a litel in fere and serue it forth.[21]

Rabbits were considered a rare and highly prized commodity in the later Middle Ages and were frequently on the menu at Acton in 1412–13, though none was eaten that year between April and August. In 1417–18 Alice's steward accounted for thirty-one delivered to the larder for the Christmas feast from the warren at Bures, and another eighty-two from the Acton manor. The following year the nets used for snaring them with ferrets had to be repaired. Rabbits, unlike hares, were not indigenous to Britain and had been introduced by the Normans in the thirteenth century. Initially they found the climate inhospitable and were largely confined to specially created warrens on land that was fit for nothing else. Warreners were employed to feed them in the winter and create artificial burrows to ensure successful and safe breeding. For many landowners rabbits were an important cash crop, though it appears Alice bred hers just for home consumption, exploiting the potential of otherwise barren land.[22] Conygarths (rabbit warrens) were still popular in Suffolk a century or so later, even celebrated one might say, as the following description makes clear:

Of the harmlesse Conies which do delight naturally to make their aboad here, I must say somewhat more, for their great increase, with rich profitt for all good housekeepers, hath made every one of any reckoning to prepare fitt harbour for them, with welcome and entertainment, from which it proceeds that there are so many warrens here in every place, which do furnish the next marketts . . . from whence it is that none who deems their houses well seated, who have nott to the same belonging a comonwealth of Conies, neither can hee bee deemed a good housekeeper that hath not plenty of these at all times to furnish his table.[23]

Fresh seasoning and herbs were used to flavour meat and fish and were either purchased from local producers, such as the onion and garlic accounted for in the Household Book, or sent over from the garden. Produce from the latter is mentioned in Alice's accounts but was estimated to have been worth less than in her grandmother's time when the yield was valued at 13s 4d. Peas grown on the home farm were delivered to the manor kitchens to mix with grain for a pottage or thick vegetable soup, a traditional supper dish. Apples and pears were grown in the kitchen gardens, and wild fruits and salads probably gathered too. Evidence now suggests that the consumption of fruit and vegetables was much higher among all social classes during this period than had previously been suspected:[24] analysis from cesspit drains demonstrates, for example, that strawberries were frequently eaten and in very large quantities.[25]

On average the Acton steward accounted for an annual sum of 52s spent on spices and dry products which works out at ½ oz of spice a day.[26] Spices in store included nuts and dried fruit, rice, saffron, cinnamon, pepper, ginger, cloves, mace, salt, sugar, honey and soda-ash or 'sandres' (cedar-wood), which may have been used for colouring like the saffron. Brightly coloured food was fashionable and was often blue as well as red and yellow. In comparison with the purchases made by Lady Margaret Cromwell for a similar size household in 1418, Alice's food may have been quite highly spiced and colourful.[27] What is particularly noticeable about her provisioning is the large quantity of mustard seed bought and the pittance of sugar, which might reflect an idiosyncratic taste for savoury

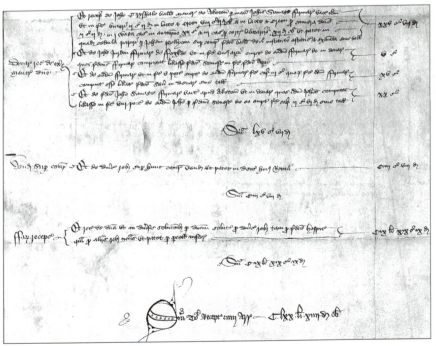

Steward's account for the Acton household, 1418–19, showing a total of £170 14½d received, mostly from Dame Alice but also from sales of wool, empty barrels and dairy produce.

flavours rather than a sweet tooth. It may also indicate the absence of a consistent provision of confectioneries, desserts and sweetmeats though some must have been made with the large quantities of honey purchased for the household. Honey was also used to preserve fruit and vegetables to provide a more balanced and varied diet during the winter months.[28]

Generally, however, we might conclude that dinner in Alice's hall was not so different to that in other gentry households. Nor did she stint herself as is demonstrated by her indulgence in rich and luxurious food on days traditionally held as feast days: on Shrove Tuesday (7 March) in 1413, for example, she served seven guests (none of whom could be considered social equals) and ten of her household capons, cony and heron, with a dessert to follow made of the eggs and milk she purchased that day. On the following day, Ash Wednesday, the household enjoyed 200 oysters, 200 whelks, half a flathe, 11 plaice and 2 haddocks, as well as the herrings, salt fish and stockfish that were the usual Wednesday fare. This feast cost Dame Alice one-tenth of her monthly expenditure on food. Though Ash Wednesday was traditionally a fast day, it was also the anniversary of the thirtieth day after Sir Guy Bryan's death and this important commemoration was marked with a special menu. Similarly large quantities of good fresh fish, butter and cream were ingredients for the meal served on Wednesday 31 May, the day on which prayers were said for Alice's parents-in-law.

Bread and ale were always home-produced at Acton, providing an average helping of one 2 lb loaf and about 3 pints of ale per person for each meal. Both bread and ale would have been consumed at breakfast and supper as well as at the midday meal. Many more white loaves were baked than brown suggesting that everyone at table ate white bread and the brown was sliced and used as trenchers, which might later have been sent out to the poor. The ale was a little weaker than that served in other households, though the quantity of a gallon per person a day was standard. In some larger households like that of Elizabeth Berkeley ale was purchased when needed rather than home-brewed.[29] Alice's social peers would have drunk wine at dinner, the average consumption of which was between a third and a quarter of a pint daily per person for the entire household and visitors. Since not everyone would have been offered it as a high proportion of the diners at Acton were farm labourers, it appears there was plenty of wine for important guests.

More red wine was consumed at Acton than white. The average annual purchase was three and a half pipes of red wine and two hogsheads of white. A pipe at 105 imperial gallons contained double the quantity of a hogshead. White wine soured more quickly than red and so was often bought in smaller containers. Alice occasionally bought white wine by the quart, which suggests something of a superior quality, as well as sweet white wines from Gascony, Malmsey (Spanish or Italian), and Romeney (from Greece). No mention is made in the Household Book of any consumption of these latter three wines, nor of the barrels of unspecified wine that she bought from time to time: she probably offered these to those particular guests she entertained in her chamber. These pipes and hogsheads were vast containers and transportation costs were high. Richard Mody once claimed 18d in expenses for going with a cart and seven horses to Colchester to collect a pipe of red wine. When Alice purchased wine from her Ipswich wine merchant, the appropriately named John Joye, she had to pay over 3s for delivery.

Of the £160 annual household expenditure accounted for by the steward William Burgh in 1419, approximately 50 per cent was spent on the household livery and wages, 45 per cent on food and the remainder on miscellaneous items such as candles, kitchen utensils and household repairs. This figure, however, does not include stock items like carcasses of meat and preserved fish, which in another account were valued at £44. When the sum of £47 is added, which was the value of the grain used for ale and bread accounted for by Burgh, then it would seem Alice spent more than half her total income on maintaining her household, and twice as much on food as on wages and livery. These figures are higher than those estimated as average for the period, which suggests that people dined well at Acton and Alice spent more time 'at home' than did many of her contemporaries.[30]

Heads of households travelled to supervise their estates, negotiate business, maintain their patronage, purchase luxury goods, visit friends and relations, go on pilgrimage and for entertainment. One of Elizabeth Berkeley's journeys in 1421 was a three-day hunting excursion with her daughters in the Forest of Arden,[31] and Lady Margaret Cromwell's steward settled an account from the custodian of her goshawk.[32] But there is no evidence that Alice went hunting. Nor is it possible to tell from the Household Book when she left the manor on a visit, since her steward invariably prefaced each daily entry with the formula, 'The Lady took her meals with the household: in addition . . .' and then added the names of guests. However, the composition of the guest lists, the plain food served and small number of horses stabled on some days, as for example 7–10 December 1412, suggest Alice was away from Acton occasionally enjoying a neighbour's hospitality.

Travelling was expensive and carriages and horses valuable assets. Lady Alice West left her daughter-in-law a 'chariot', which appears to have been quite ornate with tooled leather trappings, and in 1355 Elizabeth Burgh had a great carriage with 'covertures, carpets and cushions' that she bequeathed to her daughter.[33] Women sometimes bequeathed horses to friends: in her will of 1408, Lady Elizabeth Zouche left her squire a palfrey called Bos, a white palfrey to her chaplain and her 'chief' palfrey, Lyard darundell (a dappled grey), to a relative Sir Richard Arundell.[34] There is no mention of a carriage in Alice's accounts but she may have ridden or used a covered cart. The Acton bailiff frequently accounted for the costs of repairs to carts, saddles and horse-tack and the steward bought stirrups in London. Travelling by wagon sounds somewhat rustic but it would have been upholstered with fleece or tapestry and covered cushions, and elegance and show displayed by the trappings: Alice had black and red linen saddle cloths and red ornamental ribbons, not extravagant perhaps but stylish. It was also common for women to be carried in litters or travel on horseback. It appears that leather breeches were sometimes worn by ladies who rode astride.[35]

Oats, hay, vetch and peas grown on the estates were sent daily to the stables to feed the Acton horses and those of Alice's visitors. A blacksmith received an annual stipend and payment had frequently to be made for veterinary services,

Two ladies riding astride, from Queen Mary's Psalter, c. 1320.

though not always profitably: in 1412 Alice paid 3s 4d to treat a horse bitten by a snake at Lavenham but it subsequently died. In the absence of a Marshalsea's account there is no evidence of how many horses Dame Alice owned, though she may have occasionally hired some as was common practice. Elizabeth Berkeley often hired horses for her frequent journeys, which made good economic sense since a tenth of her annual household expenditure went towards maintaining her stables.[36]

In the 1390s Dame Alice travelled quite frequently. Between Easter 1392 and Michaelmas 1393 she was in London with a large retinue and twenty horses. She also went to Penshurst in Kent and it appears that in later years she went provisioning to the Stourbridge market, some 20 miles away. However she travelled, her presence among her caparisoned horses and liveried retinue must have evoked excitement and interest. Her arms and lineage would have been recognized in the Suffolk villages through which she passed. She associated with and entertained many of the powerful local officials and gentry in the area and her wealth and hospitality would have increased her reputation at a time of growing social mobility.

In the early days before she settled in Suffolk, Dame Alice appears to have used her London inn quite often. Acquired by Lord Bryan in 1388 and given to her sometime before his death in 1390, the inn called 'Cornerhalle on the corner' was in the parish of Holy Trinity the Less in Vintry ward, probably at the junction of Old Fish Street and Knightrider Street where the entrance to Mansion House underground station is today.[37] Having a base in London was common for members of Alice's class, useful for business as well as pleasure and also provided storage space for goods purchased in bulk.[38] Whether Alice was ever a lady-in-waiting or attached to Richard II's close circle of friends cannot be verified, but no doubt having an inn enabled her to maintain social contacts and entertain. She also used it for business: in 1400 she purchased livery cloth in London and her receiver settled a medical bill for her there. However, in later years city life may have lost its appeal, or possibly it did not make economic sense to keep a house just for an occasional visit and by 1428 the inn was being rented out.[39]

The entertainment of social peers, neighbours and workers was a general obligation in all households. Like her contemporaries, and despite the importance of maintaining a hierarchy, the daily Acton guest list regularly comprised a mixture of all social ranks. Certain feast days were marked by special celebrations, related to the religious and agricultural calendar. Luxurious food was provided for feasts such as Candlemas on 2 February and the Annunciation on 25 March regardless of whether important guests had been asked to dine. As already noted, the dinner immediately before the forty days of the Lenten fast, when neither meat nor dairy produce could be eaten, included several rich dishes. Alice's steward once purchased 5 gallons of olive oil for use at Lent instead of butter and fat, since dairy produce was prohibited at this time. As we saw, no special guests were invited to the feast on Shrove Tuesday but a harper came to entertain the company and help boost the household morale before those lean days ahead.

A more understandable occasion for jubilation was the dinner on 29 April 1413. Guests that day included the harvest-reeve, ten ploughmen, ten of the household manor and a minstrel to lead the celebrations. Ploughing was arduous work and a significant event in the agricultural calendar. This was also the last Saturday before May Day, even then an important rural holiday in celebration of summer and communal life.[40] Traditionally it was a time of parish festivities and while no special dinner was served at Acton on 1 May, the dinner two days before may have marked the occasion. Another minstrel with his companion visited on 27 July when the only other guests were Alice's shepherd John Fouler and his wife. Lamb was served for dinner that day, just the second that month (it had not previously been eaten since mid-February), so it is reasonable to speculate that this festivity may have marked the end of a successful lambing season. Another possibility is that the minstrel had been invited to honour the feast of Richard II's queen, Anne of Bohemia, or the festival of the Seven Sleepers whose legend was current at this time.[41]

Christmas was both a public and private festival. On Christmas day a harper came to amuse Alice's guests and household and stayed for over a week. While the guest lists for the end of December are generally unremarkable, with the exception of one day that will be discussed in Chapter 6, on 1 January 1413 over 300 people, described as 'tenants and other strangers', were invited to dinner together with more than a dozen of Alice's chosen friends. It is unlikely that on this day everyone was able to eat in the great hall but we can imagine the crowd pushing, shoving and jostling in the manor courtyard, and queuing for a morsel of meat. There were swans, joints of pork, mutton and beef, geese, conies, veal, suckling pig and capons, as well as an ample supply of bread and ale. And we may also imagine, standing on a trestle table away from the smoke of the roasting joints, a Frumenty made with cracked wheat, chicken broth and the 12 gallons of milk that had been purchased that morning, sweetened with almonds, egg yolk and saffron – a special symbolic winter porridge, rich with the promise of the return of spring.[42] The cost of this New Year's feast was 15s, excluding the large quantities of stock delivered from the kitchens, a third of the total purchases for the month. Such feasts were traditional in all households in the later Middle Ages, a distribution of largess to everyone in the local community to celebrate the arrival of a new year, a short respite before returning to the demanding work of farming and estate administration.

Apart from such traditional festivals we can only speculate about the degree of jollity or restraint in Alice de Bryene's household. A harper was employed twice in 1412–13 to entertain guests and minstrels came four times. Minstrels may also have provided such entertainment as acrobatics, juggling and story telling, while the harper was employed to make more serious recitations.[43] Besides the music, the reciting of romances, singing of carols and dancing of roundels (contemporary music scores and illustrations in illuminated manuscripts testify to the frequency of such entertainments), guests must have amused themselves discussing public and local events. An incident in 1405 would have kept the company interested for days: sometime that year a dragon appeared near Bures just a few miles from Acton. It was obviously a drama of great significance that apparently became known nationally as well as locally, being recorded by a contemporary chronicler in graphic detail:

Close to the town of Bures, near Sudbury, there has lately appeared, to the great hurt of the country-side, a dragon, vast in body with a crested head, teeth like a saw and a tail extending to an enormous length. Having slain the shepherd of a flock he then devoured very many sheep. Then came forth in order to shoot him with arrows, the workmen of the lord on whose domain he had concealed himself, being Richard Waldegrave, knight; but the dragon's body, although struck by the archers, remained unhurt, for the arrows bounced off his back as if it were iron or hard rock. Those arrows that fell upon the spine of his back gave out as they struck it a ringing or tinkling sound just as if they had hit a brazen plate, and then flew off by reason of the hide of this great beast being impenetrable. Thereupon in order to destroy him all the country people around were summoned. But when the dragon saw he was about to be assailed with arrows, he fled into a marsh or mere and there hid himself among the long reeds; nor was he any more seen again.[44]

Readers may recognize the spectre of those beasts, jaguars and wild cats that are apparently still occasionally sighted roaming the English countryside today.

Once the minstrels had played and the gossip been savoured, the household would have had to make their own entertainment. Bowls and boardgames, such as chess, 'tabler' and 'merles' (which were both like backgammon) were also played. Sermons and stories of saints recounted by visiting clerics at dinner, with their morals and mixture of folklore and Christian dogma, would have enthralled the listeners. But in the winter afternoons when it grew dark and there was little work to do on the farms, people must have looked for other amusement with only the crackle of a fire and flicker of candleflame for accompaniment. Story-telling, word games, quizzes and riddles require no props but a lively imagination; as pastimes they are still common in isolated rural communities. Perhaps that is how John Pellican, Alice's long-serving officer, acquired his name. Pelicans were not known to roam the lanes of medieval England, even if dragons did, but

St George slaying the dragon, from an East Anglian manuscript of the mid-fourteenth century.

some people would have heard the myth about the bird that killed its fledglings, then later pierced its breast and revived them with its own blood. The pelican was also the symbol of Christ in Christian iconography and depicted in numerous churches. Was it for this reason that John Pellican acquired his name, for selfless service to others in his role as custodian of Alice's household, or might he have had a long beak and a great pouch under his chin?

Although the majority of Alice's guests were labourers or officials connected with the estates and much of the daily routine must have been taken up with the maintenance of the household and the farms, this is not to presume an absence of sophistication and culture in the Acton household. Most likely Dame Alice's first language would have been French: her father, stepfather, father-in-law and husband all came from the military elite, an international class in which French would have been the lingua franca. Letters addressed to her were in French, as was the inscription on her personal seal and she also owned books written in French. While the use of the vernacular was becoming well established in the early fifteenth century, French remained the language of convention and polite society. But even if Alice de Bryene still adhered to a past tradition she probably also kept up with contemporary culture: her stepfather Sir Richard Waldegrave had travelled with Geoffrey Chaucer in the 1380s, so she may have enjoyed English poetry as well.[45]

The priests, friars and clergy who visited Acton played an important part in the dissemination of information and their presence at the dinner table on days when specific saints or liturgical events were celebrated would have contributed both to the edification and entertainment of Alice's guests and to the prestige of her household. Religious sensibility and a show of piety were essential features of the medieval household, and the ownership of books and public patronage would also have enhanced the reputation of the householder, factors we shall look at in later chapters. Yet despite the fact that that were several chaplains and chapel clerks in Alice's retinue (once four chaplains are specified as well as some clerks of the chapel, whose responsibility it was to look after the vestments, vessels and any portable altars that may have been used when the householder was travelling)[46] nothing suggests that her household was more pious than many others would have been at this time.

The ambience of the Acton household was coloured by a policy of self-sufficiency. Since Alice's estate administration was largely centralized and it appears she travelled infrequently by the time she was fifty, she and her household

The Swinburne Pyx, c. 1310–25, which may have belonged to Dame Alice's grandmother. The Nativity scene on the left is the same as that depicted in her Book of Hours (see p. 147).

would have spent a large proportion of their days on routine domestic and managerial matters, supervising menus, compiling guest lists, dealing with correspondence and general maintenance. Wood for the bread ovens and roasting the meat was cropped and delivered from nearby woods and cloth purchased to clean kitchen utensils and the windows when they were blackened from the cooking of joints and smoking of bacon. Coarse cloth was bought for straining milk and cheese was made. The bake oven had to be repaired frequently and the millstones for grinding the household grain sharpened and reset. Grease, or 'flotys', from the joints of meat was collected and used for frying food or sold, old wine barrels were also sold or refashioned for use in the household for grain storage, laundry, wash or bath tubs and buckets. Clarified fat or tallow was saved to make candles.

In the accounts of Lady Margaret Cromwell a tailor was employed to make clothes and money spent on dyeing worsted and livery cloth and for the cost of shoes.[47] No such items appear in Alice's accounts, though a guest named William Taylor, who cannot otherwise be identified, called three times in 1412–13, twice when local women were also invited who may have helped with the sewing. The tanning of ox, bull and cow hides and the preparation of calves' skins seem to have been undertaken outside the household and the leather hides would then have been used to make shoes, horse tackle and for binding books. The rabbit furs which were issued to the household also had to be cured, a highly skilled and specialized task before being fashioned into accessories by Alice and her household. It seems likely that these furs were from the grey rabbit, most common in East Anglia, and prized for warmth rather than display like the silver-grey and black rabbit.[48] Fleeces, woolfells and lambskins were also issued to the household for stuffing cushions, lining clothes or carded, spun and woven for tapestry and embroidery work.

Just before Christmas 1412, John 'th' Lych' was a dinner guest at Acton. Leeching was a common medical practice, as much a preventive measure by drawing off excess blood to balance the humours, as a cure for a specific illness. Bloodletting, the analysis of urine and taking the pulse were the three major diagnostic tools of the medieval physician and the actual time of drawing blood usually depended on a favourable conjunction of the planets.[49] In 1418 Lady Margaret Cromwell paid a barber to bleed her. Alice's 'leech' visited only once during the year so presumably she and her household were in reasonable health and whatever other ailments they may have suffered from would have been treated with home remedies made from spices, herbs or wild flowers. The large quantity of mustard seed in the store cupboard could have been pulverized for poultices and plasters or distilled to make a variety of useful prophylactics, and the sugar used for numerous potions.[50] The Acton steward once accounted for ½ lb of 'greynes' bought at the Stourbridge fair. These were 'grains of paradise' from a West African spice plant related to pepper and cardamom and used both for seasoning and as an opiate to make medicine.

Our introduction to Alice's household has focused on her daily routine, her retinue, hospitality, the kind of meals served and lifestyle in general. We have then looked behind this display to view the domestic scene. Perhaps this presents a rather monotonous picture of matronly pursuits, baking and brewing and evenings spent sewing by candlelight, but closer scrutiny at the guest list for 1412–13 enables us to see Dame Alice more clearly by the company she kept and illustrates a different scene.

CHAPTER 5

Men at the Table

John Gower, poet and contemporary of Chaucer, wrote, 'You know that there be three estates of men'. These were the clergy, whose business it was to pray and care for the spiritual well-being of the community, the warrior class, who defended the people and the land, and the labourers, who toiled to support the other two estates.[1] This description of the social order was not new: it was the basis of society as described in Plato's *Republic* and is still discernible in some primitive communities today. Although these distinctions were beginning to fragment by the end of the fourteenth century, each 'class' is quite clearly represented in Alice de Bryene's guest list for 1412–13. A closer examination of the reasons why visitors came to the Acton manor can tell us something about the way women fitted into the hierarchy even though they were not specifically included in the description.[2]

THE CLERGY

Clerical visitors comprised the lowest number of those of the three estates invited to Acton, and totalled less than 5 per cent of all Alice's guests. This is perhaps surprising and even more unusual is the fact that very few appear to have been complete strangers to the household. This challenges the notion of large bodies of mendicant friars preying on the hospitality of wealthy estate owners. Between the end of October 1412 and early May 1413, the only unnamed clerical guests about whom it is difficult to speculate were a 'certain' chaplain, four priests, three friars and a clerk. We have no way of knowing whether the two sisters who stopped on their way from Canterbury on 20 June were nuns, or siblings returning from a pilgrimage.

A degree in theology and subsequent appointment to one of the top posts in the Church could lead to an important position in service to the Crown – Simon Sudbury, consecrated Bishop of London in 1361, became Chancellor of England twenty years later. Those in the lower secular orders might also spend little time on

A friar from an illustrated manuscript of
The Vision of Piers Plowman, *dated 1427.*

parochial duties and looked for support in the households of the aristocracy or landed gentry as chaplains, stewards and trustees. Rectors and parish priests were in theory more concerned with pastoral care but in order to supplement their incomes often spent much of their time actually cultivating their own pastures and plots of land. Of the regular religious, nuns and monks were generally enclosed and rarely left their cloisters, while the friars whose vocations were apostolic, pastoral and contemplative worked in the community, especially in the urban areas, and had to support themselves on alms.

The most frequent religious guests at Acton were friars, understandably perhaps because of their need. They always came in pairs. Their mobility ensured that when they visited they would have been full of *omnes rumores patriae* – 'all the gossip of the countryside' – with which to regale the company at dinner. Most frequent were the Dominicans from Sudbury, an order known for their erudition, who called most months of the year and often several times a month. Alice made them an annual grant of grain and may have contributed in cash and kind each time they visited, when with few exceptions high status food was included on the menu. Their relationship with the family was of long-standing and they had been patronized by both Alice's grandfather and stepfather, who left money for them in their wills.[3]

The dates of the visits of the Sudbury friars provide some insight into their relationship with Alice and the Acton household. When they called on 7 October 1412, for example, it was the fifty-first anniversary of Alice's father's death, and they also came to commemorate the death of her mother seven years previously on 10 June 1413. On both occasions they stayed overnight. Their arrival on 15 February may have been connected with the celebration of Sir Guy's 'month's mind', the series of rituals held to commemorate specific anniversaries such as the seventh and thirtieth day after a person's death. Other dates must also have been significant and despite the presence of Alice's chaplains, these friars played an important part in assisting in the celebrations of family feast days, household and religious rituals such as Pentecost and Easter, and the Rogation days when traditionally the parish boundaries were beaten or defined. Their presence at Acton on these particular occasions can be seen as an acknowledgement by Dame Alice of the valuable work they performed in the community.

To the west of Acton was the Augustinian priory of Clare. Founded in 1248, it was rebuilt in the 1360s by Elizabeth de Burgh who was patron for fifty years. Originally 'friar hermits', the Austins soon became an active mendicant order, were famous for their teaching, lecturing and writing and, from the evidence of endowments, appear to have been especially appealing to women.[4] Their visits to Acton generally coincided with special feast days and were marked with festive food, such as suckling pig, expensive fresh fish and cream to make rich sauces. The 28 February was the date of the translation of St Augustine's relics from Africa to Sardinia, a significant date in the Austin liturgical calendar. They made another visit on 25 March, the date of the celebration of the Annunciation of the Blessed Virgin Mary to which one of the two chapels at Clare was dedicated. Their third visit on 12 July poses something of a riddle. It was the feast day of St Edburga, Abbess of Minster-in-Thanet in 716. Now this erudite Edburga had no specific connection with the Austin order. They did, however, celebrate the festival of another St Edburga, a seventh-century nun whose relics had been translated to Bicester, a house of Austin canons, on 18 July 1182. To add to the confusion there was a third St Edburga, celebrated on the same day.[5] Three saint Edburgas with festivals just six days apart is sufficient reason for imagining some stimulating conversation at the dinner table. There appears to be no idiosyncratic reason for the visit of the Austin friars on 21 October, a day sacred to St Dunstan and St Ursula, though both had exciting and detailed hagiographies which would have interested fellow guests.

The friars who came from Babwell had a longer journey, from just outside the city bounds of Bury St Edmunds by the toll-gate. They were Franciscans and their popularity in the neighbourhood is evidenced by numerous bequests in wills, including those of Alice's friends and neighbours like Sir Thomas Clopton and John Rokewode.[6] They visited only once in 1412–13 on 7 February, the day after the anniversary of Sir Guy Bryan's death, but like the Clare and Sudbury friars they were annual recipients of Alice's charity. The Ipswich friars, who were guests on 27 November 1412 and 14 September 1413, the feast day of the Exaltation of the Holy Cross, do not appear to have been regularly patronized by Dame Alice, though she instructed her bailiff at Raydon to make them a grant of wheat in 1431–2, the fortieth anniversary of her grandmother's death. There were Dominican, Franciscan and Carmelite houses in Ipswich and it seems likely that they came from one of the two latter orders, who were also beneficiaries under Alice's stepfather's will.

The friars from Colchester travelled in pairs as was usual, but on three of their four visits in 1412–13 they arrived with a clerk as well. Once again there is no direct indication to which order they belonged, Franciscan, Dominican or the Crutched friars, though the latter is most probable: the Crutched or Crossed friars, who followed the Augustinian rule, ran the hospital of the Holy Cross in Colchester, the patronage of which had been granted in 1400 to John Doreward, one of Alice's friends.[7] No special guests were invited to join the Colchester friars, although the provision of good food suggests they were expected. Two of their visits coincided with days sacred to Gilbert of Sempringham and William of Rochester, both twelfth-century English saints. St Gilbert was the only English man to have founded an order and nine of the thirteen Gilbertine monasteries were double monasteries supporting nuns as well as lay brothers.[8] St William, a fisherman from Perth, was almost an accidental saint, who had devoted himself to the care of orphans and the poor. He was murdered by a young companion on his way to pilgrimage in the Holy Land.[9] If the Colchester friars had to sing for their suppers it would have been to interesting melodies.

Contemporary opinion about the activities of the friars was often fiercely critical: Walsingham wrote of the Franciscans, 'with the intent of gathering money, they who have sworn to persevere in poverty . . . call good evil and evil good, leading astray princes by adulation, the people by lies and drawing both with themselves out of the straight path'.[10] Wyclif commented more specifically on their social behaviour saying they liked, '. . . to speke before lordis and sitte at mete with hem'.[11] Certainly Dame Alice fed her mendicant friars well and we may guess they left with bulging purses. In return they brought news and gossip of the world beyond the boundaries of her East Anglian estates, like the two friars from Hereford who were made welcome on 20 May with select company. These friars timed their visit to coincide with the feast day of St Ethelbert, titular head of Hereford cathedral and a popular saint in both Gloucestershire and East Anglia.[12] As lady of a Gloucestershire manor, some of whose retinue came from the environs of the Welsh Marches, the friars must have known they could count on Alice de Bryene's patronage. No doubt her other guests were expected to contribute alms, but they would have benefited from the opportunity of discussing matters beyond the confines of the local environment.

The dates of the friars' visits to Acton were connected with specific anniversaries celebrated in the household, important events in their own liturgical calendars and wider cultural concerns. The Austin friars from Norwich came on 29 September: Michaelmas was traditionally the day for settling accounts, but the Austins' main chapel at Norwich was also dedicated to St Michael.[13] Their earlier visit on 11 May was on the day sacred to St John of Bridlington, a popular contemporary saint. As we shall see the guest list that day indicates that company was specifically invited to enjoy the after-dinner entertainment.

Friars fulfilled many of the roles of the modern mass media and might also be compared to travelling libraries: their stories of saints and religious events were part of the cultural heritage that must have been particularly welcome to women. Less involved generally with the world of business and public activities, women of the landed classes had more time to cultivate their spiritual interests, and such knowledge was to be gained not only by reading but also by listening. As we have seen the friars' visits generally coincided with special dates in their liturgical calendars, suggesting that rather than being invited they gave advance warning of their intention to come. Nevertheless, they seem to have been made welcome by Alice.

Well-travelled and well-educated clergymen brought news and stimulating conversation together with their parochial and theological concerns and must have helped enliven many a long rural evening. But a table is not blessed if it has fed no scholars: the Masters John Gaky, John Graykil and Thomas Jordon may have been three such guests.[14] It does not appear that Alice made any special preparations for their visits by asking any of her social peers to dine and the Masters may indeed have been guests of her chaplains. But the fact that pigeons were on the menu on each occasion suggests she made an effort to welcome them. Pigeons were also served on 25 October 1412 when two Oxford clerks visited Acton. It was the day dedicated to the saints Crispin and Crispinian. Had they come three years later the reason for their visit would have been clear for that was the date of Henry V's victory over the French at Agincourt, against all odds. In 1412 these saints may not have been significant cult figures – they were in fact third-century Roman martyrs and patrons of cobblers, shoemakers and leatherworkers. Subsequently, however, they were much celebrated for what was believed to have been their divine intervention in France: Agincourt was a psychological victory and became a matter of nationalistic pride. We cannot guess the business of the clerks who came from Cambridge, Maplestead and Batesford, but those from Bures, Foxearth and Waldingfield would have been known by the Acton household and familiar with some of Alice's tenants.

Rectors came for a variety of reasons, but rarely it would seem to mark specific religious festivals. One came from Withersfield, 15 miles due south of Acton. It would appear to have been a rich living judging by the will of Thomas Grey, rector in 1395, who left various instructions about gifts for the fabric of the church where he wanted to be entombed, including a Jesse window in which he was to feature kneeling upon his armorial shield with a roll in his hand. He also ordered decorated tiles for the chapel where he was to be buried, in a tomb of fine marble bearing an image in his likeness.[15] The Withersfield incumbent in 1412–13 made two visits to Acton in October and April, remaining there for nearly a fortnight on each occasion. It is difficult to gauge his interest in the care of souls and whether the gifts of green peas that Alice made him periodically represented charity to the man or his parishioners. He certainly spent time on secular matters; Alice bought a carthorse and plough beast from him. She also did business with the rector of Stanstead, who called four times that year and sometimes sold large quantities of grain to the Acton household. The rectors from Lidgate and Wolverstone came from further afield and little appears to connect them with Dame Alice, although Wolverstone was only a mile away from her Wherstead manor.

Closer connections can be made with the last two rectors from Stansfield and Middleton. Alice's relative, John Rokewode, was patron of the Stansfield church until 1416 when the advowson was shared between William Rokewode and two of her close friends Sir Robert Corbet and Sir Andrew Boteler.[16] To welcome the protégés of acquaintances helped to strengthen bonds of alliance and friendship. The Middleton rector was her own protégé since she owned the patronage of the Middleton church and on one of his visits *Sir* Richard Harlewene, who later acceded to the rectorship, was also a guest;[17] we may guess that the two men had much to talk about. If a rector were fortunate in securing several livings he might appoint a priest to serve mass for him in one of his churches. *Sir* John Brook, Alice's steward until 1417, had been the parson of Polstead church, the patronage of which was held by the Waldegraves.[18] The two Polstead chaplains who dined at Acton may have been his guests but Alice's stepfather also had a chantry there.[19]

On 31 May, the day sacred to St Petronella, two priests arrived from Lord Bryan's collegiate chantry in Devon: it was the day set aside for masses to be sung for the repose of his soul and that of his last wife, Lady Elizabeth Montagu. Their journey to East Anglia of over 350 miles would have taken them about two weeks. Nevertheless, they came to mark this special day with Dame Alice who fed them on crab, sole and other fresh fish together with whatever accompanying sauce or confection had been concocted with the cream and butter she purchased that day. Then without even resting for the night or stopping for supper, they mounted their horses and rode away.

Clergymen often visited with business to discuss connected with the secular rather than the spiritual world. Those from the higher ranks with more education than the simple parish priest were frequently appointed as trustees and executors. *Sir* Richard Mauncell, who was invited to dine with Dame Alice four times in 1413, epitomizes such men who served their patrons in a variety of ways. He was an executor of Alice's stepfather Sir Richard Waldegrave, a trustee for his son, and acted in this capacity for other local gentry like William Clopton. As well as this it appears he held a variety of rectorships.[20] On one occasion *Sir* Nicholas Blundell, another Waldegrave feoffee, was a dinner guest when Mauncell was at the table and we may guess that their visit had something to do with family trusts which they needed to discuss with Alice. Other clerics who visited, such as *Sir* Peter Crek, parson of Assington in 1427, would also have acted as trustees.[21] The visitor who came from the household of the prior of Stoke-by-Clare might have been collecting rent as the priory held the head leases of Alice's Weston manor at Foxearth and a tenement in Bures.[22] The prior of Hatfield Peverel who dined at Acton on 26 October in the company of Alice's council came from the Benedictine priory that owned both the rectories of Acton and Assington. More pertinent was the fact that every year the Acton account rolls included a 5s fee paid to the bailiff of Hatfield Peverel who held courts for Alice at Bures.[23]

In providing hospitality and catering for the various needs and interests of her clerical guests, Alice de Bryene is unlikely to have been dissimilar to other hostesses of her class. The reasons for their visits were manifold, whether charitable, spiritual, social, commercial or administrative, and it would be hard to imagine that they experienced the Acton household as much different from others they visited. Even if business was not discussed at dinner but privately with Alice in her chamber, the presence of clergy at her table would have enhanced her honour. Above all the household and the religious community were essential features of the social order. Although women had no official place in the Church, unless they took vows, as heads of households they played significant roles as hostesses to ecclesiastics.

KNIGHTS AND SOCIAL PEERS

The knights who were guests at Acton no longer defended the realm with the steel of their swords, though in their youth many had joined military campaigns abroad and on crusades, but rather with the metal of their minds and the growing sense of their obligations as Members of Parliament. The Crown's increasing need to fund the French wars by levying taxes had become one of their chief public concerns. As representatives of the people in their shires it was important for them to sound out local opinion and assess the most efficient and equitable way of collecting revenue. Meeting with owners of large estates can also be seen as a public relations exercise: to be successful in their roles it was essential that they had the support of those who would be affected by the measures they were called upon to implement. And even if widowed estate owners like Alice de Bryene may not have had political power and administrative roles in the civil service, they belonged to the same social order as the knights and were bound together by mutual self-interest despite the fact that their roles in society appeared to be different.[24]

In the year for which there are records, five Members of Parliament came to dine with Dame Alice. With one exception they were all roughly the same age as she was or even older and would have shared similar experiences relating to the shrinking labour market and changing economic circumstances brought about by the decrease in population in the aftermath of the plague. They would also have experienced the upheavals at the end of Richard II's reign and the subsequent unrest after Henry IV's accession. Although there may have been personal reasons for their visits, they must also have been interested in her views as a local estate owner. Moreover, some of them were distantly related to Alice and therefore bound by the common interests of their kinship.

Sir John Howard is the epitome of this type of man. On the death of his father he inherited property in Norfolk and then, through well-planned marriages, accumulated substantial estates in Essex, Cambridge and Suffolk, the counties which he represented in Parliament in 1397, 1407 and 1422. He sat on numerous royal commissions, was a justice of the peace in Essex and Suffolk and sheriff in Essex, Hertfordshire, Cambridge and Huntingdon. Powerful and wealthy it was noted of him in 1420, when in dispute with one of his wife's kinsmen, that he was 'weel ykynde and of gret allyaunce' and could raise support 'as weel of lordys of estate as of othre as knyghtis and squyers'.[25]

In common with other men in his position, alliances were strengthened not only by acting as a trustee for neighbours, a service he performed for and with other

Richard II is delivered to London, from a History of Richard II, begun on 25 April 1399.

acquaintances and relatives of Dame Alice, but also through marriage and social networking.[26] Alice's stepfather had acted as Howard's attorney in the late 1390s, and in 1402 Howard joined the council of Joan Bohun, Countess of Hereford, which may have been where he and Alice met. But it is just as likely that their acquaintance was cemented by his second wife, whom he married in about 1396. She was Alice Tendring of Stoke-by-Nayland, just a few miles from Acton, and a close relative of William Clopton, another of Alice's guests in 1412–13.[27]

Sir Robert Corbet, another justice of the peace, sheriff and commissioner, was one of those for whom Howard acted as trustee. Like Howard he had acquired substantial properties in various counties through judicious marriages, enabling him to represent Wiltshire in the 1385 and 1397 Parliaments, and Hertfordshire in 1402 and 1404. On his father's death in 1404 he inherited the Assington manor in Suffolk. In 1412 he was over sixty and had been widowed for the second time. He was a frequent visitor to Acton, dining there on five different occasions in one year, three times apparently staying the night although his manor was less than 5 miles away. So what might he and Alice have talked about as they enjoyed 'supper and extras' in February, July and September? Sir Robert had been one of Henry IV's chamber knights and was also quite close to Henry V. Apart from bringing news from the royal Court, there seems to have been more than mere gossip in these tête-à-têtes: Corbet, it appears, was prospecting for another rich widow. In 1414, the year after his visits to Alice, he was elected to represent Suffolk in the April and November Parliaments, though he spent most of that year in Shropshire. It was here that he successfully wooed his third wife Joan Knightley, the twice-widowed daughter of a wealthy mercenary captain. They married in 1415.[28]

John Doreward from Bocking in Essex made only one visit to Acton in 1413. Many times a Member of Parliament for Essex, justice of the peace and sheriff, he had a high political profile and as a lawyer was frequently retained as councillor and feoffee to members of the aristocracy including Joan Bohun.[29] Like many of his contemporaries, strategic marriages played an important part in the accumulation of his property, a policy he followed for his children.[30] Doreward probably formed part of Alice's council, giving her advice on legal matters, though there are no charters or documents to confirm this. His absence at the dinner she hosted for his wife Lady Isabel, with Ralph Chamberlain and her half-brother in July 1413, might in part be explained by the fact that Doreward had been elected as speaker of Henry V's first Parliament in May that year, but we may guess that Lady Doreward talked about her husband's appointment with Alice's other guests over the meal.

Sir John Ingoldisthorpe (Ingysthorp, Ingilstrop' and Ingelstrop in the Household Book) was Member of Parliament for Suffolk in 1404 and Norfolk in 1414, and also had numerous official appointments in those two counties as sheriff, escheator and commissioner. Through his wife Elizabeth Burgh he inherited substantial properties in Cambridge, Yorkshire and Somerton in west Suffolk, not far from Acton:[31] Alice's stepfather, as kinsman of Sir John Burgh, had helped oversee their marriage settlement.[32] These are sufficient reasons for explaining his friendship with Alice but there were other connections too: in 1386 he had enlisted in the naval force of Richard, Earl of Arundel where he would have met Alice's brother-in-law Sir William Bryan. Relationships between Ingoldisthorpe and the Bures appear to have been of long standing too: in 1389 Alice's grandmother paid a Matilda Inglisthorp, who must surely have been a relative, to stay one week at the Acton manor to help the household staff.[33]

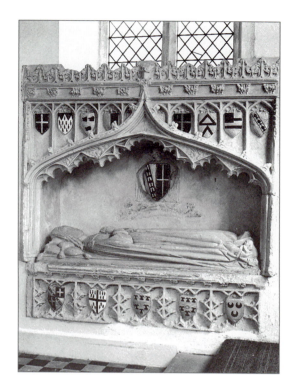

The tomb of Alice Boteler, a close relative of Sir Andrew Boteler, c. 1410, at All Saints, Newton, Suffolk. The shields bear the arms of Bures, Waldegrave, Corbet and Boteler among others.

The most frequent of these visitors, and probably the youngest, was Sir Andrew Boteler. Like Doreward he had close connections with the Court, having begun his career as an esquire in Richard II's household, and later was retained by Henry IV. He represented Suffolk in the Parliaments of 1404, 1410 and 1421 and maintained close connections with many of the local gentry as feoffee of their trusts and executors of their wills.[34] His estates were very close to Alice's, at Bulmer in Essex, Newton, Chilton and Great Waldingfield in Suffolk and he also had property in Acton. It is possible that they may also have been distantly related. Boteler evidently enjoyed a very lavish lifestyle and on occasion visited with his wife and a large retinue of squires, a maidservant and chaplain, even once staying the night. In keeping with Boteler's apparently luxurious standards, high status food was always on the menu when he called, except on 21 March which may have been a sudden, unplanned visit. Henry IV had died the previous day and it is quite possible that the news had already reached Acton, for messengers could travel as much as 60 miles a day.[35] The King had been ailing for some time and the manner of his death was quite dramatic. It seems he had swooned while making an offering before the shrine of Edward the Confessor in Westminster Abbey. Carried to his deathbed, his confessor asked him to repent both for his share in the death of Archbishop Scrope and for his usurpation. Henry said the Pope had given him absolution for the first, and his sons would never permit him to make restitution for the second.[36] Boteler's brother-in-law was one of the new King's close personal friends, so he and Alice would have had plenty to gossip about.

They may have had other interests in common. When Boteler dictated his will in 1429 his spiritual concerns were paramount as can be deduced from the provision he made for two priests to sing masses for seven years, 'for the sowles of me and my frendys'. He asked to buried close to the image of Mary Magdalene at St Gregory's in Sudbury, feeling in need perhaps of her patronage having sired only one child – an illegitimate daughter. His wealth and status did not blind him to a sense of obligation to the community: he left gifts of money to numerous churches and to various orders of friars including those patronized by Alice. Further provision was made for the poor and needy on his estates and he instructed his feoffees to free all the bondmen on his land after his death.[37]

If his will demonstrates Sir Andrew's anxiety about his soul's salvation after death it appears he was no stranger to the need for pious reflection during his lifetime. In 1430 Master John Burt, a chaplain of Bury St Edmunds, was accused of associating with heretics and charged with having possession of a book called *Dives et Pauper*, containing errors and heresies. Burt denied knowing that it was considered heretical: it actually recounted the dialogue between a rich layman and a well-read mendicant priest, exposed the practical meaning of the ten commandments, contained political and social commentary and articles on folklore, astrology, iconography, witchcraft, warfare and trade. Burt claimed that he had lent it to a friar preacher in Sudbury to make a copy for Sir Andrew Boteler.[38] There is no evidence that Boteler was a lollard knight but he obviously had wider interests beyond politics and local administration, something he may have shared with Dame Alice.

In order to organize local government effectively, these knights of the shire needed to keep in touch with local feeling, common living traditions and customs. They would all have been conscious of Alice de Bryene's standing as an important landowner in Essex and Suffolk, aware of the influence she had and the patronage she could dispense. Like other women in her situation, she too must have gained from the acquaintanceship: these were men of the world, educated, informed and generally highly motivated. Let us not presume a surfeit of small talk at the Acton dinner table, but eavesdrop for a moment on some stimulating conversation between good companions. There would have been much to talk about: political and religious developments, recent births, marriages and deaths, local scandals, old friends and enemies, the price of labour and corn and shared memories of the past.

Neighbouring gentry dined at Acton too, men like her relatives William Rokewode (elected to represent Suffolk in the Parliament of 1417) and Thomas and William Sampson, William Clopton, Gilbert Debenham, Sir Guy Corbet (half-brother of Sir Robert), Ralph Chamberlain, John Goldingham, William Hervy and Richard Appleton. While they were not knights or Members of Parliament, they were involved in local society, as commissioners, fellow trustees and executors. They were influential, not only because their widespread interests linked them to more powerful men, but also because they were responsible for electing the parliamentary representatives of their counties. Women too sometimes brought their influence to bear when it came to electing candidates: in 1455 Eleanor, Duchess of Norfolk, wrote to John Paston asking him to support one of her husband's nominees.[39]

Other male guests who can be included in this category are some of Alice de Bryene's superior tenants like Thomas Lodbrook who paid her an annual rent of over £25 for the Layham manor, and tradesmen and business partners such as William Boteler, Gilbert Morell and John Joye. The latter not only supplied the Acton household with wine, but was also a collector of taxes and customs in Ipswich on the export of cloth and subsidies of wool – no doubt a useful person to know. Alice's invitations to these men are a reflection of the new status of tenants and increasing social mobility. Nor should we forget the frequent visits of some of the executive staff on her estate team, her receiver Morgan Gough and auditor John Holbrook. While they may not all have been her social equals, they would have owned property and can hardly be included in the traditional concept of the third estate.

Business and affairs of state were not the only dishes to be savoured at the Acton dinner table. On 26 February 1413 John Talmache was invited to dinner and returned several times the following week. His father who had been married to Margaret Waldegrave, possibly Alice's half-sister, had died on 19 February.[40] The Talmaches held the manor of Bentley and property in Wherstead and also paid Alice an annual 28s rent for land at Acton. While there may have been a new lease to negotiate, there seems to have been more to these meetings than routine organization; the fact that clergy also joined the party and on one occasion, the eighth day after Talmache's death, two minstrels came to perform suggests that Alice had time to be sociable, to commiserate and offer some sympathy perhaps after the day's main business was completed.

Knights, defenders of the realm, from a Flemish manuscript of the 1340s.

The men who made up the second estate no longer played such an important part in the physical defence of the people and the realm but continued to have a role in protecting their interests. Like other women Alice de Bryene availed herself of their services and used their skills to implement her projects. Over the years she would have associated with many others with business to discuss. Let us join her at the manor for dinner on 6 September 1434 and meet those guests she has invited to talk about her most recent scheme. She is now over seventy and has been managing her estates alone for nearly fifty years. But the hourglass has turned, the sands are running out and the time has come to mark the achievements of her life and seek intercession for the smooth passage of her soul into the next world. She has decided to set up a chantry in her local parish church by endowing a priest, with the income from some of her property, to hold masses for her in perpetuity.[41] To ensure the success of this venture she intends to appoint twelve trustees.[42]

We will see just one familiar face at the table, that of Sir John Howard, the only one of her distinguished visitors of 1412–13 who was still alive. With him are several local commissioners and trustees: a lawyer, Robert Cavendish, younger brother of William Cavendish, a guest at Acton in 1413; Thomas Milde of Clare, who was responsible for supervising her courts; Thomas Hardekyn, a tax collector; John Coo, trustee of her half-brother; William Ingesthorp, a stranger but possibly related to Ingoldisthorpe, the Member of Parliament; and William Sampson, most likely a close relative and the only one of her family to act in this capacity for her.

Four of the other five trustees are more closely connected with her household: Henry Pethirton had been retained by her for over forty years and may even have been one of her husband's retinue; Richard Andrew was engaged as the Acton household steward in 1428; *Sir* John Chetylbere, her previous steward, who seems to have remained in her service as one of her chaplains; and Robert Holyere who had been appointed parson of Raydon church by Alice in 1423. Presiding over this meeting was Geoffrey Bryce, Master of St Gregory's College in Sudbury. Bryce had served at St Gregory's church since 1411 and also commanded the loyalty of some of Alice's friends acting, for example, as trustee for Sir Andrew Boteler.[43]

The calibre of the men of the second estate that Alice de Bryene appointed as her trustees demonstrates the type of patronage she was able to dispense, and gives us further insights into her activities. Women of her class had the authority, power, connections and social prestige to command respect and employ their male social peers. They also had important roles to play as hostesses in social networking, by providing a space for people to meet. A widow's household may have been especially significant in this respect as neutral ground, for generally widows were less involved in dynastic schemes or ambitious and competitive enterprises. As disinterested parties they had more opportunity to develop objective viewpoints, a valuable asset. And for knights like Sir Robert Corbet, hungry for a well-heeled companion, an invitation to dinner at Acton with Dame Alice may have held out the promise of added spice and flavour until the meal was over.

THE THIRD ESTATE

The majority of Alice de Bryene's guests, those who were seated at the lower tables, were farm hands and labourers. Her officials and estate managers were usually described by their titles; others can be identified from the annual account rolls. The frequent visits of the harvest-reeves, bailiffs, millers, herdsmen, rent collectors, haywards, carters, ploughmen and maidservants indicate that she was continually engaged in matters connected with the management of the estates. Apart from farming, the maintenance of buildings and machinery was a frequent concern. Builders and craftsmen were invited to dine as well, like the carpenters who were hired from 15 to 17 February 1413 to repair the ploughs, and the hellier and his mate who came the following week and worked almost continuously until July retiling the manor roof.

A glance at the names of some of the other guests tells us of the numerous jobs undertaken by those of the third estate. John Tyler called in October, and again in December: in 1419 he and his son came to lay tiles at the manor and repair the great oven. That same year Thomas Meller, the household miller, set and sharpened the millstones, while William Coupere made new hoops and repaired various household vessels. There were others who came to dinner in 1412–13 whose names are suggestive of their occupations but these cannot always be verified, such as Thomas Baker, John Chaundler, Ralph Chepherd, Katrina Carter, Peter Fuller, John Fysscher, Richard Hawkyn, Agnes Lavender, William and John Mason, Richard Mower, Richard Plowryght, Roger Potter, John Ropere, Thomas Slauter, John Skynner, John Smyth, William Taylor, William Throscher and Thomas Weymaker.

It is evident from Alice's stewards' reports that terms of employment varied. Skilled craftsmen like John Tyler and John Crab, the carpenter, both earned 3*d* a day, while their sons, who assisted them, took home a penny less. However, all were fed at the manor: dinner was often part of a worker's remuneration. This was likely to have been a practical measure since those coming from distant villages would not have had time to go home for a meal. Similarly the scores of anonymous visitors who stayed to eat, the numerous 'boys' from the adjacent villages of Babwell, Boxford and Sudbury and the men from further afield – Ipswich, Lavenham and Colchester – must usually have been engaged on terms which included a place at Alice's table. It appears that such casual labourers were employed in a number of different ways, many of which may not have been too demanding.[44] In the spring of 1405, for example, some boys were paid to frighten away the birds in the newly sown fields: one penny was not a bad rate for spending the morning throwing stones, waving sacks and making a fearful noise with whatever resonant material was at hand at the crows in the cornfield, followed by bread and ale and the occasional titbit in the hall of Alice's manor. At other times when workers did not eat at the manor they were paid 2*d* extra in lieu of a meal. Some jobs like shoeing the horses or mending a saddle were paid not on a daily rate but as piece-work.

Occasionally tenants of smallholdings came to dine. They did not always remain closely attached to the land. William Goodrych who visited only once in 1413 had rented a property since 1394. In subsequent years he occasionally helped with the harvest and appears to have had gleaning obligations. But farming is an unreliable business and being tied to a tenancy might not have suited him, whereas an income from trade may have seemed more dependable and certainly affords a greater sense of independence. Hard work on his own land and casual jobs for Alice enabled William to pay his son's apprenticeship fees and John became a carpenter, occasionally employed at the Acton manor. Others benefited from employment with Alice at the manor. Peter Monk was another tenant who frequently worked at Acton in the early 1400s. Soon he was being retained for an annual £4 wage to shoe the plough beasts. By the 1420s his son was also working on the estates.

Two families typify the potential rewards of the relationship between Dame Alice and her workers, positions which may have been sought and given at the dinner table. In 1400 she employed a carter called Richard Strutt, who was also a tenant; another tenant, Ralph Strutt, was her swineherd in 1410 and there was a John Strutt on the plough team in 1426. The Strutts were obviously keen to advance one of their family and in 1419 Alice engaged Robert Strutt in the household, as one of her 'inhewys' staff. By 1430 he was renting a tenement for 20*s* and on the regular payroll as her granger. William Bregge, the Acton ploughman, also found employment for his children on Alice's estates: his son William worked as a swineherd and Margaret his daughter was the manor maidservant.

The farm workers and labourers who dined at Acton, if not regular members of her farm staff, were at least employed on a casual basis. A closer scrutiny suggests that dinners were provided for workers as much for mutual convenience as for good relationship or charity. When estate staff were invited, even from the lower ranks, we may guess that there was usually some business at stake. Many it appears were also subsistence farmers and any surplus or deficit was handled under the aegis of Alice's estates. She bought their surplus stock and purchased grain when the levels in her barns were getting low. They hired her carts and bought her wool when they had saved sufficient money from working in her fields. We can only guess at the degree of social intercourse between those of the third estate and the

A labourer, from an illustrated manuscript of
The Vision of Piers Plowman, *dated 1427.*

clergy and Alice's peers sitting at the top table. However, even if there were little direct conversation, when they came to dine they would have been part of the household. Despite their inequalities, they could no more have survived without Alice de Bryene than she could have without them.

While women were not specifically represented in the description of the three estates it is evident that they played significant roles. Even if not enclosed in nunneries some women were exceptionally pious, for example, Lady Margaret Hungerford.[45] A few others such as Margery Kempe strove to walk on Mary's path. While Margery's insistence on her right to seek God in her own way, in the public world rather than a recluse's cell, incurred hostility, accusations of heresy and condescending ridicule ('Woman, give up this life that you lead, and go and spin and card wool, as other women do'), many clergymen in high positions respected and supported her.[46] For the rest, in Martha's role, women mediated their relationships with the Church through patronage, and their social and business relations with clergymen helped to support many of them in their vocations.

Few women may have aspired to the warrior class, though there are several examples of women who did actually undertake combative roles to safeguard their own property and that of their husbands.[47] They also promoted their male relatives' interests and careers by social networking, and as heads of households appointed and employed men to act for them in official capacities. Women of the third estate toiled as did their husbands to support themselves and their families, even if their labours are not always so apparent. A survey of the women who visited Alice in 1412–13 gives further examples of women's relationships with the men of the three estates and also shows how diverse many of their labours were.

1. Marriage, the exchange of rings and vows, from a Norwich manuscript, c. 1400.

tres moi damoifele/ eft ce donc verites
En fin le weil sauoir/ qment wous le faues
ame tel wous dirai quant wous le demandes

2. Five dancing women accompanied by a man playing the lyre, Flemish, 1338–44.

3. Old Wardour Castle, Wiltshire, built by Lord John Lovell who obtained a building licence in 1393.

4. *Cooking for the household, Flemish, 1338–44.*

5. *Detail of the Gough Road Map, London and the Home Counties, anonymous, mid-fourteenth century. (East is at the top.)*

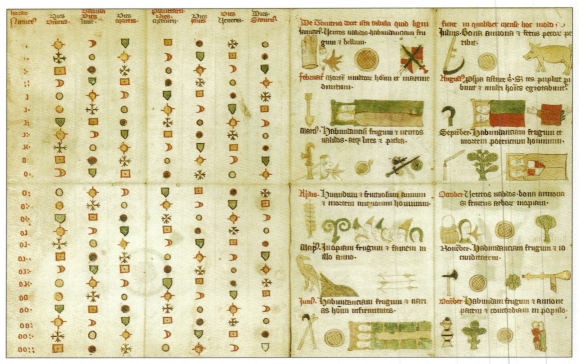

6. *Astrological and calendarial chart of the mid-fourteenth century. The right section illustrates prognostications for each month of one year.*

7. *St Petronella, whose feast day Dame Alice celebrated on 31 May, from a late fifteenth-century Book of Hours.*

8. *Alice de Raydon's Book of Hours, depicting the owner kneeling at prayer by the side of the Virgin Mary and Jesus, East Anglian,* c. *1320.*

9. *Lord John Lovell receiving his lectionary from the Dominican painter Sifrewas, c. 1400.*

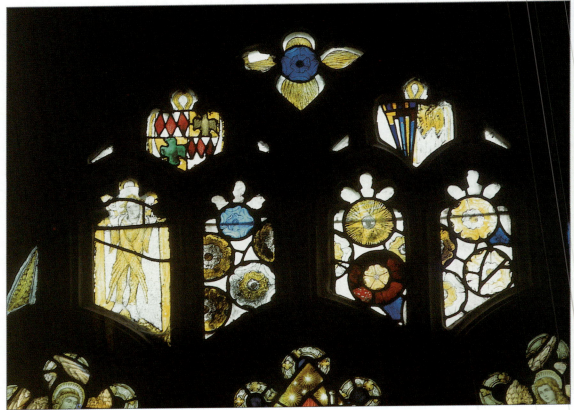

10. *East window of St Mary and St James, Hazelbury Bryan, Dorset. Alice de Bryene's arms are at the top right and those of John Montagu at the left.*

11. Part of the overpainted medieval rood-screen, St Peter and St Paul, Foxearth, Essex, depicting (from the left) the saints Helena, Mary Magdalene, Dorothy and Apollonia.

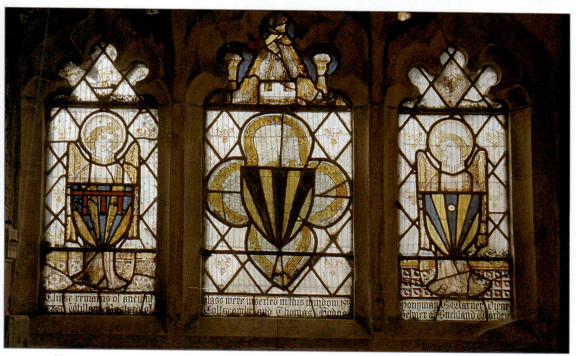

12. Arms of Lord Guy Bryan (centre), Sir Guy (left) and Sir William (right) in the bell tower of St James the Great, Slapton, Devon. The window was inserted in 1919 using fragments of medieval glass found in the chantry ruins.

13. Agricultural workers in the manor fields, English, c. 1390s.

CHAPTER 6

Women at the Table

In common with other contemporary household accounts there is a dearth of women at Acton, both in the household and at the dinner table. A similar scarcity is noticeable in the works of Chaucer and Shakespeare. This might give the impression that there were far fewer women than men in the later Middle Ages, but such an imbalance would not make empirical sense. No doubt the same proportion of male and female children were born then as are today. However, the apparent disparity in numbers between adult males and females should not be entirely ignored. It has been suggested by research in later centuries that in rural economies in particular infant boys were favoured over girls since their potential as long-term economic producers was more highly valued: if food was scarce and there were many mouths to feed, sons were fed before daughters. This bias still holds true in some agricultural communities, for example in parts of India and China, where there has been occasional evidence of more direct intervention such as the exposure of baby girls.

Nevertheless, there must have been plenty of women in the Middle Ages and if they are generally invisible, it does not mean they were not there. Much recent research has been devoted to resurrecting the circumstances of their lives, succinctly summed up in the phrase 'private wives, public husbands'.[1] Continuing significance is attached to the methods of record keeping and the inferior position of married women under the law, which conceal women's activities in the public sphere, but we need to be wary of concentrating our focus only on public roles. Women in the unrecorded privacy of their own homes would often have been busy and yet made many other contributions to the family economy and the communities in which they lived, the nature of which can partly be deduced from a survey of those who did and those who did not dine with Alice.[2]

Of the total named dinner guests throughout the year, including those described for example as 'a woman from Nayland', just over 8 per cent were women, not quite double the number of visiting ecclesiastics. In comparison with the overall averages, women were more likely to be invited on Sundays than men, but otherwise in order of preference for the rest of the week, they came like the men more frequently on Thursdays, Tuesdays and Mondays when meat was served, with a lower attendance on the fish days, Wednesdays being much more popular than Fridays and Saturdays. However, to conclude that Sundays were holidays and therefore women were free to do as they liked would be rather hasty.

The most frequent women guests on Sundays were the wife of Robert Dynham, Agnes Whyte who was married to Alex, and the wife of John Whyte, another Agnes. Dynham was Alice's chamberlain and the Whytes were engaged in various aspects of the household catering. In fact both John and Alex Whyte had served as pastry cooks at different times and all three men were likely to have been occupied in the household at dinner time. The presence, therefore, of at least one of these women on most Sundays is suggestive: it might be seen as a compensation, a way of fostering marital relationship on at least one day of the week, which also incidentally provided an opportunity for the women to savour their husbands' cooking and be waited upon by them. The circumstances of their visits on other days indicate that Dame Alice relied on them to help entertain some of her guests and also enjoyed their company. Both Robert Dynham and Alex Whyte had worked for her in the early 1390s before she finally settled in Suffolk so their relationship dated back many years.

It was not unusual for the wives of male retainers to act as companions or maids to the mistress of the house: of the six 'gentlewomen' in Elizabeth Berkeley's household in 1421, three were wives of members of her husband's retinue.[3] It may have been felt that such arrangements made for more stable relationships and helped to promote conjugal fidelity among the household servants. There is no evidence that the Dynham and Whyte women were formally retained by Alice, although occasional reference is made in the bailiffs' reports to Agnes, the lady's *cameraria* or chamberwoman, who was sometimes issued with grain to feed the manor poultry. This could have been one of the Agnes Whytes who occasionally helped her mistress with a variety of small domestic tasks. In any event all three couples enjoyed rent-free accommodation, and Alice occasionally bought produce from them, such as honey or lambs which were most likely part of these women's contribution to the family economy.

The only women permanently resident in the Acton household were Alice's maids: sometimes she had only one while on another occasion the steward accounted for wages of two. In the list of wages these women were always noted first. They are described as *ancillae*, meaning handmaiden or more formally translated as maidservant or lady's maid. No other description is given and we might guess that their roles fell somewhere between companion and servant. The specific wages of Dame Alice's *ancillae* are not given in the accounts, although as previously noted they received the same clothes allowance as her chaplains and squires, the other superior members of the household. In 1418 Lady Margaret Cromwell's 'gentlewoman' received an annual salary of 13s 4d (1s 8d less than her butler and baker), and her handmaid was paid 9s. The chamberwoman was paid 6s 8d as was one of her garth-women (a garth is a yard or enclosure, so such a servant may have been engaged to look after the poultry and the herb gardens), while the two other garth-women received 5s.[4] These latter servants probably only worked part-time. Tending gardens may well have been a job where women were able to find part-time employment as it was seasonal and could be done at odd times.[5]

Female servants were often engaged for only a short period, another reason for their comparative invisibility. Traditionally their terms of employment were annual and hiring dates varied according to regional custom,[6] although such contracts related more to agriculture labour than household companions. Since most women expected to get married short contracts were convenient. While appointment to a household post or as a farm-hand constituted a full-time job for a man, guaranteeing him a permanent wage, on marriage women assumed a new identity as *materfamilias* or *domina domus* and had to attend to their own families and domestic chores.[7] Service in a household was a way for a young woman to learn essential household skills and earn money for her dowry or as her own personal nest egg: Elizabeth Lovell had a maidservant called Elena Borley to whom she bequeathed a bed, a tunic and 40 marks for her marriage.

Adam and Eve at their traditional tasks, early fifteenth century.

Young women may also have joined a household temporarily for different reasons, for instruction, safe-keeping or to make new social contacts. In 1469 Margaret Paston wrote to her son John asking him to arrange for his sister Margery to stay with Lady Oxford or Lady Bedford. Margaret wanted her daughter out of the house because she had fallen in love with the bailiff, though she put the matter rather differently, 'for we be eythere of us wery of the othere'.[8] A couple of weeks after Easter 1412 the Acton steward noted that Agnes Sampson, daughter of Dame Alice's cousin Margaret, had come to join the household. Her name was noted before the list of guests for just a few weeks and then it seems she became one of the anonymous members of Alice's retinue. In any event it appears she left the manor sometime that summer, since her name was recorded a few months later as a visitor for one day only, significantly at Michaelmas when accounts were settled. Many years earlier between 1391 and 1394 the two young Filliol heiresses came to live at Acton. In their case it seems unlikely that they were engaged as maidservants: their particular circumstances will be discussed in more detail in the next chapter. However, these examples demonstrate that medieval women are generally more visible in the public world of a large household than in the privacy of their own homes.

Matchmaking is traditionally considered the domain of women. Agnes Sampson's short residence in the Acton household would have given her the opportunity of meeting potential partners in an appropriate environment. Once a suitable relationship had been established, negotiations about the marriage settlement could begin. These could be quite protracted and did not always succeed: diplomacy was an important feature.[9] The dinner Dame Alice hosted for Lady Doreward, Ralph Chamberlain and Richard Waldegrave on 1 July 1413 is significant in this respect. Isabel Doreward came with several of her household and a son and his wife who may have been the daughter of Ralph Chamberlain. In any event Elizabeth Chamberlain married one of Lady Doreward's sons,[10] and one of her daughters married the son of Sir Richard Waldegrave at about this time.[11] Whether or not these marriage alliances were discussed over dinner that day, the occasion would have provided an opportunity for various potential in-laws to meet each other.

Like the two Agnes Whytes, Margaret Brydbek was often invited to dine at Acton on Sunday and occasional weekdays. Once she came with a maidservant and another time with a daughter. Most months of the year she was a guest at least twice, except in July and September when she made single visits and in August, October and November when she did not come at all. Two years later Alice granted her alms of half a bushel of dried peas. Her husband is not mentioned, although ten years previously a John Brydbek had been paid in grain for his services as a human scarecrow.[12] It seems then that Margaret was an impoverished widow who was offered succour at Alice's table. The single visits of

A woman shearing sheep, from a fifteenth-century Latin Psalter.

two other women from Margaret's household, her daughter and servant, and the absence of all of them during some of the busiest months in the agricultural calendar, suggest they were occupied with their own household or employed to help others. It would not have been unusual for poor widows like Margaret Brydbek to have had a female servant: the daily tasks of even a very modest household, collecting firewood and water, looking after animals and a plot of land, cooking, brewing, baking and spinning could not have been easily undertaken without help. Several other widows like Margaret Archetin, Hawis Astle and Hawis Clerbek were guests at Acton, but whatever their individual circumstances the infrequency of their visits indicates they had busy lives.

Peasant women and the wives of smallholders are naturally pastoralists, for rearing sheep, carding and spinning wool, and working in various aspects of the dairy trade such as making cheese, are all jobs which can be done on a part-time basis and at or close to home.[13] Women were also employed casually when specific seasonal tasks were required like weeding, sowing and gleaning. Many of the female relatives of Alice's tenant farmers or workers were engaged for odd jobs.

Both Alice Peyton and Alice Fouler, wives of the Acton shepherds, helped by sowing seed, and stooking (stacking sheaves) at harvest time. These women very rarely dined at Acton but Alice also bought lambs from the Foulers, which were probably reared by the women. When John Fouler died in about 1430, his widow lost the right to free accommodation that had come with his job, but was able to pay the rent herself.

Margaret Fouler, the shepherd's daughter perhaps, assisted Edward Christmas one year rethatching some of the estate cottages, but whereas he was paid 4*d* a day with dinner, she only earned 1½*d* but was also fed. Sometime later Petronella Fouler earned the same daily rate, but there is no indication in either case whether these women were working a full or part-time day, nor exactly what their jobs were. There is evidence that in the years following the plague epidemics some women earned as much as men working in the fields at harvest time. However, these women are visible because they were fined, as were the men, for taking wages in excess of those laid down by the Statute of Labourers, which attempted to regulate pay demands at a time of labour shortages.[14] Generally, it would seem that while women were able to find seasonal jobs alongside men, it was usually more menial work and they were paid at a lower rate. If Margaret and Petronella's 1½*d* wage was for just half a day, it was still less than the top rate for a man's work, but no doubt many women were grateful, then as now, for the opportunity of some part-time work once their own daily chores had been completed. Nor were such jobs necessarily short-term: Alice Peyton was employed for thirty-five days sowing seed and Petronella worked for twenty-six days.

The disparity of wages for men and women is reflected in the grain liveries paid to the Acton farm workers, which averaged 4 quarters 2½ bushels per employee each year. The bailiffs received the most: their liveries came to 6 quarters 4 bushels, exactly double that awarded to the manor maidservants. This was probably fairly standard practice, since it was recommended in *Husbandry*, a medieval didactic tract, that as maidservants had special perks from looking after the milch cow and the poultry and may have been allowed to take home milk and eggs, a livery of a quarter of corn every sixteen rather than twelve weeks was considered appropriate. They were, however, expected to work as hard as the men.[15] The manor maidservant at Acton was invited to dine nearly every week, usually on Tuesdays, which must have been a part of her remuneration; she also received an annual clothes allowance of 6*s* 8*d*.

There are numerous references to women's casual labour in Alice's bailiffs' reports and also to the purchase of stock, usually from men though occasionally from women. In 1415–16, for example, Alice bought oxen, rams and ewes from her cousin Margaret Sampson. Another traditional way of supplementing the family income on a part-time basis was by brewing ale.[16] Little equipment was necessary, just large pots, a ladle, vat and straining cloth, all of which were likely to have been in most peasant kitchens. Often it seems women lent each other the necessary utensils and took it in turns to do the brewing. Such items were occasionally bequeathed by poor widows to close friends.[17] Various women are mentioned in the Layham court rolls, of which Alice held the jurisdiction in 1413, for breaking the assize of ale – an occasional fine worked out cheaper than acquiring a licence.[18] Women also earned extra money by weaving, spinning and carding wool, but these types of home-based self-employment leave no visible record. Providing accommodation was another way of earning extra money at home: Alice Mabbell charged 16*d* a week per head for two boys to board with her while they attended the Lavenham grammar school during the Easter and John the Baptist terms at Dame Alice's expense.[19] The potential flexibility of these kinds of jobs suited the circumstances of women's social and biological lives, an aspect of female employment that is a feature of the labour market today.

Curious absentees from the Acton dinner table are any female relatives of the Deyes. Deye is an old English word that originally meant a kneader, then a woman or man having charge of a dairy. The Deyes were frequent visitors to the manor and had long-standing connections with Alice on her various estates, renting land, doing casual jobs and working in the household. John, Peter, Richard and Robert were all dinner guests in 1413 and John's son later became Alice's harvest-reeve. She often bought stock from them, particularly calves and dairy items, yet no Deye woman is mentioned as having visited that year. Presumably some of these men were married or had mothers, sisters or daughters who may have been occupied milking cows and making cheese and butter. Alice Seg' did not dine at Acton in 1413 either, though in 1420 she was employed to look after the dairy herd at Bures. She was once issued with 7 yards of linen cloth, which at 8*d* a yard was a superior quality to the coarse 'polltrid' used for straining milk and other liquids, and may have been part of her livery as a dairy maid.[20]

Of the dozen or so anonymous women who dined at Acton in 1412–13, 3 came at Christmas, 2 on Easter Monday, 1 at the end of July and 2 at the height of the harvest season. The dates of their visits suggest they came to the manor to earn some money, selling trinkets, hawking goods and locally grown produce or helping with the extra work necessitated by seasonal festivities and feeding the boon-workers in August. A meal at the manor was part of their wage. Three days before Corpus Christi, which in 1413 was followed by the vigil of the Nativity of John the Baptist and Midsummer's Eve (24 June), all significant festivals, six women who had spent the morning gathering herbage and grasses dined on bacon and pigeon at Alice's table. It was traditional around the time of great feasts to change the floor coverings of the public reception areas of a household; indeed in some of the more isolated *pueblos blancos* (white towns) in Andalucia, patios and pavements are still strewn today with sweet-smelling foliage at Corpus Christi, as were the floors of homes in the west of Ireland early in the 1900s. On 29 December 1412 one Agnes Lavender and her daughter, employed no doubt to help with the extra Christmas laundry, had dinner at Acton. These one-off jobs could only be fulfilled by those who did not have permanent paid employment outside the home.

Looking for extra work on a casual basis or selling home produce was not the only reason for a woman to visit. On 20 October 1412, three weeks after the end of the financial year, the wife of Thomas Pepyr came with one of her household to dine with Alice. No one else of that name visited that year and the only mention in the Acton records of someone with a similar name was John Pypere, the tenant of Alice's Thorp Morieux estate in 1428. Taking into account the vagaries of medieval spelling, they could have been members of the same family. Six months later Thomas Payn's wife arrived with a maidservant and stayed the night. Thomas Payn rented land at Bures and in 1428 John Payn, possibly a relative, had the lease for the Wherstead manor. If Mistress Pepyr and Mistress Payn were wives of superior tenants, which seems possible, then their invitations to Acton are suggestive. Either they came as representatives of their husbands to settle accounts or Alice wanted to have the opportunity of meeting them, though it might be naive to imagine that this was only in the interest of sociability and good relationships – it would have given her the chance to assess them personally, woman to woman.

Wives of some of Alice's other tenants of smaller properties were also invited periodically during the year such as Joan Berner, Isabel Chapman, the wife of John Frend, Rose Gryffyn and Alice Lorkyn. Maud and Joan Archer, relatives of one of Alice's tenants who was employed to do a variety of casual jobs and rented the dairy herd, seem to have been dependable women on whom she relied for extra help at busy times of the year, before the New Year festivities and at the beginning of the ploughing and harvest season. The wife of John Saltwell also came several times with her husband in August 1413. Saltwell had helped with the harvest at Acton in the 1390s and later was engaged to do carpentry work.

During the harvest season it must often have been necessary to repair scythes, sickles, rakes and carts; his wife may have helped him or assisted with the feeding of the boon-workers. It can be argued that within this environment men and women played complementary roles according to their responsibilities and capabilities and it would not have been unusual for householders to employ the female relatives of their workers at busy times .

Other women who dined at Acton seem to have come as representatives of their male relatives or have been invited as a way of cementing relationships and extending patronage. On 25 April 1413 Robert Cawston's daughter enjoyed a feast of veal, suckling pig, capon and pigeons held in honour of St Mark. The records show that Cawston was involved in the wool trade and frequently bought fleeces from the Acton manor, although he himself did not visit at all that year. William Boteler's wife also visited at the end of December and stayed a few days in January, though Boteler himself is never once mentioned as a guest. Yet he and Alice concluded many business deals together, buying and selling produce, stock, grain and wool. It would be interesting to know whether these two women came because their male relatives were otherwise occupied, to do business on their behalf.

Both of these women arrived on their own, as did Alice Growlond, Alice Wysman and Alice Nowers. John Nowers, who did not visit in 1412–13, was the keeper of the Acton pigeons and appropriately, since she may have helped look after them, pigeons were on the menu when Alice Nowers came to dinner. All three women are likely to have lived nearby, as did those wives and daughters of Alice's friends who frequently visited on their own, while other female visitors came from much further afield. The 'woman of London' who arrived on 13 January with her maidservant and a household member may have been returning home after staying with friends or relatives for the Christmas season. No further description of her is given and it would seem that she was exercising the traditional right of travellers to request hospitality along their way. She, like the two 'sisters of Canterbury' who enjoyed Alice's goodwill five months later, would have been a welcome guest bringing news and gossip from the larger world beyond the small Suffolk community. These latter two visitors were apparently quite intrepid since no man or household member is mentioned as accompanying them.

Women appear to have been as mobile as men at this time, if they were free from home-based responsibilities. Those who are only identified by the villages from which they came travelled an average of 4 miles to Acton, the shortest journey from Sudbury being about 3 miles and the longest from Bures 6 miles. The anonymous men who dined at the manor generally came from further away. Recent research has shown that this trend predominates in our contemporary society: women generally work closer to home than men. If Alice's female guests walked to and from the manor, the journey would have taken them at least an hour each way, a significant amount of time in terms of the jobs they could have been doing at home. Sometimes they must have been able to hitch a ride in a cart or anyhow join a group walking along the way. In 1413 Margery Kempe travelled extensively to various religious and pilgrimage centres, including York, Bridlington, Norwich, Lincoln and London, before setting off for the Holy Land. She was usually accompanied by her husband or maidservant. When she left England that autumn, her extravagant behaviour alarmed her travelling companions who often abandoned her, but within a short while she found a new guide or group of pilgrims with whom to travel.[21]

While individuals and pilgrims might join up and travel together, relying on numbers for safety, for single men were as vulnerable as women, those with more money or business to attend to took many of their household with them. Elizabeth Berkeley journeyed from Gloucestershire to Essex in 1421 with 32 in her retinue, 57 horses and 11 hackneys but this was for a two-month stay and she took chattels, staff and provisions with her.[22] Lady Joan Swinburne, who stayed with Alice de Bryene on the nights of 4 and 5 September, was accompanied by her son, a maidservant, a chaplain, 2 squires, 4 valets and 2 boys. She was the second wife of Sir Robert Swinburne, a Member of Parliament for Essex between 1377 and 1390, and had been widowed since 1391. A wealthy woman in her own right, Lady Swinburne had four sons and two daughters. Her stepson Sir Thomas Swinburne had earlier tried to oust her from some of her late husband's estates and had been forced to produce securities for over £1,000 as a guarantee not to molest her, her servants, children and tenants. His death on 9 August 1412 may have freed her from the worry of continuing litigation but not from other responsibilities. It seems likely that one reason for her visit was to oversee the construction of her late husband and stepson's double brass and altar tomb in St Peter's church at Little Horkesley, just a few miles from the Acton manor. Even if she had not been particularly fond of her stepson, contemporary etiquette demanded that she involve herself with these last rites.[23]

Alice and Joan Swinburne were old acquaintances and distantly related through the marriage of Lady Joan's stepdaughter, another Joan, to John Rokewode.[24] Agnes Rokewode, the wife of their son William, was a frequent visitor to Acton and dined with her family there the day before Lady Joan's arrival. Since a greater selection of high quality food was served on this occasion than the following day, it could be that the Swinburne party was expected but had been delayed. But whatever the circumstance of her visit, Lady Joan did not rest long at the manor and left after dinner on 5 September. Although she and Alice would have had much to talk about, sharing many common experiences and concerns, leisure was not really a fifteenth-century concept and Lady Swinburne's short stay was likely to have been a combination of both business and pleasure.

However, other visits had a more personal intent. Alice's sister-in-law Lady Joan Waldegrave arrived on 14 February with her maidservant, a son, a squire and three household members, but without her husband. It was in fact the only time that year that she came without him. She stayed for two nights and apart from some workers and two friars the only other guest was Alice's cousin Margaret Sampson. The first day of her visit was St Valentine's Day. Chaucer, in his *Parlement of Foules* written in 1382, said this was the day, 'whan every foul cometh there to chese his make', but was not very optimistic about the favourable outcome of this courtship. Although he satirized the tradition of romantic love, the birds attending the Court of Nature to choose their mates sang a sweet farewell to winter and heralded the arrival of spring:

> Now welcome, somer, with thy sonne softe
> That hast thes wintres werdes overshake
> And driven away the longe nyghtes blake.
> Saynt Valentyn, that art ful hy on lofte
> Thus syngen smale foules for thy sake.[25]

No mention was made in *The Parlement of Foules* of the tradition of sending love tokens – that was first recorded by Lydgate at the beginning of the fifteenth century.[26] But even if a recitation of Chaucer's poetry and tales of courtly love helped to enliven a dreary afternoon at the end of winter, the occasion may have been one of mixed emotions: Alice's husband had died on 6 February, and the seventh day after a death was one marked by special celebrations. The actual anniversary of Sir Guy's death does not appear to have been commemorated by any public ritual at Acton, though the absence of any significant guests on that day and the following week suggest that it was honoured in private. But the eighth day, after the time set aside for private mourning, was the one Alice de

Bryene chose to share with close female relatives. Two friars from Sudbury arrived the following day, as well as another member of the Waldegrave household, and greater quantities of fresh fish were purchased than usual. The friars were still there on the final day of Lady Waldegrave's visit when a great feast was held with swan, heron, suckling pig and capons on the menu.

The administration and management of estates and care for workers and tenants were a continual concern and responsibility for women running their households. Family was important too as the circumstance of Lady Waldegrave's visit demonstrates. It has been argued that the social networks of peasant widows tended to be more independent of kin[27] and, although this may have been true of gentry and noble women as well, families of the wealthier classes were often physically separated by geographical distance and had interests and business in different parts of the country. Alice's sole surviving daughter did not visit in 1413, possibly hampered by child-bearing and the responsibilities of managing her own household and estates. However, by returning to her birthplace when she was widowed, Dame Alice did have close relatives nearby. One of her most frequent women guests was her cousin Margaret Sampson.[28] She was invited every month except in April and August, many times spending the night at the manor though she cannot have lived far away since she sometimes came for just the day. In November 1412 she stayed for ten days when Morgan Gough, a former trustee of Lord Bryan and probably Alice de Bryene's new receiver after Micheldever's death, came for a week. He was certainly an honoured guest since high status food was on the menu every day of his visit and a fresh pipe of red wine was opened in his honour. He also brought a chaplain and two household members with him.

The occasions of Margaret's visits demonstrate how much Alice relied on her relative for support to help entertain certain guests, even if she may have been something of a country cousin compared with those ladies of the nobility with whom Alice must have associated when she was married. The only time Margaret's husband accompanied her was during the New Year celebrations; otherwise she came alone or with household members, and once only with an unnamed son and daughter. This son may have been Thomas Sampson, one of Alice's chantry trustees, whom we met in the last chapter. Sometimes it appears that a woman was invited to represent Dame Alice while she was away, as on 2 May 1413 when the wife of John Whyte came to dine with various estate workers. This was Hock Day, and Alice held the jurisdiction of the Hock Day court in Acton, which she may have attended;[29] it was also the anniversary of her stepfather's death, an occasion she would certainly have commemorated, probably with her half-brothers. It would have been natural to call on a female friend to preside over the dinner table in her absence.

The support of female relatives and friends at times of private significance is natural for women sharing subjective, emotional experiences. Female companionship must also have been welcome in a household dominated by men and at the dinner table where the majority of the dinner guests were male. Social interchange, gossip and entertainment were important factors as well. On 11 May 1413 Margaret Sampson was invited to dine with both the Agnes Whytes and Isabel Chapman. The other principal guests were the rector of Withersfield, who had come on one of his protracted visits, and two Austin friars from Norwich. This was the day dedicated to St John of Bridlington,[30] whose shrine Margery Kempe went to visit a few weeks later.[31] An Austin friar who had died in 1379, his reputation as a wise and beloved superior and deeply religious man must have been instrumental in precipitating the manifestation of numerous miracles near his tomb immediately after his death. Canonized in 1401, details of his life were bound to excite the imaginations of those who were virtually his contemporaries. Everyone loves a story about a modern hero and it is perhaps not surprising that Alice chose to share the visit of the Austin friars, who came to celebrate St John of Bridlington's feast day and may even have known him, with some of her close women friends.

If listening to and telling stories is considered the province of women, then it would have been interesting to eavesdrop at Alice's table on 29 December 1412 when at least twelve women sat down to dinner together, with eight household members and a harper. The only other named guest, significantly if he lived up to his name, was Richard Scrivener. It seems likely that Alice de Bryene invited these ladies to help with the preparations for the forthcoming New Year feast, decorating the hall, making garlands, wrapping gifts, preparing sweetmeats, setting up the trestle tables and composing wordgames, mummeries and riddles. It may have been hard work but enjoyable too and the company dined well on beef, mutton, bacon, goose and conies.

Of course these women must have gossiped over the meal that day. The gossip was an important figure in the later Middle Ages, from the word godsib (sibling) or godparent, denoting the spiritual affinity of the baptized and their sponsors. More significantly a gossip was a woman who attended a close friend when she was in labour and often assisted at the birth. Such women were part of the informal domestic webs of information and power, passing on their wisdom and experience with little respect for hierarchy, though at the same time they adhered

St John of Bridlington who died in 1379 and was canonized in 1401, from the Duke of Bedford Hours, c. 1400.

*'Of a feast we sing', from a late
medieval music score.*

to traditional and conservative concepts and their opinions must often have been
prejudiced. Many of their 'old wives' tales' consisted of practical advice on sex,
rearing animals, horticulture, cures and the interpretations of dreams and
omens.[32] Predictably 'women's tongues' were usually conceived as being divisive,
the ready butt of medieval misogyny, though it was not until the mid-sixteenth
century that the gossip became a pejorative figure.[33]

Garrulous women were considered to be idle. Just as the majority of medieval
women are invisible, so too their voices are muffled. But one woman's voice comes
clearly to us across the centuries with words that speak chapters. At noon in
August 1570, Jone Tetterell, widow, was challenged by her fellow reapers as they
took a lunch break from their work in the Acton cornfields; they wanted to know
to whom she would give her chattels on her death. She replied that they would
easily be given away since she had so little. Then John Jyan said to her, 'Then
I pray you give them to William Tetterell, your son's son', and she answered that
that was what she would do, whereupon her grandson William came over to her,
pulled off his cap and thanked her.[34] Her will was proved eighteen months later.

In the trust deed executed before her death, in which the income from certain lands was reserved to fund her chantry, Alice de Bryene excluded the income from a property called Struttes during the lifetime of a woman named Alice Davy to whom she had granted the land. Davy is a fairly common Suffolk name, although no Davys visited Acton in 1413. However, in 1428 a Thomas Davy rented Alice's mill at Raydon. Her distant relative John Rokewode left 13s 4d to Alice Davy of Stansfield in his will of 1415, which was probated in 1423.[35] He also left money to various religious orders and to Thomas Davy who was the Stansfield rector:[36] Alice Davy might have been his sister who kept house for him. On the other hand, she could have been one of Dame Alice's permanent companions for whom she wanted to provide after her death, or possibly a god-daughter.

There is no specific mention of any of Alice de Bryene's god-daughters dining at Acton in 1412–13, though she is likely to have had many. The agreement of wealthy women to undertake the sponsorship of the children of their dependants bridged the gulf in the social hierarchy. Such relationships enlarged the social network and were usually taken seriously. In 1420 Matilda Bowes, wife of Sir William Bowes, left sheep to three of her god-daughters who were all named after her. Another god-daughter also called Matilda, daughter of Sir Robert Hilton, received two books, one called 'ye gospelles', the other 'Trystram'.[37] Alice's daughter Elizabeth left twenty marks towards the marriage of her god-daughter, Alice Sampson, in her will.

The women who visited Alice in 1413 are representative of the entire social spectrum from those six nameless females enjoying a meal after a morning of gathering rushes to the well-to-do Lady Joan Swinburne who arrived with a large retinue for a very short stay. As we have seen wives came without their husbands and daughters without their parents; some in fact visited as representatives of their male relatives. The absence of certain men is also indicative of different gender roles. The infrequency of William Rokewode's visits in 1413 compared with those of his wife can be explained by his public duties: he had been appointed as escheator of Norfolk and Suffolk that year and was also involved in administering the will of his uncle, Sir Thomas Swinburne, whose interests in France involved prolonged and complicated negotiations.[38]

This survey of Dame Alice's women guests sheds some light on their activities. Their comparatively infrequent presence at the dinner table must often have been because they were busy cooking their own meals and looking after their homes, children, land and animals, while their male relatives were working for Alice or

Man asleep in a cornfield.

selling the family produce. This did not, however, exclude the possibility of negotiating their own deals or doing so on behalf of their menfolk. While their domestic responsibilities usually kept them at home, they were on occasion as mobile as men and as capable of undertaking the same tasks, whether it was breeding stock, working in the fields or overseeing the construction of a family tomb. On occasion it appears they were invited to help entertain important guests: at other times they came to be entertained. As well as this we may surmise that some of them found time to be sociable and sympathetic, characteristics that conform to traditional gender concepts.

CHAPTER 7

The Wider World

Reviewing further details of Alice de Bryene's life can tell us something of a medieval woman's work in the wider world beyond her household and estates, the extent of her authority and the contributions she made to society. Much has been written about peasant and urban women in this period and their economic roles, and the lifestyles of aristocratic and noble women have also been described,[1] but the activities and occupations of gentlewomen with large estates and an ample amount of expendable income are less well documented. It must be apparent by now that such women were not just rich and idle, though their labours tend to appear less productive than the jobs of their poorer country cousins or towndwellers, since they were often carried out in the household or within the realm of service to the rural community. This might have earned them prestige and provided them with stimulation and satisfaction but their activities cannot be measured in economic terms.

There has been a tendency to lump together the pastimes of women of the landholding class whether they were dowager queens, countesses or country gentry. In this type of exercise women like Alice de Bryene appear to have had rather minor roles, humdrum lives and little public influence, compared with ladies of the upper echelons of society. They did not have that kind of spectacular wealth that enabled a lady like Elizabeth de Burgh, Lady of Clare, for example, to found a college at Cambridge.[2] Nor were their social connections and fortunes sufficiently attractive to ensure that through marriage or in widowhood they would be in a position to wield significant influence and patronage.

One of the problems inherent in attempting to assess the contributions these women made to society and their access to power is the distinction that has been drawn between public and private spheres.[3] The review of the position of the medieval household made in earlier chapters and more specifically the description of Dame Alice's estates, lifestyle and guests reveal the difficulty in separating these two spheres, since the household was a woman's workplace. A further distinction needs to be drawn between the economic life in the urban centres and the body of rural dwellers. About 90 per cent of the population lived and worked in the country at this time and much of their life was governed by the demands of the land and the rhythm of the seasons.

To run a household meant developing managerial skills in many diverse areas, employing and supervising staff, organizing guest lists, meals and festivities and maintaining social networks. Heads of households were major employers and by their engagement of labourers and purchase of produce for consumption in the household they played a significant role in stimulating the economic life of the community. Decisions also had to be made about expenditure, repairs and renovations, and rebuilding needed to be overseen and litigation dealt with. Examples are often cited of women who actually undertook the physical defence of their properties, like Margaret Paston who wrote to her husband in 1448 to send arms so she could protect one of their manors in his absence. It appears to have been such a commonplace occurrence that in the same letter she also asked him to buy almonds, sugar and material for clothes for herself and the 'childer'.[4]

Households were the nerve-centres of estate management which required a basic knowledge of husbandry, agriculture and local manorial custom. Labour and tenant relationships had to be managed and both rights and obligations acknowledged and fulfilled. Also widows like Alice had all once been married women with family relationships to maintain, children to advance in society and their own property rights to protect. All these aspects of work were part of the daily occupations of a woman of the landholding class, but she had other tasks and interests beyond the household and 'busying herself in the family interest'.[5]

MANORIAL OBLIGATIONS

One of the privileges of lordship was the right to exercise authority in the manor courts and collect revenue from fines, as well as for keeping records of the proceedings. This right automatically descended to a woman on the death of her husband. By the end of the fourteenth century the old structure of obligations that the vassal or bonded servant owed his landlord was fast diminishing in favour of leases and wages. However, certain manorial services still existed between some tenants and their landlords. There were payments such as the entry fine levied before a new tenant could take over a lease, 'merchet', the sum payable on the marriage of a bondman's daughter and 'heriot', a kind of death duty usually in the form of cattle or sheep, which was due to the lord on the death of a tenant. As previously noted, Alice did not always enforce this latter obligation: the old beast worth 4*s* was returned to a widow at her Bures estate. She did, however, collect the fine due to her when a marriage was contracted between the daughter of John Wysman, one of her few remaining bondmen at Acton, and the son of her 'supervisor', Thomas Malcher.[6]

Alice inherited rights in the manor courts at Oxenhall in Gloucestershire, at Sutton Poyntz in Dorset, at Wherstead, Layham, Acton, Bures and Raydon in Suffolk and at Foxearth, Liston and Pentelow in Essex.[7] Revenue came from fines levied in the manor courts for minor misdemeanours such as trespass and from manorial dues, though on most of Alice's estates nearly all customary labour services were commuted to cash or commodity rents. While a landlord, whether man or woman, might be present at the manorial court, in most cases a steward was instructed to oversee the proceedings. There is no evidence that Dame Alice ever attended the courts over which she had jurisdiction but she was obviously aware of what went on, and occasionally instructed her steward to waive her rights when, for example, one of her relatives let his animals stray on her land.[8] At an earlier date when manorial payments were more lucrative since there were many more bondmen, Elizabeth de Burgh enjoyed an annual revenue of over £100 from her numerous courts and seems occasionally to have been present, at least to accept the entry fines of leading vassals.[9]

EXECUTORSHIP OF WILLS

Appointing women as executors of relatives' wills is often cited as evidence of affection and trust, as well as an acknowledgement of their administrative abilities.[10] Alice acted in this capacity for her husband and father-in-law and probably also did so for her stepfather and stepgrandfather. Lord John Devereux appointed his daughter Jane as his executor, although his son was alive at the time,[11] and Alice's granddaughter Maud named her mother as one of her two executors.[12] It is likely to have been a pragmatic decision too for women were essentially home-based and would have had more time to concentrate on and deal with ongoing routine and administrative detail. Supervising the execution of a will was not only a matter of fulfilling the deceased's last wishes, but settling his debts as well. Alice had a copy of a letter addressed to all Sir John de Sutton's executors, who were unnamed, by one of the clerks who had compiled the accounts for various of his manors.[13] It was an appeal for money owing to him and for expenses incurred in the course of his work. The clerk complained that all he had so far received from the executors was 'un gowne de noir drap' – black

Arms of Sir Guy Bryan now in the United States of America.

clothes to wear at his late employer's burial. We may guess that it was a woman who ensured this essential detail was observed in time.

In the case of winding up large estates the work involved was likely to have been considerable.[14] Sir Guy Bryan's death abroad in 1386 may have absolved Alice from making funeral arrangements, but there would still have been obits of some kind to organize, the 'month's mind' and various other anniversaries to observe. Possibly a monument of some sort would have been erected at the Bryan chantry at Slapton and other memorials made. There is evidence that there was once a window bearing Sir Guy's arms in Allhallows Church in Sudbury[15] and it is probable that Alice commissioned and installed others to commemorate him in places where he had close connections. In the same church the arms of Alice's father and grandfather were also once displayed.

There might also have been a memorial mass if the relatives and executors had wished. This would have presented a logistical exercise in itself if it included masses at various churches and the distribution of clothes, ale, meat, alms and candles to the poor. These celebrations were an essential obligation on the part of those who headed large households, a display commensurate with their 'honour' from which all those connected with the family could expect to benefit. Nor can we discount the possibility that Sir Guy's remains were interred at the Slapton chantry: that had been the wish expressed in his will and it was not uncommon for bodies to be embalmed or stripped of flesh and the skeleton or heart dispatched to the favoured place of burial.

Though Sir Guy's will was unusually brief and simple, Alice appears to have been quite conscientious in fulfilling it. She did at least rectify one of his omissions and in employing members of her husband's retinue provided for their future. There were other administrative matters to be dealt with as well in the execution of a will. First the deceased's personal seal had to be surrendered and then the will authenticated before letters of administration could be issued and probate granted. Sir Guy's will was probated on 30 March, some seven weeks after his death. If there were several executors, as in Lord Bryan's case, those who opted out of the administration were required to appoint a proctor. Then an inventory had to be compiled, special commissions undertaken where indicated and final accounts drawn up before letters of dismissal could be issued.

Of the six executors appointed by Lord Bryan before his death in 1390, Sir Robert Fitzpayne and John Lord Devereux were dead three years later, Sir John Chandos died in 1397,[16] Micheldever in 1400 and Walter Trote in 1402, leaving Alice as the sole executor. The litigation with Sir William Bryan and Lord Bryan's numerous financial deals[17] meant it was unlikely that his will could be discharged quickly and in fact seven years after his death there were still outstanding matters that Micheldever in his own will asked his executors to settle.[18] A recognizance for £500 given to Alice and Micheldever in 1393 by the London merchant Bartholomew Bosano indicates either that she and Micheldever were in business together, or that just the two of them were acting as executors of Lord Bryan's will even though two other executors were still alive.[19] In 1405 when Dame Alice was the last surviving executor there were still matters to be dealt with on the late Lord Bryan's estates.[20]

FINANCIAL AND LEGAL AFFAIRS

There is evidence that many women were active in the business world. Women in towns, especially London, are particularly visible in this context since they were able to take advantage of the *femme sole* status and trade independently even if married.[21] Margery Kempe is a notable example of a married women who set up her own

The sole surviving impression of Alice de Bryene's seal attached to a deed, dated 10 February 1394, in which she appointed an attorney to act for her at Foxearth.

business in King's Lynn, brewing ale and grinding corn though both enterprises failed.[22] Perhaps more remarkable is the fact that her financial independence enabled her to discharge her husband's debts, a bargain she struck with him in return for his agreement to join her in taking a vow of chastity. Before leaving for her first pilgrimage she asked her parish priest to make a public announcement from the pulpit that she would personally settle any claim made against her husband.[23]

Despite the Church's ruling on usury, women were moneylenders as well as men. There is one mention in Micheldever's receiver's accounts of a 30*s* debt collected by him in 1395 on Dame Alice's behalf from the late Donald, a surgeon.[24] Alice's grandmother owed debts of 40*s* each to several women, not all of whom can be identified as widows or tradeswomen.[25] Peasant women too are known to have been in the moneylending business.[26] It is apparent that women on Alice's estates were economically active. As we have seen she entertained the female relatives of some of her business associates and concluded deals with them. In about 1425, for example, she paid Margaret Chamberlain, who seems to have been a relation of her London agent and steward Richard Chamberlain, for livery cloth.[27]

As property owners widows needed to be *au fait* with practices in the world of real estate. There are indications that Alice bought property, for example the land at Polstead in Suffolk that she designated for the trust she set up to finance her chantry, which appears not to have been part of her original Bures' inheritance and was probably acquired by her for her own use.[28] It is also possible that she acted as a mortgagee, which would explain her interest in the Thorp Morieux estate mentioned in Chapter 3. While custom generally prevented women from acting in executive roles on their own behalf, Alice was able, like other women of her class, to appoint attorneys to act and litigate for her.[29] Similarly, she enfeoffed various trustees with her manor at Sutton Poyntz, a common device used by lawyers to effect tax evasion, ensure a particular descent or give protection against claimants.[30] When she was awarded joint custody of property devised to her daughters by Lord Bryan, it was an acknowledgement of her interest in her daughters' inheritance, and her administrative and executive capabilities.[31]

Once a will had been proved women often had to protect their property rights and nearly every death was likely to prove a hurdle to a straightforward inheritance. A stepson like Lady Joan Swinburne's or a brother-in-law such as Sir William Bryan ensured that widows had to be continually vigilant. Just three months after Sir Guy's death Alice went with Lord Bryan to the King's Court at Westminster to confirm that she held the charter relating to the manor of Sutton Poyntz which was part of her jointure and register her life interest in it.[32] While a jointure was settled on the wife at the time of her marriage, dower was that portion of the husband's property, usually a third, that came to a widow for the rest of her life on her husband's death. Such settlements caused endless problems. In 1412, twenty-five years after Sir Philip Bryan's death, his widow Joan and her third husband sued Alice's daughter Philippa and her husband Henry Scrope for dower at Puncknowle in Dorset, which Philippa had inherited more than twenty years before.[33] In fact Philippa had died in 1406 so it would seem that Scrope had continued to occupy the property and had not acknowledged Joan's third interest in it.

Recourse to lawyers in the Middle Ages was as time-consuming and expensive as it is today. Christine de Pisan writing in 1405 advised women to attempt to settle matters amicably rather than go immediately to the law courts, pointing out that they would be taken advantage of because of their inexperience.[34] Advice and mediation could be sought from the widow's council or approach made to influential friends. The only specific reference to Alice's council is the provision of furs granted to her council members in the stewards' reports, but we can presume she consulted many of her influential dinner guests, such as Sir John Howard, and made approaches to people who had access to those with whom she had to negotiate. While she must often have paid for advice, she may also sometimes have used gentle persuasion to get close friends or kin to help her.

Shortly after Alice's grandmother died in 1392, Lord Devereux wrote to her widower Sir John de Sutton about property that his wife had alienated or transferred which by right formed part of Alice's inheritance.[35] He explained his interest in the matter quite candidly, namely that his son had married one of her heirs, and asked de Sutton to assist him and send all the necessary documents post-haste. In September of that year the escheator of Essex was ordered to give Alice possession of her properties and she paid a half mark's fine to delay paying homage and fealty until the following Easter.[36] Since Alice had a copy of the letter Devereux wrote we may guess that she had asked him for help, an approach that was obviously effective and economically sound and should not be viewed as a display of a lack of autonomy or initiative.

Securing the inheritance was only one task. Assistance might also have to be given to help children in their legal entanglements. Evidence from Micheldever's receiver's accounts of 1391–1400 demonstrates that Alice travelled quite often during this period. In September 1391 she visited Devereux's Penshurst castle and went again sometime between Easter 1392 and Michaelmas 1393. While she may have been visiting her daughter there, the sudden death of Lord Devereux in February 1393 meant that further help would have been needed to protect her daughter's inheritance. Philippa and her husband were potentially a very wealthy couple but both were still underage. The revenues of the Bryan manor of Puncknowle and the Devereux manor of Donington in Buckinghamshire were quickly taken into the king's hands. The custody of the rest of Lord Bryan's estates, which had been held by Lord Devereux, was awarded to Richard II's brother John Holland, Earl of Huntingdon.[37]

Alice was fortunate that her stepfather, Sir Richard Waldegrave, had managed to keep a foot in both political camps during the troubled years of Richard II's reign. His position close to both the king and the opposition must have been useful to Alice as far as the custody of her daughter's estates was concerned. However, her presence in London in 1392, 1393, in the summer of 1394 and again in October the following year suggests that she too may have been busy whispering in official ears, if not to ask for *douceurs* (favours), at least to prevent *douleurs* (sorrows). The next few years culminating in Richard II's 'tyranny', deposition and murder were precarious times. Waldegrave finally severed his relationship with the king in November 1397, and would no longer have been able to make representations for Alice. Though Philippa was now a widow she was at least old enough to secure possession of her inheritance.[38] At about this time Micheldever accounted for a sum of over 11s for doing some business on Philippa's behalf.[39] Probably this had something to do with Philippa's inheritance but the fact that Alice paid for it suggests that if she had not actually initiated the action she took responsibility for it. It is also apparent from the same receiver's accounts that Alice had custody of certain Bryan properties pending her daughter's majority.

Families usually tried to ensure that a daughter's property, whether it was her jointure or land she had inherited as an heiress, reverted to the bloodline on her death if she died childless. Various legal devices were used to protect this interest. However, during his lifetime the rents and profits of the wife's estates were deemed to belong to her husband. When Alice's son-in-law Robert Lovell found himself in financial straits because he had pledged large sums on Prince Henry's behalf he was forced to mortgage some of his wife's property to settle outstanding debts.[40] This may have given Lovell some temporary relief but he continued to be financially embarrassed, claiming as late as 1427 that Henry V had been indebted to him for many years for £2,230. On his death in 1434 chattels to the value of £150 were confiscated in settlement of a debt. It seems to have been a fairly motley collection of goods that were surrendered: granted there were some silver goblets and spoons, pewter vessels, a pair of beds with silk hangings, a pipe and a hogshead of wine, but there were also carts, a wagon bound with iron, a plough and household utensils worth £20, hardly selling off the family silver.[41] Nevertheless, one may imagine that Lovell's widow was active in deciding which items she could most easily do without.

If a woman were keen that her heritage and patrimony would revert to her children or her family of origin on her death, then she needed to be vigilant and aware of her husband's intentions. However, a different situation might prevail, either because she could be easily manipulated or if her loyalty lay more with her husband's family. Alice's great-granddaughter Avice allowed her husband, James Ormond, Earl of Wiltshire, to entail her estates to his heirs in default of their having children of their own.[42] There is plenty of evidence of Earl James' rapaciousness and dynastic ambitions for his own bloodline,[43] which in the event only partially succeeded, but he would not have been able to go so far without his wife's agreement.

THE POLITICAL ARENA

The political situation was bound to reverberate on women's lives. While military action, the war with France and Richard II's deposition may not have had a direct effect on the household, discussions and speculations about the implications of any new development in the political arena must often have been made at the dinner table. Few women would have been spared the loss of a relative or close friend during the turmoil of these troubled times. The execution of her son-in-law Henry Scrope was one tragedy that Alice would have had to have endured: the murder of her husband's cousin John Montagu, 3rd Earl of Salisbury, was another. Montagu, a close friend of Richard II, had failed in his attempt to muster Welsh support for Richard on his return from Ireland in 1399. Nevertheless, he was included in a general amnesty given to Richard's supporters by Henry IV in 1400. But his misguided attempt with the Earls of Huntingdon and Kent to seize Henry at Windsor on Twelfth Night sealed his fate and he was murdered by a mob in Cirencester. Their reward for this act of citizens' arrest and popular justice was an annual grant of four does for the men, six bucks for the women and a tun of wine each. Montagu's body was buried at Cirencester Abbey but his head was sent in a basket, with Kent's, to the king.[44]

Christine de Pisan, whose son had served in Montagu's household, wrote of him: '. . . he was so humble, sweet and courteous in all his ways, and had every man's voice for being loyal in all places and right prudent. Full largely he gave and timely gifts. He was brave and fierce as a lion. Ballads and song and roundels and lays right beautiful he made. Though but a layman, still his deeds were so gracious that never, I think, of his country shall be a man in whom God put so much good and may his soul be set in Paradise among the Saints for ever.'[45] There is no record of what Alice thought of him, but it would appear that she made a public declaration of their kinship: parallel to her arms impaled with those of her husband in the east window of Hazelbury Bryan church, of which she was patron, are those of John Montagu. It was a statement not only of family loyalty but also arguably of political sympathy, a bold act since Montagu's loyalty had cost him his head.

EDUCATION AND LITERACY

Despite the general restrictions on women exercising executive powers in public office, their position as members of the landholding class, with the subsequent administrative responsibilities that such ownership involved, raises the question of their education, general competence and expertise for such roles. Margery Kempe blamed the failure of her business enterprises in part on lack of experience, and Christine de Pisan warned women against initiating legal action without recourse to professional advice since they were likely to be naive about such matters. However, few women or men of this class would have been strangers to the legal implications inherent in property ownership. Since land was the basis of wealth and of fundamental importance, it is hard to believe that landowners were ignorant or indifferent about such matters and prepared to leave all decisions and actions in the hands of their officials and council members. Widows who had opted for autonomy and independence would have been especially sensitive to the need to acquire the necessary skills to protect their interests.

There was virtually no formal education for women at this time, or indeed for most men unless they were destined for the Church, except in a few of the aristocratic households where daughters as well as sons might have tutors. Didactic literature recommended little more than the acquisition of feminine virtues and basic household crafts. However, young girls would have learnt many diverse skills from their mothers, surrogate mothers or patrons who, in their natural role as teachers, could impart essential knowledge relating to all aspects of house keeping, hospitality, medical care and husbandry.[46] Such education was likely to have been essentially pragmatic. Alice had young women living in her household from time to time who would have learnt from her example, but there are indications that she may even have made a profession of teaching.

In contemporary Royal Household accounts ladies with the title of *magistra*, *magistrix* or *maitresse* (which can all be translated as 'teacher') are occasionally recorded. They were usually the wives or widows of courtiers.[47] The household of a widow with no sons may have been considered a particularly suitable training ground and secure haven for female wards. Sometime between 1391 and 1394 two young heiresses were living with Alice de Bryene, and it appears that she and Joan Bohun, Countess of Hereford, had been in some negotiations about the arrangements for their forthcoming marriages. Richard II in a brief letter to Alice, written before 1394, explained that he was uncertain about the details, asked her to ignore his previous letters and continue the negotiations with the countess to their mutual satisfaction.[48]

The two girls, Joan and Anne, were about thirteen and nine when their father John Filliol died in 1391. He had been a business associate of John de Sutton, Alice's stepgrandfather, and was a wealthy man.[49] There is no evidence of whom

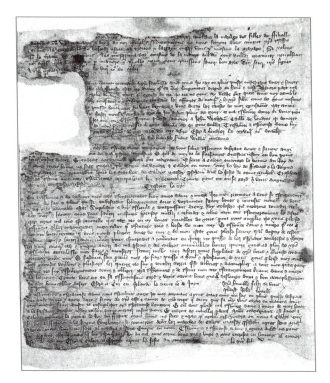

*Page from Alice de Bryene's
Letter-book written in French,
c. 1385–1400.*

had bought the wardship of his daughters before their proposed marriages to two of the king's squires but it is unlikely that they were lodging with Alice only for safekeeping. Probably, like Agnes Sampson, they were staying there for instruction as well. Apart from learning about routine household and estate management they may have had the opportunity of acquiring other skills such as reading and writing. This would have been particularly useful for young women of the gentry class, like Agnes, whose income on marriage might have been insufficient to employ a full-time scribe.

The letters cited throughout this book belonged to Alice de Bryene and were copied on both sides of one sheet of paper that appears to have been part of a larger collection. They were all written in French. The diversity and scope of the letters, ranging from requests to executors for payment of debts, affectionate letters from sons-in-law, advice about household management and problems with inheritance, could have been used to teach young women to read, speak and maybe even write French. They would also have given them an opportunity of learning about the many different tasks that they might have to undertake when running their own households, a much more personal and related exercise than that to be gleaned from devotional or formula books.[50] Such formal collections did exist and were used to train young men in business methods and the art of correspondence.[51]

The use of the vernacular was growing in this period for certain government directives, private correspondence and wills, where previously French had been used. But even if English was becoming the medium of preference, French was still regarded by many as the language of convention and polite society,[52] dating back to the time of chivalry and the military elite. The continuing circulation in the fifteenth century of manuals to teach the '*douce Français de Paris*', the French equivalent of the Queen's English, demonstrates the desire to have models to help maintain such an accomplishment.[53] If Alice were using her collection of letters to teach young women to read and write French, it is likely that they already had the basic tools of literacy in English and were keen to acquire more polished social skills. Dame Alice's adherence to a past culture is also suggestive of a conservative outlook. Maintaining traditional values is a further contribution that women, and especially widows, may have made to society.

Latin had been used throughout the Middle Ages and continued to be so in later centuries for ecclesiastical matters and in legal departments. All Dame Alice's account rolls were written in Latin, a reflection of the fact that in general her stewards were recruited from the clerical class. Daily prayers and the liturgy in her chapel would also have been conducted in Latin and we know that she, like many other women, owned devotional books in Latin.[54] It has been claimed that comprehension of the Latin language was rudimentary in nunneries at this time and knowledge of syntax poor,[55] but since the content of both account rolls and religious books, and indeed property charters and enfeoffments, was both fairly simple and formulaic, it could soon have been learnt and understood in principle, though we should not presume that this implied a fluent mastery.

Such 'pragmatic literacy' as a tool of trade has been discussed in terms of the ability to read, but not necessarily to write.[56] All wealthy householders employed scribes or clerks to deal with their records, correspondence and even to copy books. This did not appear to have presented much anxiety in the contemporary mind, much as before the advent of personal computers executives were quite content to let their secretaries type letters and contracts for them. The advantages of women being able to read were recognized in the upper classes of society: in 1397 Henry Bolingbroke purchased primers and 'ABCs' for his two daughters, who were five and two-and-a-half years old at the time; and in 1483 it was widely

tatiu ir ctcbicati ut s.   cptons.   ct famuna. uō q̃ quīſ familian

A lady dictating to a secretary.

expected that a knight's daughter should learn to read although 'as for wrytynge it is no force yf a woman can nought of hit, but as for redynge I saye that good and prouffytable is to all wymen'.[57]

However, increasingly people were developing their own writing skills and there were obviously occasions when correspondents wanted to add something personal, an indication not only of a growing wish for privacy but also, often, of affection. Sometimes all that was autograph was literally that, a signature at the end of a letter. At other times it was something more intimate. Elizabeth Stonor in the 1470s frequently wrote her own letters and if they were dictated she usually added the last sentence herself: once it was an allusion to something she and her husband seem to have shared in private, 'My owne good [husb]ond I se well ye [re]membre the putting at . . . out of the bed whan you and I lay last togedyr.' On another occasion her final addition had a familiar and revealing ring, 'And Cosen, heras ye wryte to me that I have no leysyr: truly I have been crised and besy, ellys I wyld have wryte to you or thys tyme.'[58]

Alice not only educated women: she also paid for two young boys, Robert Hole and John Baker, to attend the nearby grammar school at Lavenham.[59] Judging by their names they seem to have been local lads connected with the estates whom she thought might benefit from an education. In 1401 a Robert Hole was paid 4*s* for gathering thatch. Several employees called Baker worked for Alice or rented land on her farm at Foxearth. In 1427 she appointed a John Baker as rector of the

Foxearth church of which she was patron.[60] If this was the same man for whom she had paid to have lessons at the grammar school, then her investment was worthwhile.

RELIGIOUS PATRONAGE

Some widows in Alice's position inherited the advowson of parish churches on the death of their husband. Alice was patron of the churches in Hazelbury, Foxearth, Raydon and Middleton. This gave her rights and obligations. Church buildings had to be maintained and in some cases even rebuilt, though this was not necessarily the responsibility of the patron unless ambitious plans were made. Generally, only the chancel was the responsibility of the patron. However, the installation of stained-glass windows, decoration of walls and rood-screens, donation of vestments, altar-cloths and chalices enabled a woman to commemorate her family and friends and leave the individual mark of her own pious sentiment. The right to present to a benefice was also a means of providing support for a clerk in the service of the household, or for friends or relatives who were in holy orders. Incumbents could be selected to further a widow's particular interest in the 'cure of souls', whether it inclined more to religious, social or educational sensibility. This type of religious patronage had a much wider effect than that which could be dispensed in the household's private chapel.

Patronage could also take a more collective form. The gild associations, to which many women in the urban areas had access, served as a vehicle for protection in trading practices as well as a form of social security, by providing financial assistance in times of need and towards the expenses of a funeral with contributions from all gild members. Some gilds were formed specifically for religious purposes with a patron saint whose festival was celebrated, either in a private chapel if it were a rich gild, or at a service in a local church if the gild were less prosperous. There is evidence that women also clubbed together to raise money to commission and install stained-glass windows in honour of their particular patron saint or gild.[61]

Commissioning works of art was only possible for very wealthy people. Few women could afford to commission literary or devotional books, let alone an illuminated Book of Hours, like the one owned by Alice de Raydon, an ancestor of Dame Alice.[62] Elisabeth de Vere, Countess of Oxford and granddaughter of Alice's trustee Sir John Howard, was one of Osbern Bokenham's patrons. The thirteen Lives that made up his collection *Legendys of Hooly Wummen*, completed

*Nativity scene from Alice de Raydon's
Book of Hours, c. 1320.*

in 1447, had a particular appeal to women.[63] Bokenham, who wrote in 'Suthfolk speche', joined the order of Austin friars when he was eleven and was at the Clare Priory, close to Acton, from 1427 for some years, so he may even have been a guest at Alice's table.

The political influence and social contributions made by middle-class philanthropic women in the Victorian era are well documented.[64] Such activities are not so easily discernible in the medieval period but should not be discounted. Talking with guests of all social ranks at the dinner table or in the environs of the estates widened the perspective of the landlord, whether a man or woman. Women, and especially widows, had more time for this type of social interchange and their life experiences of marriage, motherhood and widowhood, which would have marked fundamental changes in their outlook, must generally have given them a more empathetic understanding of the differing tensions in society. The diversity of their tasks within an apparently narrower world than that familiar to men would also have facilitated a depth of understanding and compassion beyond the immediate concerns and traditional view of the average male estate owner.

Even if a woman's personal intervention was circumscribed by collective hierarchical and patriarchal attitudes and customs, she could authorize her male peers to initiate her actions and in her discussions with them would have had different insights to voice. The importance of lordship and honour would also have guaranteed that women of the landholding class, and particularly widows, could exercise some influence, enjoy respect and be treated as equals even if they were different from men. All the evidence suggests that they were as capable as men in the performance of both their private and public duties. That they had less formal authority need not have meant that they were disempowered and unable to influence contemporary opinions. We just do not hear them speak.

CHAPTER 8
Considerations for the Afterlife

Medieval women are most visible when dead. Their presence remains in their effigies or brasses and in their testaments or wills. The images by which they were commemorated can tell us much about their self-perception, or others' perception of them, while from their wills we can learn of some of their interests during their lifetimes and the actions they hoped would be initiated after their deaths. Unfortunately, while this may provide a clear picture, it is circumscribed by myopia. This limited vision is due partly to the fact that we only see what is there and our focus is drawn to the many ecclesiastical records that have survived. The tendency to concentrate on female piety whitewashes women with the same brush used to portray the purity of the Virgin Mary as a compensation for the original sin of Eve. Contemporary cultural norms, however, did lay great stress on religion and piety and women were also expected to fulfil charitable roles.

Some women were pious but not necessarily more so than many men and it may not always have been their primary concern. On Wednesday 13 January 1389 Alice's grandmother Alice de Sutton appears to have been pricked by her conscience after the Christmas revelries, or a Pepysian review of her assets in the new year, and started to contemplate her debts. The list she had drawn up is surprising.[1] As previously cited, there were several unpaid bills from tradesmen and women, which was not so unusual as it was customary for the wealthy to live off credit. But what is remarkable is that she had apparently not fulfilled the terms of her first husband's will. Sir Andrew de Bures had died twenty-nine years earlier. Bequests of cash to various friends, household members and estate staff at his numerous manors had not been paid. Nor had she distributed the £20 that he had asked be given to deserving paupers in various towns in the area. Finally, she had neglected to pay the Sudbury friars a grant of 10 silver marks that they might pray for his soul, the souls of his parents, of some of his friends and various other Christians.

Both men and women generally concurred with the belief in the efficacy of post-mortem prayers as a way of purchasing remission from time to be spent in purgatory for their sins on earth. Unfulfilled obligations and uncharitable or

Old Age, from The Romaunt of the Rose, *late fifteenth century.*

malicious acts might in this way be purged more swiftly. Moreover, the benefit was also held to accrue to those performing the required obsequies who in their turn, when Death came to gather them, must have hoped for similar indulgences from their heirs and friends. These 'legacies of guilt' could be a burden on descendants,[2] even when provision was made for them by the deceased in their wills, and it would be unreasonable to suppose that Alice de Sutton's oversight was an exception. The road to hell is paved with good intentions indeed, especially when they are left too late or for others to carry them out.

Conscientious individuals could travel a different path. Provision in wills for post-mortem indulgences may have been a last resort for some, while a charitable act performed during a person's lifetime was a more certain and highly recommended route along the straight road and through the narrow gates that led to heaven, a sentiment expressed on a fifteenth-century encaustic tile at Great Malvern Abbey:

Consider man thy life
May not endure for ever
What thou dost thyself
Of that thou art sure
But that thou entrusteth
To thy executors care
If it be of any avail
Tis but a matter of chance.[3]

Such deeds are less apparent than fine tombs or pious statements in wills, but a few examples of Alice's charity may give us an insight into the way and to what extent some medieval women fulfilled their social and religious obligations.

In the 1390s Alice's receiver accounted for various sums of money granted to help the poor on her West Country estates. A recurrence of the plague, freak weather conditions and a dearth of corn made 1390 and 1391 particularly difficult years.[4] Lord Bryan's death at this time might have inspired charitable gestures, but a grant of 20s to two poor men at Oxenhall was especially generous. At about the same time Alice approved a smaller grant to a pauper at Hazelbury and also made a contribution to the relief of poor tenants in Sutton Poyntz. Tenants at other Bryan manors benefited from a 10s award in 1396–7, the tenth anniversary of Sir Guy's death, which was noted in the accounts as being 'part of the expenses of the Lady's indulgences'.[5] Between 1416 and 1419 she continued to subsidize the needy on her Gloucestershire farm, although this may have stemmed less from charity than necessity on an estate where there still seem to have been many bonded servants who might have been unhappy about the terms of their leases.

No such arrangements are apparent in East Anglia, though some poor people were given sustenance at Acton. Their names make it easy to identify with these local indigents and suggest they were destitute rather than merely impoverished: Adam Blindman, Agnes Shepherd, John Wafer, Thomas Grye, Bartholomew Hykyn and William Prat, shunned perhaps by family and friends for his feeble-mindedness, all received aid.[6] Other recipients of Alice's charity, such as Ralph Strutt and Edward Thurgor, who had both occasionally worked for her, may temporarily have fallen on hard times. The average handout was actually quite constrained, about half a bushel of grain each, which worked out at a couple of weeks' meagre sustenance.

The Foxearth and Bures' bailiffs also occasionally accounted for grants of grain and dried peas given to paupers on these estates. But they were not the only benefits Alice's paupers received. Each year at Acton one of the 'poor of the household' was granted the use of a cottage worth 2s annually and land nearby, valued at 2s 6d, was given rent-free to other needy people.[7] This was a practical solution, providing both shelter and land on which crops could be grown, fostering responsibility and self-sufficiency so that people might learn to fend for themselves rather than become too dependent and live off charitable handouts.

Many householders kept special almoner's accounts that specified the annual sums paid in charity. Thus Lady Margaret Cromwell spent a total of 9s 5d in 1417–18 in oblations and alms though the recipients are not named.[8] No such account exists for Acton. It was also common practice to send left-over food out to paupers, and almsgates are mentioned for some residences where these offerings were made. Once again there is no such evidence for Alice's manor but she did apparently make an annual distribution of bread on Maundy Thursday in 1412 and 1413, a day marked even now by symbolic royal charity, when at least thirty extra white loaves above the daily average were sent to the table from the pantry and hence, we may presume, to the poor.

This award like others she made may have been customary. As her mother and grandmother had done before her, she gave all her permanent farm workers a penny at Christmas and Easter, 'beer and cheer' money, with double for her bailiffs. In the accounts it is noted as an oblation for the workers' *sedlopum* or seedbasket, an obligation which still exists today in the form of the Christmas box. Similarly they received a penny or ha'penny for candles on 2 February at Candlemas, the day dedicated to the Purification of the Virgin Mary. This was the day when all the church candles needed throughout the year were consecrated. Parishioners were obliged to process with a candle and offer a penny to the priest at mass, a financial obligation that Dame Alice partly fulfilled for her employees.[9]

Alms giving was as much a part of the social fabric of medieval life as an idiosyncratic expression of religiosity. It is not always easy to differentiate whether the giving of charity resulted from the necessity to conform to social tradition or from genuine piety. It might be argued that Alice's liberal hospitality at Acton indicates a generous nature, but as we have seen, although she fed a quantity of anonymous people from nearby villages, it was often on days when specific provisions were purchased. Many of the unnamed guests may also have been seeking casual work, although those coming from as far away as Ipswich were probably travellers. Otherwise it is difficult to assess whether her hospitality was solely a charitable gesture, except perhaps for the meals she gave to widows like Margaret Brydbek, the *extraneo* who arrived on 9 September 1412, the 'wayferour' who called the following January, the half dozen-odd unnamed clerical visitors and the clerks who came from Oxford and Cambridge – impoverished students perhaps. Such an insignificant percentage of her total annual guest list could hardly be called openhandedness in comparison with a lady like the Countess of Warwick, who apparently found place at her table nearly every day for hungry people such as the 'two pilgrims at the gate'.[10]

Another way of dispensing charity was to make contributions to the Church. We have already witnessed the comings and goings of various friars and ecclesiastics, some of whom were recipients of Alice's alms. Most years the Franciscan friars of Babwell, the Austins of Clare and the Dominicans from Sudbury each received an average handout of four bushels of barley or wheat, quantities that would make 30 gallons of ale or 125 2 lb wheaten loaves, the minimum basic sustenance for one man for two months, alms which might be viewed as moderately generous but certainly not lavish. One year some Ipswich friars also received grain, while Alice occasionally instructed her agent in London to make a grant of 6s 8d to the Carthusians.[11] Such diffuse donations conceal any personal affiliations and might be cynically viewed as an insurance strategy to spread the risk and provide the widest possible cover for an uncertain afterlife. However, most of these religious orders had been previously patronized by her family and such non-partisan distribution could also be seen as more effectively charitable.

These appear to have been standard annuities but Alice did occasionally respond to particular circumstances that reflected her personal interests and concerns. In 1404 Roger Brunch, the Acton bailiff, sent a quarter of wheat down the road to the Acton church: the belltower was being repaired that year, though whether the grain was actually dispensed to the workers for their daily bread or sold to raise money for wages and building materials we have no way of knowing. Two years later the work was still unfinished and Brunch accounted for a further quarter of grain given by the lady for the 'fabrick' of the church, together with the usual four bushels granted to the three orders of friars. This additional largess may have been stimulated as much by the deaths that year of both Alice's mother and eldest daughter, as the uncompleted repairs.

The granting of grain may not have been a great sacrifice to a successful farmer, but gifts could take, quite literally, a more concrete form. The reconstruction and redecoration of churches was another way of fulfilling social duty and giving alms to the Church, an act that was presumed to reflect the piety of the donor. It also provided opportunities for self-aggrandizement and self-proclamation. In Langland's *Piers Plowman*, the Lady Meed, who represented the profit-motive, is absolved from her sins by a friar-confessor who tells her:

> We have a wyndow a-werchynge,
> Wole stonden us ful hye,
> Woldestow glaze that gable and grave there thy name,
> Sykir sholde thi soule be hevene to have.[12]

St Mary and St James, Hazelbury Bryan, Dorset, rebuilt in the 1400s under Alice de Bryene's patronage.

Alice had inherited the patronage of several churches and rebuilding works at St Mary and St James', Hazelbury, carried out in the early 1400s, must have involved her in considerable expense. Built in the perpendicular style, the church is a particularly well-proportioned piece of work with beautifully designed buttresses and certain similarities to Wells Cathedral and Sherborne Abbey. There is little doubt that Dame Alice was responsible for most if not all this work, which was completed under John Tonkere, her rector of 1426. His initials appear on a shield on the north wall. Her own modest autograph is to be found in the upper lights of the east window, where her arms – those of the de Bures with two lively lions impaling her husband's consisting of three azure piles and a red label to differentiate them from Lord Bryan's – are displayed. This small window is hardly ostentatious, even if the building is an excellent example of its kind.

Alice was also patron of St Peter and St Paul's at Foxearth. Little remains of the original decoration of the medieval church, which was restored in Victorian times by John Foster, the incumbent in the mid-nineteenth century who was a member of the Oxford Movement. If Alice made any contribution to the fabric or furnishings of the church it is now hidden from us, except possibly for the medieval rood-screen, which was overpainted in the last century. Saints commemorated on it represent a medley of cults that, while popular figures in this period particularly in East Anglia and Devon, might be indicative of personal affiliations. It is worthwhile then spending a few minutes studying the screen, for saints had important intercessory powers, and devotion to them was another way to alleviate problems on earth and help speed the soul to heaven.

As on many medieval screens, both the Blessed Virgin Mary and Mary Magdalene are represented: virgin mother and penitent whore, they enjoyed universal patronage and were especially popular with men. Of the four other female saints, Apollonia, Barbara, Dorothy and Helena, the first three were all virgin martyrs of dubious authenticity. It has been argued that part of their appeal originated in their defiant defence of their chastity, but while this may have attracted many men and such troubled women as Margery Kempe, who fiercely concurred with the ecclesiastical view that virgins were more beloved by God than widows or wives, it is questionable whether all women adopted them as role models. The stories of their lives, however, abounded in exciting and prodigious incident, providing the same sort of stimulation and entertainment as popular romances and some public figures do today.[13]

Whatever the collective view of these particular saints, details of their cults do show a personal connection to Alice de Bryene. Apollonia and Dorothy are also to be found in the east window of Torbryan church in Devon of which Lord Bryan and Elizabeth Lovell were patrons. The continuing family devotion to particular saints was an important aspect of spirituality. Moreover, St Dorothy was venerated on 6 February, the date of Sir Guy's death, and would have been chosen to commemorate him. St Apollonia's festival, three days later, was another significant date in the celebration of the 'month's mind', part of those obsequies deemed essential to ensure the ultimate salvation of a person's soul. At Acton in 1413 this day was marked with festive food. Apollonia was said to protect devotees from toothache, a useful lady to have on your side when tooth-pulling was one of the services offered by barber-surgeons.[14]

The two other Foxearth saints, Barbara and Helena, also appear on the Torbryan screen. St Barbara was commemorated on 4 December, a day which does not appear from the household accounts to have been of any special significance. But as patroness of miners, fire-work makers, artillerymen, stone-makers and fortifications, she must have had a following in the Bryan family especially as it was believed she also protected against sudden death, lightning, subsiding mines, cannon-balls and impenitence, a good friend for those engaged in warfare. St Helena's feast day was on 18 August, the day after Lord Bryan's death: the mother of Constantine the Great, she would have been an inspiring figurehead for women. It may also be a significant fact that legend recorded she was the daughter of King Coel of Colchester, and therefore a local heroine.[15]

The six male images were conventional cult figures, with a couple of exceptions. First portrayed is Jesus, next to whom is St Alban, founder of the Benedictine Abbey at St Albans. On his right is St Walstan, a local East Anglian saint. Legend records he was born of royal blood at Blythburgh in Suffolk in the tenth century. Renouncing his claim to the throne, Walstan espoused a life of poverty and worked as a reaper. He refused his employer's offer to be his heir and requested instead the gift of a cow in calf. Subsequently, two calves were born that later, on his death, drew his cart through the solid walls of Bawburgh church leaving behind visible traces of the wheels. On his feast day 'all mowers and scythe felowes sekynge him once a year' gathered at his Bawburgh shrine.[16] As patron of the harvest, he understandably enjoyed a following of labourers, farmers and estate owners.

The next saint Felix, depicted with an anchor, gave his name to the port of Felixstowe on the Suffolk coast. An obscure figure, his cult is often confused with other Romans of the same name. He was probably venerated on 15 July. The anchor emblem suggests he was patron of sailors and might, therefore, have been one of Lord Bryan's personal saints. The fifth figure, St Edmund, is shown holding a sceptre and orb which identifies him as the patron of Bury St

Edmunds; on 20 November 1412, which was his feast day, swan was served at Acton. Last is St Augustine in whose hand is held a heart of fire which confirms that he was Augustine of Hippo, the philosopher and inspiration of the Austin order, rather than St Augustine of Canterbury.[17] If Alice and her chaplains were responsible for choosing which saints to portray, we see here a nice balance of the traditional and personal, reflecting in part an intention to commemorate Sir Guy and various family saints, together with respect paid to local tradition as is suggested by the choice of St Helena, St Edmund, St Felix and St Walstan.

St Mary's at Raydon is a simple Norman church with some fine late medieval additions. The patronage had been in the Raydon family for more than a century

Interior of St Peter and St Paul, Foxearth, Essex, which was restored in the Victorian era.

when it passed to Alice's grandmother. Though Alice de Sutton may have been lax in executing the terms of her first husband's will, she did make contributions to the Raydon church by paying for candles, a custom that Alice continued when she gave 12*d* worth of wax to the altar. This was in 1432, the same year that she granted grain from the Raydon manor to an order of Ipswich friars. It was the fortieth anniversary of Alice de Sutton's death and these alms would have marked the occasion.

Observing anniversaries was another way of reducing expiation in purgatory as well as securing indulgence for the donor. As we have noted in our survey of clergy visiting Acton in 1412–13, Alice took this task seriously. Nor were such rituals only conducted in the household: her West Country receiver accounted for an annual payment of 13*s* 4*d* for the cost of contributing to Sir Guy's memorial masses at the Bryan chantry at Slapton, except in 1392–3 when she paid 24*s*. This larger, but hardly exceptional, sum may have been in honour of his fortieth birthday. These obituary services were often quite complex and an occasion for public display commensurate with the social standing of the deceased. One year at Acton Alice provided lengths of wool-russet and bowls for thirty-six paupers and commissioned her carpenter to make and erect a cross at the Acton cemetery. At about the same time she paid two men to clear the hedges around the cemetery and the Acton manor garden. We may guess that this marked a special anniversary or possibly her sponsorship of the traditional Palm Sunday observances, a ceremony that involved a special shrine being erected in the churchyard on which the church's principal relics were displayed.[18]

Should we now ask whether Alice was a pious lady, 'a model East Anglian matron',[19] fussing over her alms-basket and the niceties of religious observation? It is unlikely that anyone would have asked that question when she was alive, circumscribed as all their lives were by the Church. Also, piety is difficult to gauge, for what we may recognize as benevolence and virtue is not necessarily complemented by an inner religious attitude. There is some evidence that she fulfilled a few of the seven corporal acts of mercy, which were to feed the poor, give drink to the thirsty, house the stranger, clothe the naked, visit the sick, relieve the prisoner and bury the dead. But in terms of plain piety we have little to inform us of the state of Alice's soul. It would appear she paid such dues as were deemed necessary to qualify for currency in the economy of salvation: she paid her tithes, gave alms, observed anniversaries. She was certainly charitable but not excessively so, just as much perhaps as was demanded by her position in the community. In common with other medieval households she had private

St Sytha, patroness of domestic servants and housewives, from John Lacy's Hours, 1420.

chaplains and singing clerks, and celebrated mass in her own chapel, but that is not evidence of spirituality. She observed standard religious practice but probably no more than her next-door neighbour. It is even difficult from the material we have to establish any specific religious cult or affiliations, but let us sift through the grain once more, separate the tares from the wheat and gather our harvest in.

In the household accounts some religious festivals are noted at the head of a particular day, but the practice is inconsistent, reflecting perhaps the particular devotion or impulse of the steward. Vigils of only six Apostles are mentioned and all the Marian feasts, with the exception of the Annunciation which, nevertheless, judging by the menu in 1413, was maintained as a feast day. All the traditional holy days, such as All Saints, Corpus Christi and the Nativity, were celebrated. The presence of visiting clergy and special food occasionally indicate that a particular saint was venerated, as on 27 April in 1412 and 1413, the day dedicated to St Sytha. She was patroness of domestic servants and housewives who invoked her help when they had lost their keys, and was depicted in churches in Oxford, East Anglia and the West Country.[20]

Obligatory fasts like the Ember Days, which were the Wednesday, Friday and Saturday immediately after the first Sunday in Lent, Pentecost, the Exaltation of the Holy Cross and St Lucy's day, were observed; and it would appear from the consistently lower figures for supper served on Friday evenings that many in the household fasted then as well, unless it was their traditional night out and then quite the opposite may have been the case. During the harvest in August, Alice's boon-workers worked on two of the four Sundays, while members of the household appear to have had every Sunday off; this may have had less to do with a Sunday observance than good labour relations. Nothing in particular informs us of the existence of a private devotion or special attachment to a particular saint, other than those examples noted. Even the names of Alice's daughters had social rather than religious connotations – Philippa being named possibly after Edward III's queen, and Elizabeth for Alice's mother-in-law.

However, she would have been unusual had she not done something to ensure a safe deliverance at the Last Judgement. Long widowed with little immediate family and sensitive to contemporary fashions, a chantry foundation was a practical way to guarantee post-mortem prayers.[21] To have left it so late might be indicative of a lack of anxiety about the afterlife or the fact that she was just too busy to contemplate death. The terse idiom of her trust deed without any preamble or invocation, despite the fact that it was written in the first person, is a reminder that this was essentially a legal document and not a statement of religious solicitude. References, however, were made in it to another charter drawn up for her trustees with further details about her will, which probably contained specific instructions about her funeral such as the type of mass to be sung, alms given and clothes her cantarist and chaplains were to wear.

In the deed the land entrusted to fund her chantry priest was meticulously specified, provisions made for the appointments of new trustees and directions given as to the safe keeping of the charter. Ultimately, the responsibility lay with Geoffrey Bryce, Master of St Gregory's College, and was to be passed to his successor at his death. For a fee the Master was to select a suitable chaplain to celebrate divine service daily in perpetuity, at St Mary's chapel in Acton, for the souls of Alice, her parents, husband and all her ancestors. If a suitable priest could not be found, the trustees were to sell the land and dispose of the proceeds as they deemed most fitting. It is interesting to note the nice balance between lay, clerical and household members in her choice of trustees, selected presumably to represent her various different interests.

All contingencies appear to have been covered and we must conclude that Alice was conscious of the problems inherent in relying on others to fulfil post-mortem wishes. Her apparent disregard of communal charity and prayers for friends and all Christians in favour of a few family members is in line with late medieval spirituality when, it has been argued, there was a shift of emphasis in formal acts of charity.[22] The omission of prayers for the soul of her elder daughter is striking, though it is possible that Alice had already made arrangements for masses to be celebrated for her in the church where she was buried. The appointment of trustees, all carefully selected, excluded the necessity of obtaining a mortmain licence which might have led to problems, and in choosing Bryce as chief trustee she secured a sympathetic mediator when it came to seeking consent from the diocese. In all, her chantry deed speaks of expediency rather than affectivity, a reflection perhaps of her idiosyncratic behaviour and particular practice of piety.

This practicality stood Alice in good stead. Her chantry survived until the Reformation when the income from her trust was said to have been worth nearly £9 a year. Outrents absorbed some of this but there was still nearly £8 for the incumbent. He was described as a 'very impotent man' of simple learning, but he might still have given a few lessons to children in the chantry chapel to supplement his income, as was fairly common practice in rural areas. No reference was made to the type of service he celebrated except that he sang mass and said prayers for 'Dame Alice' and members of her family. One silver-plated chalice weighing 6 ounces and worth 6s, together with other ornaments valued at 18s, had also survived the hundred-odd years since Alice was buried there.[23]

A century later William Dowsing, that 'uncompromising zealot of iconoclastic fame', was on the rampage in Suffolk, smashing superstitious images, inscriptions, windows and sculptures in any church or chapel tainted with Popery. Churches in Assington, Boxted, Bures, Clare, Layham, Nayland, Raydon, Stanstead, Sudbury and Withersfield all suffered. On 20 April 1643 Dowsing recorded that at Raydon 'we brake down an Crucifix and twelve superstitious Pictures and a Popish inscription *Ora pro Nobis*'. The following month he was at the Waldegrave chapel at Bures: 'There was a Picture of God the Father and divers other superstitious pictures, twenty at least, which they promised to break.' When the wrecking party returned neither the warden, his daughter nor servants could be found to give them the key. Dowsing's men were promised 6s 8d but orders were still given to remove the cross.[24] In all they visited 150 places in 50 days. Acton, for some reason, escaped his hammer. However, the church was not in a position to avoid the attention of a similarly minded religious enthusiast

Altar tomb of Sir Andrew and
Sir Robert de Bures, 1360/1,
All Saints, Acton, under an ogee arch
decorated with cherubs.

at some other date. The heads of the sixteen cherubs hovering on the ogee arch above the double altar tomb of Alice's father and grandfather have all been severed at the neck, and the inscriptions removed from Alice's brass, that of her great-grandfather, and her father and grandfather's double-tomb chest.[25]

From the evidence we have of Alice's charity and cares towards the end of her life, it would be difficult to conclude that religious solicitude played an overriding part. Essentially it seems she was guided by pragmatism and unlike her husband it does not appear that she was haunted by visions of hell-fire: her chantry deed lacks the urgency we witnessed in her husband's will. She had, however, lived a long and full life, while Sir Guy died when he was still in his prime. More might be learned of her personal outlook and pious concerns from a testament, that legal instrument whereby people devised their chattels and appointed executors. Widows are generally more visible as testators than married women who, since legally were considered to own no property, could not make personal bequests, though husbands sometimes permitted their wives to make wills and leave property for charitable purposes. In many such testaments and wills the preamble, initial invocation to a particular religious cult, description of the type of funeral services desired, gifts of liturgical items and distribution of moneys to individuals, churches and charitable organizations provide an insight into an individual's spiritual aspirations and subjective experience of God.

Two examples of wills made by women who were contemporaries of Alice provide a striking contrast. In 1435 Lady Joanna Beauchamp requested that her 'symple and wrecched body' be buried with 'alle the worship that to be don unto a woman of myn estate, which God knowyth wele procedeth not of no pompe and veynglory that I am settee for ynne my body, but for a memorial and a remembrance of my soule to my kyn, frendys, servantes and all others'. That 'worship' included a provision for 5,000 masses, cloths of gold to be given to each church where her body lay en route to its final entombment and suits of black for the friars attending her body. Considerable sums were set aside in alms for the poor and public works, such as road and bridge maintenance.[26] While it is arguable that this demonstrates some humility stimulated by a fear of the afterlife, the importance of her social standing, even post-mortem, was not to be ignored and no doubt Joanna Beauchamp's mourners were suitably impressed and fully conscious of her estate when they attended her numerous memorial masses.[27]

Lady Alice West, whose fondness for material possessions we have already witnessed in the description of her beds, also remembered her poor tenants with generosity and left large sums for masses to be sung for her soul, that of her husband and all Christians. But she had different ideas about the style of her final departure from this world: 'Also I wol and deuyse that, ware that euer I deye, my body be caried to the forsayd Priorie of Crischerch, pryuelich and with right litel cost, and ther-to beried att the ferst masse, with a taper of v pound wax stondyng and brennyng att my heued, and another of v pound of wax brennyng atte my fet, with-out any other cost or solempnite ydo afterward. This is myn hool wil, that this be parfourmed as hit is writen her-before.'[28]

Some had little time to contemplate death: Alice's granddaughter Maud made her will eight days before she died and, apart from the appointment of executors and directions as to her place of burial, named only two legatees, her thirteen-year-old daughter and seven-year-old son.[29] Her mother Elizabeth, who died the following year, had had more time for reflection. Nevertheless, her will, which was drawn up on her deathbed, is characterized by familial and related social concerns. She dedicated her soul to God and the Blessed Virgin, left money to Salisbury Cathedral and nineteen parish churches on her estates of which she held the patronage including those recently patronized by Alice, as well as those in Oxenhall, Bures and Acton. Such diffuse generosity might well have been stimulated by the certain presence of priests at her bedside. The clergy at the Bryan collegiate chantry at Slapton, where she wished to be buried, were well provided for and they also received a vestment embroidered with her husband's arms, a chalice and her seal. Servants and household members were remembered too and the residue of her estate left to her executors to dispose of as they thought best.[30]

The final enactment was the funeral and the erection of the monument. The place of a woman's burial, as previously discussed, was often indicative of divergent familial and affective interests. Funerals like obituary anniversaries were frequently magnificent ceremonies with provisions made for a lying-in-state in the church, the singing of the *dirige*, a night-long vigil, and the requiem mass the following morning. Quantities of expensive candles were supplied, special clothes provided for priests, retainers and mourners including the poor, who were essential attendants at the service, and sometimes details drawn up for an elaborate progress from the place of death to that of the entombment. Funerals of some noblewomen are well documented and often seem to have been designed to reflect the splendour of their public life.[31] Those of the gentry, while no less complex, were on a smaller scale and related more to their immediate community and localized concerns.

A funeral feast was obligatory. On Alice de Sutton's death quantities of stock, including eighty sheep, were sent over from the manor at Raydon to Wivenhoe, and pigs and poultry were slaughtered at Acton for the feast there. Much earlier in 1337 Dame Katherine of Norwich spent one-sixth of her entire annual expenditure hosting a feast for ninety-two guests on the anniversary of her husband's death.[32] These ceremonies could last for several weeks. When Thomas Stonor buried his mother sometime before 1425 over £30 was spent on the obsequies, which consisted of the burial rite, the service on the seventh day and the feast and distribution of alms on the thirtieth day.[33]

Whereas the final will allowed some scope for autonomy and individual action, the choice of mourning monument was more restricted. That some individuals had definite ideas about how they wished to be portrayed can be presumed from many of the surviving medieval tombs, together with instructions given in wills, though specific requests for requirements about brasses are rare. The Countess of Warwick, who died four years after Alice, wanted the figure on her tomb to depict 'my Image to be made all naked, and no thyng on my hede but myn here cast bakwardys . . . of the gretness and of the fascyon lyke the mesure that Thomas

Porchayn hath yn a lyst', and she charged that her head-band set with peach-coloured rubies be sold 'to the utmost pryse' to pay for this final extravagance.[34] Sir Walter de Manny, companion-in-arms of Alice's father-in-law, also left detailed instructions in 1371: 'And I will that a tomb of alabaster with my image as a knight and my arms thereon shall be made for me like unto that of Sir John Beauchamp in St Paul's London.'[35]

Although these are specific instructions, both suggest an absence of individual self-perception in favour of a collective stylized image, a statement not about who they were but what they represented. Few were bold enough to implement original ideas. That Edward III's Queen Philippa chose, when commissioning her own tomb in the 1360s, to be depicted realistically with ageing face and portly body rather than a bland stereotype of an idealized queen might indicate supreme self-confidence in one who was at the top of the hierarchical heap.[36] In her unique position, she could afford to be portrayed in her own likeness. Richard II used a death mask of his dead queen, Anne of Bohemia, for her effigy, which was not a flattering image but was an expression of his attachment to her and his personal grief.[37]

Tombs could be more easily adapted to individual expression. Alice Chaucer, Duchess of Suffolk, wishing to emphasize the corruptibility of the body, a popular theme in late medieval England, had herself depicted as a noblewoman on the top of her Ewelme tomb with her decaying body underneath. Brasses were literally less easily moulded to personal taste and their 'mass-production' from prefabricated brass components made in the London workshops left even less scope for originality.[38] Alice's great-grandfather's brass, a splendid depiction of a knight in late thirteenth-century attire, the details all precisely executed and finely decorated, demonstrates the preoccupation in the medieval mind with warfare and chivalry. Categorized as one of the Camoys types from the London workshops at St Paul's,[39] the figure with its feet resting on a lion cub is 6 ft 6 in. The Latin inscription on it once read, 'Robert de Bures lies here. God have mercy on his soul. Whoever will pray for his soul shall have forty days of pardon.'[40]

Alice's brass, close to his in the chapel of St Mary at All Saints' in Acton, is more modest. The figure is seen dressed in widow's attire, with a close-crimped cap and coverchet, plaited barbre to the neck and simple ungirdled gown. Her face looks earnest, her gaze direct and her hands, devoid of finger rings, are joined in prayer. A small dog, symbol of fidelity, plays at her feet. The contrast between Sir Robert's grandiose effigy and the undecorated simplicity of Alice's brass might appear indicative of the differences implied by gender roles in the Middle

Ages. But, although aristocratic women dressed as sumptuously as men, widows were not generally prone to ostentation. The ideology of chivalry ensured that men looked glorious in their working gear. Alice remains elegant in her widow's weeds. If Alice's brass is smaller and plainer than her great-grandfather's, it may reflect convention dictated by ideology or an idiosyncratic impulse. It could also be an indication of the size of her purse, or her executors' perception of its size, for such brasses could cost as much as a timber-framed house.[41] And maybe she really was 4 ft 9 in tall.

The brass figure of Alice de Bryene lies under a triple-arched canopy with the arms of Bryan, and Bryan impaling Bures at the corners. An inscription once read: '*Hic jacet Alicia de Bures filia et heres d'mi Rob'ti de Bures militis quae quondam fuit uxor Guidonis de Bryan junioris militis quae obit xi die mensis Januari anno domini mill'imo ccccxxxiv cuius anima propicietur Deus Amen.*'[42] It was recorded by a herald in 1593 but had been destroyed by 1627. Is there anything unusual about the use of Alice's maiden name and reference to her patrimony?

Detail of Alice de Bryene's brass, 1435, at All Saints, Acton, Suffolk.

Perhaps not. Another independently minded East Anglian lady, Margaret Paston, left instructions in her will of 1482 that her tomb, engraved with her arms, those of her husband and her family, should bear the inscription: 'Here lieth Margret Paston, late wif of John Paston, doughter and heire of John Mawteby squier, on whos sowle God have mercy.'[43]

But it is interesting. Though Margaret Paston acknowledged her relationship to her father, like Alice as his daughter and heir, nevertheless her married name was inscribed on her tomb. But not on Alice's. All extant documents relating to Dame Alice, her trust deed and the accounts concerning her estates refer to her by her married name. In life she remained the property of her husband; in death however she reverted to her maiden name. She had after all returned to live, work, die and be buried in the place of her birth, as indeed had Margaret Paston. It would seem then that Alice identified first of all with her father as an equal, as parent, provider, progenitor and transmitter of property, and only afterwards as a wife. The inscription on her brass could be either a reflection of common practice, or else an idiosyncratic expression of a level of independence, confidence and self-awareness.

It is time then to say farewell to Alice. Can we wish her as sometime later the affectionate Thomas Betson did William Stonor, that she might have 'hevene at your endynge'?[44] After the singing of the *dirige* and requiem mass, would Alice's chaplains and trustees have extolled her virtues, and if so, which ones? She had it appears fulfilled her public and social duties, running her estates and household and caring for those involved in them, giving alms and hospitality. In all this she may have been no different to many of her contemporaries. But there is little we can say about her private life, her subjective view of the world, what she experienced, how she felt and whether there was poetry, passion and harmony in her heart.

As she is interred in the northern corner of St Mary's chapel in the Acton church, it might be inappropriate to suggest that she had been conscious of any inequalities implied by gender, and when her brass was laid next to that of her great-grandfather it must have been done with equal pride. It is difficult not to see her finally as wedded to her household and estates and rooted to the soil. Whatever the reasons for her decision not to remarry, the half-century of her widowhood presumably brought her some satisfaction and sense of self-fulfilment. Her inheritance of the Bures' estates, together with the property in the West Country that came to her through her marriage, may have dictated her future, a life primarily as a farmer and manager of a large household: it was not perhaps such a bad life after all.

Epilogue

The days are shortening: Michaelmas has passed, accounts have been settled and winter is setting in. Waking at dawn, stiff but alert, Alice hears the early morning birdsong and sees light shimmering in the east. Rousing her maid, she dresses, takes her stick and leaves her chamber. The smell of freshly baked bread rises from the kitchens together with the sound of chattering and laughter. She descends to the great hall where last night's fire is still smouldering and the boys beginning to stir from where they have slept near the warm ashes. One springs up and unbolts the door letting in a gust of bracing air.

It is only a little distance over the moat and across the fields to the chapel of St Mary, but it takes her a long time. Her small dog shuffles beside her: they have grown old together. Silhouetted against the northern sky, you might think for a moment that you see more than a bent old lady clothed in black russet followed by her dog. For there in front, leading the way, a stern knight is marching, lion cub at his feet and two bounding ahead. Alice's great-grandfather had lions on his shield as well as one for an eternal footrest – symbols of power and might. But Alice's dog, though humble, is no less vibrant and more suited to the English countryside.

Picture her as she makes her way towards the church, hear her thoughts. Her stick sinks into the newly ploughed field. 'The soil looks good and when they have spread the dung from the cowsheds and the stables it will be rich and fertile. What are we sowing next year? It was fallow the year before. With luck we will have a long summer and a plentiful supply of wheat and barley, so I need not buy in again. How expensive it is. They will be brewing again today, I suppose. I must check the stock. It is Advent already, time of festivities, I may need to buy some more wine.

'I wonder who I should invite this year? So many of my friends are dead. It would be nice to see my granddaughter with her children but she will have her own household to entertain. I'll miss Richard and fear he may not live to see the spring. Perhaps Cavendish will come; I want to discuss my will with him. And then there's Andrew Boteler's daughter. She's inherited a fair amount of money. Will she manage I wonder? I expect so, she's had lots of experience and knows what she's doing. I'll see if I can get the minstrels we had last year, their music was lively and everyone enjoyed their mummeries. I suppose the Sudbury friars will come again and entertain my household with their tales.'

The northern door to the chapel is not stiff, but as Alice opens it a small wind blows and it shuts behind her. It takes time for her eyes to adjust to the darkness. She stands, waiting. The rising sun reaches the bottom of the eastern light and a ray shines down on the monumental brass of her great-grandfather. Nearer the altar is the double-tomb chest of her father and grandfather, neither of whom she knew. There is a space there in the middle. As the sun climbs it illuminates a bare flag-stone. 'It is here', she thinks, 'that I will be buried. My brass won't be as ornate as my great-grandfather's; my life was different. But it will tell my story, a part of my story.'

Here lies Alice de Bures, daughter and heir of Sir Robert de Bures, who was the wife of Sir Guy de Bryene . . .

Cuius anima propicietur Deus
Amen

Appendix 1

The following is a list of the account rolls relating to Alice de Bryene's estates during her lifetime held at the Public Record Office, London; many are incomplete and fragmentary and can only be dated by internal evidence. The dates refer to the beginning of the accounting year.

SC6/833/12	Sutton Poyntz) receiver's accounts		
	Hazelbury	) 1391–1400	
	Oxenhall	)	
SC6/842/25	Foxearth	1408	bailiff's account
SC6/858/16	Oxenhall	1395	"
/17	"	1396	"
/18	"	1402	"
/19	"	1412	"
/20	"	1413	"
SC6/989/1	Acton	1356	"
/2	"	1370	"
/3	"	1389	"
/4	"	1390	"
/5	"	1391	"
/6	"	1394	"
/7	"	1396	"
/8	"	1400	"
/9	"	?	"
/10	"	1405	"
/11	"	1407	"
/12	"	1409	"
/13	"	1410	"
/14	"	1414	"

/15	"	1415	"
/16	"	?	"
/17	"	1418	"
/18	"	1421	"
/20	"	1422	"
/21	"	1396	"
SC6/990/1	"	1430	"
/2	"	1431	"
/3	?	undated	"
/4	?	"	"
/5	Raydon	"	"
/6	"	"	"
/7	"	"	"
/8	Bures	"	"
/9	Acton	"	"
/10	"	"	"
/11	Bures	"	"
/12	Raydon	"	"
/13	?	"	?
/14	Foxearth	"	"
/15	?	"	"
/16	Waldingfield	"	"
/17	Bures	"	"
/18	Acton	"	"
/19	"	"	steward's account
/20	"	"	bailiff's account
/21	Bures	"	"
SC6/991/1	Acton	1417	steward's account
/2	"	undated	"/or receiver's
/3	Bures	"	bailiff's account
/4	Acton	"	steward's account
/5	Bures	"	bailiff's account
/6	Acton	"	"
SC6/1002/10	Layham	1387	bailiff's account
/11	"	1389	"
/12	"	1393	"
/13	"	1399	"

SC6/1003/6	Oxenhall	1401	"
/7	"	1409	"
/8	"	1416	"
/9	"	1419	"
/21	Raydon	1391	"
SC6/1007/3	Waldingfield	1406	"
SC6/1245/9	Bulmer	1392	"
/10	Bures	1384	"
/11	"	1410	"
/13	"	1428	"
/14	Foxearth	1373	"
/15	"	1404	"
/16	Acton	1428	receiver's account
/17	"	1431	"
SC6/1247/3	Oxenhall	1410	bailiff's account
/4	"	1411	"
/5	"	1417	"
SC6/1249/1	Acton	1398	"
/2	"	1403	"
/3	"	1411	"
/4	"	1418	steward's account, published with *The Household Book*
/5	"	1424	bailiff's account
/6	"	undated	"
/7	"	"	"
/8	"	"	"
/9	Bures	"	"
/10	Acton	"	"
SC6/1297/22	Acton	"	steward's account
DL29/430/6904	Acton	1393	bailiff's account

Appendix 2

Main references to Dame Alice's trustees,^ 1434 and visitors* to Acton, 1412–13. Relatives or people of the same surname who did not visit that year but appear in some of the account rolls are noted in brackets. Individual ecclesiastics are identified and referenced but not friars or priests.

Acton, Vicar of:* SC6/989/10,17,18,20; SC6/990/9; SC6/1245/17; SC6/1249/3,5.

Andrew, Richard:^ SC6/990/1,9; SC6/991/2; SC6/1245/16, household steward. A 'gentilman' of that name is mentioned in the Chancery Rolls of 1442 as a tax collector, *CFR, 1437–45*, p. 222.

Anton, James:* SC6/842/25; SC6/990/17,21; SC6/1245/15, ploughman (Richard: SC6/989/13, rent collector; Robert: SC6/1245/15, tenant).

Appylton, Richard* and wife,* of Essex: *CFR, 1413–22*, p. 210; BL Add 19115; Harley 891, 1449, 1560 (John: Copinger, *The Manors of Suffolk*, vol. 7, p. 289).

Archentein/in, Margaret,* widow of John(?): (John: SC6/989/8,10,11; SC6/1249/3,4, Acton tenant, casual work; Thomas: SC6/1249/3).

Archer, Joan,* John,* Maud:* SC6/989/6,8,10,11,17,18, 20, variously ploughman, rent land and the dairy (John Archer, junior: SC6/989/13; SC6/1249/2,3, tenant).

Astle, Hawis,* widow of William **Astele** (?): (William: SC6/989/6; SC6/1249/1, former Acton bailiff and cowherd; John: SC6/989/6,17; SC6/990/1; SC6/1249/1,3,5, ploughman).

Ayloff, John* of Sudbury: SC6/989/13; SC6/1249/1,4, sells cattle (Peter: SC6/1245/10, bailiff of Bures; Robert: SC6/991/1; SC6/1249/3, buys pelts, sells calves).

Baker, John:* 1. SC6/842/25, Foxearth rent collector; 2. Newcourt, *Repertorium*, vol. 2, p. 275, *CPR, 1401–5*, p. 147, Foxearth rector; 3. SC6/1297/22, student at Lavenham.

Baker, Thomas:* SC6/989/14,18,20; SC6/1249/3, Acton tenant, purchases corn and carting services.

Baker'/ton, John:* SC6/989/8,13; SC6/990/9, reaper, thatcher and buys wool.

Barbour, Geoffrey,* of Sudbury: SC6/990/19, candlemaker.

Barbour, John:* SC6/989/18; SC6/990/1; SC6/1249/3, thatcher, buys corn, sells pigs.

Barbour, Thomas:* SC6/989/17, harvester.

Berner, Joan,* John:* (Robert: SC6/989/5, buys corn, harvester).

Blundell, *Sir* Nicholas:* *CCR, 1385–9*, p. 374; *CCR, 1419–22*, p. 123; *CPR, 1399–1401*, p. 505; *CPR, 1408–13*, p. 278; Morley, 'Catalogue of Beneficed Clergy', p. 30, clerk, parson of Stansfield, Coney Weston, and Herringswell, executor of Sir Richard Waldegrave MP.

Bonys, Richard:* SC6/1249/3, mower.

Boteler, Alice,* same as 'wife of William Boteler'(?) (William: SC6/989/10,14,15; SC6/990/1; SC6/1249/3,4, buys wine for Dame Alice, supplies dairy produce, purchases wool-fells, corn, sells lambs, rents grazing).

Boteler, Sir Andrew,* MP, wife* and household:* see Roskell, Clark and Rawcliffe, *History of Parliament*, vol. 2, pp. 455–6.

Bregge, William:* SC6/989/14,16,17, ploughman (Margaret, his daughter: SC6/990/1; SC6/1245/5, manor maidservant; William, his son: SC6/989/20, swineherd).

Brook, *Sir* John: BL Add Ch 54192; Bacon Collection, MS 2256; SC6/833/12; SC6/989/3–16; SC6/1003/21; Newcourt, *Repertorium*, vol. 2, p. 363; Morley, 'Catalogue of Beneficed Clergy', p. 40, household steward, chaplain.

Brook, William,* of Holtan: SC6/989/17; SC6/990/19; SC6/1245/13, auditor, supervises courts, buys grain and cider, executor of Katherine Tendring, Howard (ed.), *The Visitation of Suffolk*, vol. 1, p. 30.

Brydbek, Margaret,* widow of John (?): SC6/989/15 (John: SC6/1249/2, human scarecrow).

Buntyng, Richard,* of Sudbury: his will, Norfolk R.O., *Norwich Episcopal Register*, DN4 Book 8, f. 242.

Bust, Thomas,* of Sudbury: his will, PRO, Prob. 11/2b, f. 81.

Carter, Geoffrey:* SC6/989/13; SC6/1249/3, tenant (Katherine: SC6/990/1; SC6/1249/5, rents land and grazing).

Cavendish, William:* SC6/1245/16; SC6/1249/4; BL, Add Charter 19122; *CCR, 1422–9*, p. 125; *CPR, 1413–6*, p. 82; *CPR, 1416–22*, p. 272; PRO, Prob. 11/3, f. 141, citizen and mercer of London, supplies household with wine.

Cavendish, Robert,^ (brother of above): BL, Add 19122; *CCR, 1419–22*, p. 347; *CCR, 1435–41*, pp. 47, 136; *CPR, 1422–9*, pp. 189, 277, 570; *CPR, 1429–36*, pp. 124, 132, 277, 345, 446; PRO, Prob. 11/3, f. 171; Suffolk R.O., 651/8–11; EL13/12/4, commissioner, lawyer, executor of Elizabeth Lovell.

Cawston, daughter of Robert:* (Robert: SC6/989/15,17,18,20; SC6/1249/5, buys fleeces).

Chamberlain, Ralph,* and wife:* SC6/1245/9; *CPR*, numerous, e.g., 1400, 1402, 1404, 1406, 1410, 1411, 1413, 1414, as feoffee, peace commissioner, Bacon Collection, MS 2275; Suffolk R.O., H1/5/5/13,17.

Chapman, Isabel,* John:* SC6/989/10,12–14,17,18,20; SC6/990/1; SC6/1249/3,4, tenants, employee, buys corn.

Chetylbere, *Sir* John:^ SC6/1249/5; SC6/1297/22; Newcourt, *Repertorium*, vol. 2, p. 497; household steward, parson of Rochford church in Essex in 1422; see also *CCR, 1435–41*, p. 490 for his later appointment in another widow's household.

Clerbek, Hawis:* SC6/989/7,8,10,19, 21; BL Add 19123; *CIPM*, vol. 16, p. 90; sells cattle (Walter, SC6/990/1).

Clopton, William* and wife,* of Long Melford: Suffolk R.O., FL509/13/11, H1/5/16/6; BL, Add 19123; commissioner, feoffee.

Cock/Cok, John:* SC6/989/8; SC6/1249/4, buys and sells produce (Robert: SC6/989/18, carter).

Colbrook, John:* SC6/989/13; SC6/1249/3, harvester.

Coo, John:^ *CCR, 1423–9*, p. 126, trustee of Sir Richard Waldegrave (there was a man of this name who rented land from Alice, see, for example, SC6/989/6,11; SC6/990/1).

Cook, John:* SC6/989/5,10, 20; SC6/990/1; SC6/991/1, rents land, buys lambs, household member.

Coppyng, John:* SC6/989/12, 13,17–20; SC6/990/1,9; SC6/1249/5, tenant, mower, thatcher, herdsman.

Corbet, Guy* and wife:* BL, Add 19124, half- brother of Sir Robert, see below.

Corbet, Sir Robert,* MP of Assington: see Roskell, Clark and Rawcliffe, *History of Parliament*, vol. 2, pp. 654–6.

Coupere, William:* SC6/991/1; SC6/1249/4, cooper.

Crek, *Sir* Peter:* SC6/989/18; Morley, 'Catalogue of Beneficed Clergy', p. 46, parson of Assington.

Dag', John:* SC6/989/5- 8,10,13,17,18, 21; SC6/991/6, SC6/1249/2,3, tenant, thatcher, 'clokke-maker' (Sebyl: SC6/1245/5,18).

Debenham, Gilbert,* esquire of Little Wenham: SC6/1245/17; Nicolas (ed.), *Testamenta Vetusta*, vol. 2, p. 210; *CPR*, various, e.g., 1410, 1412, 1431, 1440, feoffee, commissioner.

Deye, John,* Peter,* Richard,* Robert,* SC6/989/5-7,10,13,17,18, 20, 21; SC6/990/1, SC6/991/1; SC6/1245/11,15; SC6/1249/2,3, variously tenants, employees, cowherd, cattle-dealing, rent collector, household member.

Doreward, John,* MP and wife:* see Roskell, Clark and Rawcliffe, *History of Parliament*, vol. 2, pp. 790–2.

Dynham, wife,* son* and daughter* of Robert: (Robert: SC6/833/12; SC6/989/6-8,10,17,18, 21; SC6/990/1, Dame Alice's chamberlain; (*Sir* Richard: SC6/990/1; PRO, Prob. 11/2a, ff.7–9, Alice's chaplain).

Fouler, John* and Alice:* SC6/989/10,12,15,17; SC6/990/1,9; SC6/1249/3,4, shepherd (Margaret: SC6/1249/5; Petronella: SC6/989/20; Edward: SC6/990/1).

Frend, John* and wife:* SC6/990/8; SC6/1245/11,13, tenant at Bures.

Fuller, Robert,* of Assington: SC6/1245/11, buys wood (John: SC6/989/6,13,17,18, 20; SC6/1249/2, 3, tenant, cattle-dealer; Margaret: SC6/990/1).

Fysscher', John:* SC6/1245/11, tenant at Bures.

Galant, John:* SC6/989/18, tenant.

Geffrey, Thomas:* SC6/989/10,17,18, 20; SC6/990/1; SC6/1249, 3, 5, tenant, breeds and sells livestock, ploughman.

Goldyngham, John, of Essex:* SC6/990/16; SC6/1003/21; *CCR, 1409–13*, p. 115; *CPR, 1408–13*, p. 265; PRO, Prob.11/2b, f. 210, feoffee.

Goodrych, William:* SC6/989/6,8,10,11,13,15,17,21; SC6/990/1; SC6/1249/2, 3, tenant, employee (John: SC6/990/1; SC6/1297/22, carpenter).

Gough, Morgan:* *CCR, 1385–9*, p. 623; *CPR*, various, e.g., 1399, 1402–4, 1409, commissioner, feoffee, attorney, Dame Alice's receiver(?).

Gryffyn, Rose,* John,* Richard:* SC6/989/5-8,10,11,13,15-18, 21; SC6/990/1; SC6/1249/1-3, variously tenants, thatcher, carter, harvester.

Gugge, John: SC6/842/25; SC6/989/6, tenant (Semanus:* Edmund: SC6/989/21; William: SC6/990/14).

Hamerden, John:* SC6/989/20; SC6/990/1; SC6/1249/1, 3, 5, tenant, carter.

Hardekyn, Thomas:^ *CFR, 1422–30*, pp. 294, 332, collector of taxes in Essex.

Harlewene, *Sir* Richard:* Newcourt, *Repertorium*, vol. 2, p. 419, rector of Middleton.

Hatfield Peverel, Prior of:* SC6/989/13.

Hervy, John* of Lavenham: SC6/989/14,15; *CCR, 1435–41*, p. 363; *CFR, 1422–30*, p. 114, feoffee, granted subsidy and alnage of cloths, buys grain.

Hethe, John:* SC6/989/15; SC6/1249/4, blacksmith.

Holbrook, John:* SC6/990/19; SC6/1245/13,16, clerk, auditor, supervises Alice's courts.

Holbygge, William:* SC6/989/20; SC6/1249/5; SC6/1297/22, blacksmith.

Holyere, Robert:^ Norfolk R.O., *Norwich Episcopal Register*, DN4 Book 8, f. 85, DN5 Book 10, f. 601, parson of Raydon church.

Hoo, John:* SC6/990/15; SC6/991/4, rents Cramaville.

Howard, Sir John,* ^ MP, wife* (the Lady Alice) and daughter:* Roskell, Clark and Rawcliffe, *History of Parliament*, vol. 3, pp. 431–3; PRO, Prob. 11/3, ff. 48–50 for Alice Howard's will.

Inglesthorp (Ingylstrop), Sir John,* MP: see Roskell, Clark and Rawcliffe, *History of Parliament*, vol. 3, pp. 475–7.

Ive, William:* SC6/990/16; SC6/1007/3, Waldingfield tenant, rent collector.

Jerold, William:* SC6/989/16,17, thatcher (John: SC6/990/1, tenant).

Joye, John,* of Ipswich: *CFR, 1413–22*, pp. 349, 353, *CFR, 1422–30*, pp. 19, 333; BL, Add Ch.s 9672, 9678, supplier of wine, collector of taxes and customs, peace commissioner.

Kendale, William:* SC6/989/15,17; SC6/990/3; SC6/991/1; SC6/1249/3,4; SC6/1297/22, snares rabbits for table, casual work, household member.

Lalleford, John* of Bury St Edmunds: Suffolk R.O., A1/2/16/1,16.

Langham, William:* SC6/989/21; SC6/990/5; DL29/430/6904, holds courts at Wherstead and Raydon.

Lodbrook, Thomas:* SC6/1245/16, rented Layham farm (John: SC6/1249/5, 'farmer').

Lorkyn, Alice* and John:* SC6/989/13; SC6/990/14; SC6/1245/15, Foxearth tenants, buy fleeces, sell cows (Richard: SC6/1002/13).

Lowys, John:* SC6/1245/11; SC6/990/21, 'farmer' of cows at Bures (wife helps at harvest time, SC6/990/17; Richard: SC6/989/7, carpenter).

Lytleton, John:* SC6/833/12; SC6/1003/9; SC6/1247/3-5, Oxenhall bailiff.

Malcher, Thomas:* SC6/989/6,8,17,21; SC6/1249/1,3,4; 'supervisor' and overseer, Acton, sells cattle (daughter: SC6/989/7).

Materas, John:* SC6/1245/11, Bures rent collector, rents land, buys corn and wood.

Mauncell, *Sir* Richard:* Bacon Collection, MS 584; *CCR, 1419–22*, p. 123; *CPR, 1408–13*, p. 278; Howard (ed.), *The Visitation of Suffolk*, vol. 1, p. 116;

Norfolk R.O., *Norwich Episcopal Register*, DN3 Book 6, f. 271, DN4 Book 8, ff. 20, 22, DN5 Book 9, f. 23, clerk, executor of Sir Richard Waldegrave MP, rector of Toppesfield, North Wycene and Polstead.

Meller, Thomas:* SC6/989/6; SC6/1249/4, repairs mill machinery.

Milde, Thomas ,^ of Clare: SC6/1245/16; *CCR, 1413–9*, p. 372; *CCR, 1429–35*, p. 297; *CCR, 1435–41*, pp. 136, 143, 363; *CFR, 1422–30*, pp. 220, 304; *CPR, 1429–36*, pp. 132, 137, 470; Suffolk R.O., EL13/12/4, supervises Alice's courts.

Mody, John:* SC6/989/13,18; SC6/991/1, buys produce (Richard: SC6/990/8, 9; SC6/991/1; SC6/1297/22, household member, snares rabbits, buys wool, sells sheep and cattle).

Morell, Gilbert:* SC6/1249/3, buys fleeces, rents grazing. (Alex: SC6/989/13; SC6/990/1, buys sheep, sells cattle).

Mose, Robert:* SC6/989/6-8,10,12,14,15; SC6/1249/3,4, carpenter, repairs to drainage system, sells pigs, buys produce.

Munk, Peter:* SC6/989/6,7,8,10,13-15,17,18,20; SC6/1249/2,3,5, repairs carts, rents forge, buys and sells produce.

Nowers, Alice:* (John: SC6/989/13; SC6/990/6; SC6/1249/3-5, keeper of the pigeons, sells pigs, buys produce).

Payn, wife of Thomas:* (Thomas: SC6/1245/11, tenant Bures; John: SC6/1245/16, tenant Wherstead).

Pethirton, Henry:^ SC6/833/12; SC6/990/1,8,9, from Petherton in Somerset (?), long-standing household member.

Peyton, Alice,* wife of John(?): (John: SC6/989/14,15,17,18, shepherd).

Plowrygth, Richard:* SC6/989/10,14,15,17,18, 20, carpenter, mends ploughs.

Plum, John:* SC6/989/18; SC6/990/1; SC6/991/1, casual labour, buys corn, drover.

Reydon, Robert:* SC6/989/14,15; SC6/1245/11, buys produce, granted alms.

Rodelond, John:* SC6/989/7,10; SC6/1007/3, sells cattle, buys fleeces.

Rokewode, Agnes,* William,* MP, and daughter:* Roskell, Clark and Rawcliffe, *History of Parliament*, vol. 4, pp. 232–3; SC6/989/5,7,8,17,18, 20; SC6/1249/4, 5 (Amice and John: SC6/990/1).

Ryngezell, William:* SC6/989/13,17,18, 20; SC6/1249/3; SC6/1297/22, tenant, sells cows and grazing.

Sake, John:* SC6/989/5-11, 13-15,17,18, 20; SC6/990/1; SC6/1249/2-4, tenant, thatcher, casual work.

Saltwell, John,* and wife:* SC6/989/7,13,21, casual work, harvesting, carpentry.

Sampson, Agnes,* daughter of William and Margaret: BL, Add Charter 19121.

Sampson, Margaret,* and son:* SC6/989/15, sells Alice cattle and sheep.

Sampson, Thomas,^ * esquire: SC6/1297/22; *CCR, 1435–41*, p. 363; *CFR, 1420–30*, p. 114; *CFR, 1437–45*, p. 103; *CPR, 1429–36*, pp. 41, 124, commissioner.

Sampson, William:* see Agnes and Margaret above.

Scoyll, John:* SC6/989/8, 10, 13, 15, 17–19; SC6/990/1; SC6/1245/11; SC6/1249/3,5, tenant, rent collector, sells foals, buys sheep, wheat, casual labour.

Smyth, John:* 1. of Lavenham; 2. of Cavendish; 3. of Bures: SC6/989/16–20; SC6/990/14; SC6/991/4; SC6/1249/3, variously, veterinary services, smith, ploughman, sends eels from Bures' mill.

Smyth, Robert:* SC6/989/5–11,13, 17–19; SC6/991/1; SC6/1249/3, tenant, buys cattle, casual labour, household member (Margaret: SC6/989/20).

Stanstead, Rector of:* SC6/1297/22.

Stoke-by-Clare, Prior of:* SC6/990/8; SC6/1245/11.

Strutt, Robert:* SC6/989/17; SC6/990/1, tenant, granger, household member (Thomas: SC6/989/6; Ralph: SC6/989/13–15,17; SC6/1249/2,3; Richard: SC6/1249/1).

Swinbourne, Lady Joan,* widow of Sir Robert, MP: Roskell, Clark and Rawcliffe, *History of Parliament*, vol. 4, pp. 557–9.

Swinbourne, Geoffrey:* son of Lady Joan, see above.

Tallick, John:* SC6/989/5,6,8,11,17,18, 21; SC6/990/1; SC6/1249/2, tenant, sells cattle.

Talmache, John,* of Bentley manor: SC6/989/5,6, 8; *CIPM, 1405–13*, p. 367.

Teyler, William:* SC6/989/18, 20, 21; SC6/1249/2, tenant.

Thomas, William:* SC6/989/8, rents cows from Alice.

Thourgor, Edward:* SC6/989/5,8,13,21; SC6/1249/3, tenant and ploughman (John and Robert: SC6/990/1).

Tyler, John:* SC6/989/7,8,10,17; SC6/1249/3,4, casual work and laying tiles (William, his son).

Waldegrave, Sir Richard,* Lady Joan* and son:* SC6/990/14; SC6/1245/11,13; Roskell, Clark and Rawcliffe, *History of Parliament*, vol. 4, pp. 735–9.

Waldegrave, William:* see above.

Webbe, John:* SC6/989/6,7,13,14,18, 20; SC6/1003/21; SC6/1007/3; SC6/1249/4, tenant, casual labourer, builder (Andrew: SC6/990/1; Peter: SC6/1249/3).

White, 'the wife of John':* (John: SC6/989/14,20; SC6/990/1; SC6/991/1; SC6/1249/3, 4; SC6/1297/22, household member, buys and sells produce).

Whyte, Agnes,* wife of Alex: (Alex: SC6/833/12; SC6/989/8,10–15,18, 21; SC6/991/1; SC6/1249,1–4, household member, sells produce).

Wysman, Alice* and John:* SC6/989/6–8,10,13,14,17,18; SC6/990/1, tenant, smith, buys fleeces (Robert: SC6/1249/2,3).

Wythersfield, Rector of:* SC6/989/7,8,14,15; SC6/990/18; SC6/1249/1–3.

Notes

Introduction

1 *The Household Book of Alice de Bryene*, ed. V. Redstone, Suffolk Institute of Archaeology and Natural History (Ipswich, 1931).

2 See, for example, C. Dyer, *Standards of Living in the Late Middle Ages: Social Change in England* c. *1200–1520*, (Cambridge University Press, 1989).

3 E. Rickert, 'Documents and Letters: a Leaf from a Fourteenth-Century Letter Book', *Modern Philology*, 25 (1927), 249–55.

4 See P. Coss, *The Knight in Medieval England 1000–1400* (Stroud, Sutton Publishing, 1993), on the social implications of the changing role of 'knighthood'.

5 E.H. Carr, *What is History?* (Harmondsworth, Penguin, 1990), Chapter 1.

6 E. Power, *Medieval People* (London, Metheun, 1975), p. 61.

7 J. Bennett, 'Medieval Women, Modern Women: Across the Great Divide', in D. Aers (ed.), *Culture and History 1350–1600: Essays on English Communities, Identities and Writing* (New York, Harvester Wheatsheaf, 1992), pp. 147–75.

8 C. Barron, 'The "Golden Age" of Women in Medieval London', in *Medieval Women in Southern England, Reading Medieval Studies*, XV (1989), 35–58.

1. The Medieval Household

1 See PRO, SC6/989/6, SC6/991/6, SC6/991/1, SC6/1297/22. Further references for evidence relating to Alice de Bryene's household will not generally be noted but most details were elicited from the account rolls listed in Appendix 1.

2 I have identified the majority of Alice de Bryene's guests in 1412–13 from a variety of sources. Details of some of them with the most important references are given in Appendix 2.

3 A list of surviving accounts and transcriptions of several can be found in *Household Accounts from Medieval England*, ed. C.M. Woolgar (2 parts, Oxford University Press, 1992–3).

4 See Jennifer Ward, *English Noblewomen in the Later Middle Ages* (London, Longman, 1992), for a detailed description of the de Burgh household.

5 Ward, *English Noblewomen*, p. 5.

6 See, for example, L. Stone, *The Family, Sex and Marriage in England 1500–1800* (London, Weidenfeld & Nicolson, 1977), who maintains there was little affectivity in medieval families, and Barbara Hanawalt, *The Ties That Bound: Peasant Families in Medieval England* (New York, Oxford University Press, 1986), who gives evidence of strong familial ties.

7   *The Book of Margery Kempe*, ed. B.A. Windeatt (Harmondsworth, Penguin, 1985), pp. 126, 132, 238, 251, 253, 259.

8   A copy of Sir Guy Bryan's will transcribed by John Gage in the early nineteenth century is in Cambridge University Library, Hengrave Hall, Deposit 2, Collection of the Babergh Hundred.

9   PRO, Prob. 11/3, f. 171.

10 R.N. Swanson, *Catholic England: Faith, Religion and Observance before the Reformation* (Manchester University Press, 1993), p. 104.

11 R. Newcourt, *Repertorium: Ecclesiasticum Parochicale Londinense* (2 vols, London, 1708), vol. 2, p. 363; C. Morley, 'Catalogue of Beneficed Clergy of Suffolk 1086–1550', *Suffolk Institute of Archaeology and Natural History* 22 (1934–6), 40; BL, Add Ch. 54192; Bacon Collection, Department of Special Collections, University of Chicago Library, MS 2256; PRO, SC6/833/12, SC6/989/3-16, SC6/1003/21.

12 Lambeth Palace Library, Arundel Register, vol. 1, ff. 163–4.

13 *The Book of Margery Kempe*, p. 196.

14 *Chaucer's World*, ed. E. Rickert (Columbia University Press, 1948), p. 373.

15 N. Saul, *Scenes from Provincial Life: Knightly Families in Suffolk 1280–1400* (Oxford, Clarendon Press, 1986), p. 105.

16 M.W. LaBarge, *A Baronial Household of the Thirteenth Century* (London, Eyre and Spottiswoode, 1965), p. 59.

17 The Dynhams had been in Alice's service since at least 1390 and appear to have been based in the West Country. Nothing connects them with the Suffolk village of Denham. Sir Guy Bryan's Aunt Joan was married to Oliver Dinham in 1350, though she had no sons called Richard or Robert. Possibly the Dynhams came from an unidentified cadet or illegitimate branch of the Dinham family.

18 William Langland, *The Vision of Piers Plowman*, ed. A.V.C. Schmidt (London, J.M. Dent, 1995), p. 163.

19 PRO, SC6/1297/22.

20 LaBarge, *A Baronial Household*, p. 36.

21 *The Book of Margery Kempe*, p. 98.

22 *Walter of Henley and other treatises on estate management and accounting*, ed. D. Oschinsky (Oxford, Clarendon Press, 1971), pp. 403–5.

23 C.D. Ross, 'The Household Accounts of Elizabeth Berkeley, Countess of Warwick, 1420–1', *Transactions of the Bristol and Gloucestershire Archaeological Society*, 70 (1951), 91–2.

24 Ibid., p. 91.

25 LaBarge, *A Baronial Household*, p. 120.

26 *The Fifty Earliest English Wills, 1387–1439*, ed. F.J. Furnivall, Early English Text Society, no. 78 (London, Trübner and Co., 1882), p. 4.

27 PRO, SC1/51/24; and E. Rickert, 'Documents and Letters: a Leaf from a Fourteenth-Century Letter Book', *Modern Philology*, 25 (1927) p. 253.

28 Rickert, 'Documents and Letters', p. 249.

29 Christine de Pisan, *The Treasure of the City of Ladies, or the Book of the Three Virtues*, tr. S. Lawson (Harmondsworth, Penguin, 1985).

30 Ibid., p. 19.

31 *The Goodman of Paris; a treatise on moral and domestic economy by a citizen of Paris, c. 1393*, ed. E. Power (London, Routledge and Sons, 1928), pp. 93–7.

32 C. Dyer, 'The Consumer and the Market in the Later Middle Ages', *Economic History Review*, 2nd series 42 (1989), 305–27.

2. Marriage and the Family

1 J. Ward, 'Sir Robert de Bures', *Transactions of the Monumental Brass Society*, 10 (1963–5), 144–9; *CCR, 1330–2*, p. 427.

2 *CIPM*, vol. 10, p. 477; Bacon Collection, MS 2227.

3 Dorset R.O., D/WLC T296; *CCR, 1369–74*, p. 471; *CIPM, 1377–84*, vol. 15, p. 349.

4 *CIPM*, vol. 17, p. 87; V.A. Copinger, *The Manors of Suffolk: Notes on the History and Devolution* (6 vols, London, Fisher Unwin, 1905), vol. 6, p. 120.

5 *Women in England, c. 1275–1525, Documentary Sources*, ed. and tr. P.J.P. Goldberg (Manchester University Press, 1995), pp. 5–6.

6 *CCR, 1385–9*, p. 302; *CPR, 1385–9*, p. 276; N.H. Nicolas, *The Controversy between Sir Richard Scrope and Sir Robert Grosvenor* (2 vols, London, Nichols, 1832), vol. 2, p. 376.

7 S. Sheridan Walker, 'Widow and Ward: the Feudal Law of Child Custody in Medieval England', in S.M. Stuard (ed.), *Women in Medieval Society* (University of Pennsylvania, 1976), p. 163.

8 J.S. Roskell, L. Clark and C. Rawcliffe (eds) *The History of Parliament: The House of Commons 1386–1421* (4 vols, Stroud, Alan Sutton Publishing, 1993), vol. 4, pp. 735–9.

9 J.J. Alexander, 'Early Owners of Torbryan', *Transactions of the Devonshire Association*, 68 (1936), 197.

10 R.G. Stanes, 'Sir Guy Brian, KG', *Transactions of the Devonshire Association*, 92 (1959–60), 260.

11 'Is not able to give his assent since he has lost his memory', *Collectanea Topographica et Geneaologica*, ed. J.B. Nichols (8 vols, London, Nichols and Son, 1834–43), vol. 3, p. 250.

12 For an overview of Lord Bryan's life see Stanes, 'Sir Guy Brian KG', pp. 249–77. Apart from numerous notations in the Close, Fine and Patent rolls and the Calendar of Papal Registers, see also *Chronicon Angliae 1328–1388*, ed. E.M. Thompson (London, Longman, 1874), pp. 69–70; *The Anonimalle Chronicle 1333–1381*, ed. V.H. Galbraith (Manchester University Press, 1970), pp. 68, 70, 84, 91; T.F. Tout, *Chapters in the Administrative History of Medieval England: the Wardrobe, Chamber and Small Seals* (6 vols, Manchester University Press, 1920), vols 3, 4, passim; C. Given-Wilson, *The Royal Household and the King's Affinity: Service, Politics and Finance in England 1360–1413* (Yale University Press, 1986), pp. 51, 73, 156; *Testamenta Vetusta*, ed. N.H. Nicolas (2 vols, London, Nichols, 1826), vol. 1, pp. 78, 89, 96; E. Upham, *Index to the Rolls of Parliament 1278–1503* (London, imprint, 1832), p. 94; *Collectanea Topographica et Geneaologica*, vol. 3, pp. 250–62.

13 *CIPM*, vol. 16, pp. 380–2.

14 V. Gibbs (ed.). *The Complete Peerage* (13 vols, London, St Catherine's Press, 1910–59), vol. 2, p. 361.

15 *The Complete Peerage*, vol. 8, p. 585.

16 There is no direct evidence who William's patron was and he may well have been named after his maternal uncle, the 2nd Earl of Salisbury or his half-sister's uncle-in-law, William Courtenay, Archbishop of Canterbury in 1381. However, he almost certainly spent some time in the household of Richard, 3rd Earl of Arundel, to whom he once gave a piece of tapestry: see *A Collection of Wills now known to be extant of the Kings and Queens of England from William the Conqueror to Henry VII*, ed. J. Nichols (London, Nichols, 1780), p. 132.

17 *Wykeham's Register*, ed. T.F. Kirby (2 vols, London, Simpkin and Co., 1899), vol. 2, p. 378.

18 *CIPM*, vol. 16, pp. 128–9.

19 J. Rosenthal, *Nobles and the Noble Life, 1295–1500*, (London, Allen & Unwin, 1976), pp. 22–40.

20 H. Leyser, *Medieval Women: A Social History of Women in England, 450–1500* (London, Phoenix Grant, 1996), p. 117.

21 *CFR, 1383–1391*, p. 262; *CPR, 1388–92*, p. 126.

22 Roskell, Clark and Rawcliffe, *History of Parliament*, vol. 3, p. 433.

23 Goldberg, *Women in England*, p. 10.

24 See J.M.W. Bean, *The Estates of the Percy Family* (Oxford University Press, 1958), pp. 117–27 for an overview of the claimants and settlements of the Bryan estates; and Bacon Collection, MS 2358, 2371, 2903, 3173 with reference to the Bures.

25 A. Simpson, *The Wealth of the Gentry 1540–1660* (Chicago University Press, 1961), p. 91.

26 *CCR, 1374–7*, p. 229; J.S. Roskell, 'Sir Richard de Waldegrave of Bures St Mary, Speaker in Parliament 1381–2', *Suffolk Institute of Archaeology and Natural History*, 27 (1958), 160.

27 Bacon Collection, MS 2250.

28 *Inquisitions Post Mortem 1359–1413 for Gloucestershire*, ed. T.M. Blagg (6 vols, London, British Record Society, 1914), vol. 6, p. 102; *CCR, 1374–7*, pp. 278, 481; *Dorset Inquisitions Post Mortem 1216–1483*, ed. E.A. Fry (London, British Record Society, 1916), pp. 186–92.

29 *CPR, 1374–7*, pp. 160, 444; *CPR, 1377–81*, pp. 409, 449; J. Campbell-Klease, *A History of Hazelbury Bryan* (privately published, 1983), Ch. 1, p. 15, quoting the Account book of Thomas, Earl of Buckingham.

30 *CPR, 1377–81*, p. 324; *CPR, 1381–5*, pp. 285, 358, 589, 598; *Monasticon Dioecesis Exoniensis*, ed. G. Oliver (Exeter and London, Longman, 1846) pp. 322–8.

31 *Feet of Fines for Essex 1327–1498*, ed. R.E.G. Kirk (6 vols, Colchester, Essex Archaeological Society, 1949), vol. 3, p. 198.

32 Stanes, 'Sir Guy Brian', p. 267.

33 Froissart, *Chronicles*, ed. G. Brereton (Harmondsworth, Penguin, 1968), p. 331.

34 Leyser, *Medieval Women*, p. 109.

35 University of Cambridge Manuscript Library, Hengrave Hall, Deposit 2, Collection of the Babergh Hundred.

36 E. Rickert, 'Documents and Letters: a Leaf from a Fourteenth-Century Letter Book', *Modern Philology*, 25 (1927), p. 254.

37 Julian of Norwich, *Revelations of Divine Love*, ed. and tr. C. Wolters (Harmondsworth, Penguin, 1966), *passim*; *The Book of Margery Kempe*, ed. B.A. Windeatt (Harmondsworth, Penguin, 1985), pp. 58–60, 122–4, 220–1.

38 *Testamenta Vetusta*, vol. 1, p. 283.

39 Paddy Payne and Caroline Barron, 'The Letters and Life of Elizabeth Despenser, Lady Zouche', *Nottingham Medieval Studies*, xli (1997), 137, 150–1.

40 *CPR, 1408–13*, p. 278; *CPR, 1416–22*, p. 105; *CPR, 1422–9*, pp. 141, 277.

41 *Calendar of Charter Rolls, 1341–1417* (London, HMSO, 1916), vol. 5, pp. 306, 315; *CFR, 1383–91*, pp. 178, 192, 201; *CCR, 1385–9*, pp. 475–6, 604–5.

42 *CCR, 1385–9*, pp. 623–4.

43 *Calendar of Select Pleas and Memoranda of the City of London 1381–1412*, ed. A.H. Thomas (Cambridge University Press, 1932), pp. 145–6; *CCR, 1385–9*, p. 593.

44 *CPR, 1388–92*, pp. 119, 303.

45 *Calendar of Papal Registers, Papal Letters, 1362–1404* (London, HMSO, 1902), vol. 4, p. 393; *The Episcopal Register of Thomas de*

Brantyngham 1370–94, ed. F.C. Hingeston-Randolph (2 parts, London, Bell, 1906), part 2, p. 707; *The Westminster Chronicle 1381–94*, ed. L.C. Hector and B. Harvey (Oxford, Clarendon Press, 1982), p. 439.

46 *CPR, 1391–6*, p. 400.

47 *CIPM*, vol. 17, p. 363–4.

48 *CCR, 1385–9*, p. 628–9.

49 *CPR, 1381–5*, p. 565.

50 E. Rickert, 'Documents and Letters', pp. 254–5.

51 Ibid., p. 253–4.

52 *CCR, 1396–9*, p. 216.

53 *Complete Peerage*, vol. 11, p. 566. The marriage was legitimized in the Scrope manor chapel of Turnham Hall on the Ouse below Selby in North Yorkshire, J.H. Wylie, *History of England under Henry IV* (4 vols, London, Longmans, 1896), vol. 2, p. 205–6.

54 *Thomas Walsingham; Historia Anglicana, 1272–1422*, ed. H.T. Riley (2 vols, London, Longman, 1863–70), vol. 2, p. 305; T. Pugh, 'The Southampton Plot 1415', in R.A. Griffiths and J. Sherborne (eds), *Kings and Nobles in the Later Middle Ages* (Gloucester, Alan Sutton, 1979), pp. 62–89.

55 *Rymer's Foedera, conventiones, literae et cuiscunque generis acta publica*, ed. G. Holmes, 3rd edn (10 vols, The Hague, 1745), vol. 4, pp. 131–3.

56 Roskell, Clark and Rawcliffe, *The History of Parliament*, vol. 3, pp. 632–4.

57 PRO, SC6/858/19, SC6/1003/8,9; SC6/1247/5.

58 Wylie, *History of England under Henry IV*, vol. 3, p. 319.

59 *Complete Peerage*, vol. 1, pp. 247–9.

60 *Complete Peerage*, vol. 10, p. 128.

61 J. Rosenthal, 'Aristocratic marriage and the English Peerage 1350–1500: social institution and personal bond', *Journal of Medieval History*, 10 (1984), 181–94.

62 Rowena Archer, ' "How Ladies . . . who live in their manors ought to manage their households and estates": women as landholders in English society in the late Middle Ages', in P.J.P. Goldberg (ed.), *Woman is a Worthy Wight: Women in English Society in the Late Middle Ages c. 1200–1500* (Stroud, Alan Sutton, 1992), pp. 149–81.

63 H. Harrod, 'On the mantle and ring of widowhood', *Archaeologia*, 40 (1866), 308.

64 M.C. Erler, 'Three fifteenth century vowesses', in C. Barron and A. Sutton (eds), *Medieval London Widows 1300–1500* (London, Hambledon Press, 1994), pp. 165–84.

65 Christine de Pisan, *The Treasure of the City of Ladies or the Book of the Three Virtues*, tr. S. Lawson (Harmondsworth, Penguin, 1995), pp. 81, 159.

66 William Langland, *The Vision of Piers Plowman*, ed. A.V.C. Schmidt (London, J.M. Dent, 1995), p. 163.

67 C. Barron, 'The widow's world in later medieval London', in Barron and Sutton (eds), *Medieval London Widows*, p. xxxiv.

68 F.J. Furnivall (ed.), *The Fifty Earliest English Wills 1387–1439*, Early English Text Society, 78 (London, Trübner and Co., 1882), p. 4; Payne and Barron, 'Letters and life of Elizabeth Despenser', p. 144.

69 Barron, 'The widow's world', p. xxvii.

3. *Estate Management*

1 Sources for this chapter, unless otherwise specified, are the various account rolls itemized in Appendix 1.

2 PRO, SC6/1003/6.

3 *Chronicon Adae de Usk 1377–1421*, ed. E.M. Thompson (Oxford University Press, 1904), p. 229.

4   C. Allmand, *Henry V* (London, Methuen, 1992), p. 63.

5   Richard Micheldever's will, PRO, Prob. 11/2a, ff. 7–9. See also *CIPM*, vol. 17, p. 170; *CPR, 1385–92*, p. 332; *CCR, 1385–9*, pp. 87, 217, 275, 475; *CCR, 1389–92*, pp. 92, 537; *CCR, 1392–6*, p. 153.

6   G.A. Holmes, *The Estates of the Higher Nobility in Fourteenth Century England* (Cambridge University Press, 1957), Chapter 3.

7   *CCR, 1349–54*, p. 469; R.G.F. Stanes, 'Sir Guy de Bryan KG', *Transactions of the Devonshire Association*, 91–2 (1959–60), p. 271.

8   J.S. Roskell, L. Clark and C. Rawcliffe (eds), *The History of Parliament: the House of Commons 1386–1421* (Stroud, Alan Sutton, 1993), vol. 4, pp. 846–9; T.M. Blagg, *Inquisitions Post Mortem for Gloucestershire 1359–1413* (London, British Record Society, 1914), vol. 6, p. 146.

9   Carole Rawcliffe, 'Baronial councils in the later Middle Ages', in C. Ross (ed.), *Patronage, Pedigree and Power in Later Medieval England* (Gloucester, Alan Sutton, 1979), p. 88.

10 PRO, SC6/833/12.

11 See PRO, CP 25/1/323/m 106; CP 40/509/m 113; CP 40/596/m 314; CP 40/597/ m 477; *CCR, 1405–9*, p. 623; *Collectanea Topographica et Genealogia*, ed. J.B. Nichols (8 vols, London, Nichols and Son, 1834–43), vol. 3, p. 253.

12 T.F.T. Plucknett, 'The Medieval Bailiff', *The Creighton Lecture in History 1953* (The University of London, Athlone Press, 1954), pp. 1–33.

13 PRO, SC6/990/21.

14 PRO, SC6/1003/6,7.

15 PRO, C 139/70, no. 34.

16 J.M.W. Bean, *The Estates of the Percy Family* (Oxford University Press, 1958), pp. 116–27.

17 PRO, SC6/833/12.

18 BL, Egerton Roll 8333.

19 T. Hardy, *The Trumpet Major*, The World's Classics (Oxford University Press, 1986), p. 9.

20 PRO, SC6/989/3.

21 PRO, SC6/990/7,12.

22 Bacon Collection, MS 903.

23 See BL, Add Ch. 18671; Roskell, Clark and Rawcliffe, *History of Parliament*, vol. 4, p. 500; V.A. Copinger, *The Manors of Suffolk: Notes on the History and Devolution* (6 vols, London, Fisher Unwin, 1905), vol. 3, p. 204.

24 J. Rosenthal, *Nobles and the Noble Life, 1295–1500* (London, Allen & Unwin, 1976), p. 59.

25 Bishop Grosseteste writing in the thirteenth century to advise the Countess of Lincoln on estate management revealed that 10 quarters of apples and pears were needed to make 1 tun (2 pipes) of cider. Alice bought in 2 quarters and 2 bushels of apples that year, presumably to supplement the quantity that she had harvested from her own orchards: D. Oschinsky (ed.), *Walter of Henley and Other Treatises on Estate Management and Accounting* (Oxford, Clarendon Press, 1971), p. 429.

26 Oschinsky, *Walter of Henley*, pp. 3–9.

27 Ibid. pp. 275–87, 337, 382.

28 L.C. Hector and B. Harvey (eds), *The Westminster Chronicle 1381–1394* (Oxford, Clarendon Press, 1982), p. 365.

29 Oschinsky, *Walter of Henley*, p. 333.

30 R. Hutton, *The Rise and Fall of Merry England: the Ritual Year 1400–1700* (Oxford University Press, 1996), pp. 37–44.

31 *The Book of Margery Kempe*, ed. B.A. Windeatt (Harmondsworth, Penguin, 1985), p. 58.

32 A.O.D. Claxton, *The Suffolk Dialect in the Twentieth Century* (Ipswich, Boydell Press, 1968), p. 85.

33   A. Simpson in *The Wealth of the Gentry 1540–1660* (Chicago University Press, 1961), pp. 97–202, writing about the Bacon estates from material held in the Department of Special Collections at the University of Chicago Library, summarizes the movement of rents at Acton, Foxearth, Bures, Raydon, Wherstead and Waldingfield. On Henry Bures' death in 1529 they were fairly similar to Alice's time, except at Foxearth where the 40 per cent drop in value might reflect the high outrents of that manor. Sixty years later, however, the rents had doubled, and by 1654 there was an increase of 800 per cent.

4. The Gentle Lifestyle

1   E. Rickert, 'Documents and Letters: a Leaf from a Fourteenth-Century Letter Book', *Modern Philology* 25 (1927, pp. 249–50.

2   J. Rosenthal, 'Aristocratic Widows in Fifteenth Century England', in B.J. Harris and J.K. McNamara (eds), *Women and the Structure of Society* (Durham, NC, 1984), p. 36.

3   Philippa Maddern, 'Honour among the Pastons: Gender and Integrity in Fifteenth Century Provincial Society', *Journal of Medieval History*, 14 (1988), 357–71.

4   C. Ross, 'The Household Accounts of Elizabeth Berkeley, Countess of Warwick, 1420–21', *Transactions of the Bristol and Gloucestershire Society*, 70 (1951), 81–105.

5   J.C. Ward, *English Noblewomen in the Later Middle Ages* (London, Longman, 1992).

6   PRO, SC6/1297/22. Further references for evidence relating to the lifestyle at Acton will only be noted if it was not elicited from the account rolls in Appendix 1.

7   G. Holmes (ed.), *Rymer's Foedera, conventiones, literae et cuiscunque generis acta publica* (10 vols, The Hague, 1740), vol. 4, p. 131. The fact that Scrope's will was never proved, since his lands and chattels were forfeited, means that Alice may not have actually received any of his bequests, but it does give us an idea about the Acton lifestyle.

8   M.W. LaBarge, *A Baronial Household of the Thirteenth Century* (London, Eyre and Spottiswoode, 1965), p. 141.

9   *The Paston Letters and Papers of the Fifteenth Century*, ed. N. Davis (2 parts, Oxford, Clarendon Press, 1971), part 1, p. 216.

10   LaBarge, *A Baronial Household*, p. 139.

11   PRO, Prob. 11/3, f. 171.

12   F.J. Furnivall (ed.), *The Fifty Earliest English Wills 1387–1439*, Early English Text Society, 78 (London, Trübner and Co., 1882), p. 50.

13   LaBarge, *A Baronial Household*, p. 123.

14   Furnivall, *The Fifty Earliest English Wills*, p. 6.

15   H.J. Yallop, 'Slapton College', *Transactions of the Devonshire Association*, 92 (1959–60), 142.

16   PRO, Prob. 11/1, f. 53, John Filliol's will.

17   *The Paston Letters*, part 1, p. 217.

18   C. Dyer in *Standards of Living in the Late Middle Ages: Social Change in England c. 1200–1520* (Cambridge University Press, 1989), p. 58, calculated that 20,133 lbs of meat was consumed in Alice's household in 1418–19. I have used that figure and divided it by the number of guests in 1412–13.

19   C.M. Woolgar, 'Diet and Consumption in Gentry and Noble Households', in R.E. Archer and S. Walker (eds), *Rulers and the Ruled in Late Medieval England* (London, Hambledon Press, 1995), p. 22.

20   PRO, SC2/203/10.

21   *Curye on Inglysch*, ed. C.B. Hieatt and S. Butler, Early English Text Society (Oxford University Press, 1985), p. 112.

22 M. Bailey, 'The Rabbit and the Medieval East Anglian Economy', *The Agricultural History Review*, 36 (1988), 1–20.

23 R. Reyce, *Suffolk in the Seventeenth Century: the Breviary of Suffolk (1618) with notes by Lord Francis Hervey* (London, John Murray, 1902), p. 35.

24 Nicole Crossley-Holland, *Living and Dining in Medieval Paris: the Household of a Fourteenth-Century Knight* (Cardiff, University of Wales Press, 1996), p. 116.

25 P.W. Hammond, *Food and Feast in Medieval England* (Stroud, Alan Sutton, 1993), pp. 93, 101.

26 Dyer, *Standards of Living in the Late Middle Ages*, p. 63.

27 Evelyn Price, 'Ralph Lord Cromwell and his Household' (unpub. MA thesis, University of London, 1948), Appendix 3.

28 Crossley-Holland, *Living and Dining in Medieval Paris*, pp. 121, 125.

29 Ross, 'The Household Accounts of Elizabeth Berkeley', p. 99.

30 C. Given-Wilson, *The English Nobility in the Late Middle Ages: the Fourteenth Century Political Community* (London, Routledge, 1987), p. 93; C. Dyer, *Lords and Peasants in a Changing Society – the Estates of the Bishopric of Worcester 680–1540* (Cambridge University Press, 1980), p. 202.

31 Ross, 'The Household Accounts of Elizabeth Berkeley', p. 89.

32 Price, 'Ralph Lord Cromwell and his Household', Appendix 3.

33 J.J. Jusserand, *English Wayfaring Life in the Middle Ages*, tr. L. Toulmin-Smith (London, Fisher Unwin, 1925), p. 99.

34 P. Payne and C. Barron, 'The Letters and Life of Elizabeth Despenser, Lady Zouche', *Nottingham Medieval Studies*, xli (1997), p. 144.

35 LaBarge, *A Baronial Household*, p. 141.

36 Ross, 'The Household Accounts of Elizabeth Berkeley', pp. 86–90.

37 See Alice's Inquisition Post Mortem at the PRO, C139/70, no. 34. In M. Lobel (ed.), *The City of London from Prehistoric Times to c. 1529*, The British Atlas of Historic Towns (3 vols, Oxford University Press), vol. 3, Map 3, Ormond's Inn, which belonged to James Ormond, Earl of Wiltshire and husband of Alice's great-granddaughter, is shown at the corner of Knyghtryderstrete and Garlicke Hill, right next to the corner of Olde Fysshestrete.

38 Caroline Barron, 'Centres of Conspicuous Consumption: The Aristocratic Town House in London 1200–1550', *London Journal*, 20 (1) (1995), 9.

39 PRO, SC6/990/3,19; SC6/991/2; SC6/1245/16,17. In 1428 it was rented to William Alees, draper, and in 1431 to John Sturgeon, mercer. The annual rent was £6 13s 4d.

40 R. Hutton, *The Rise and Fall of Merry England: the Ritual Year 1400–1700* (Oxford University Press, 1996), pp. 27–34.

41 William Langland, *The Vision of Piers Plowman*, ed. A.V.C. Schmidt (London, J.M. Dent, 1995), p. 231.

42 For a contemporaneous account of a New Year's feast, the anonymous writer who described the festivities of Arthur's court at Camelot must have been drawing on experience as well as imagination, though Alice's celebrations would certainly have been less elaborate: *Sir Gawain and the Green Knight, Pearl and Sir Orfeo*, tr. J.R.R. Tolkien (London, Allen & Unwin, 1975), p. 26.

43 LaBarge, *A Baronial Household*, p. 178.

44 *Annales Johannes de Trokelowe*, ed. H.T. Riley, Rolls Series (London, Oxford University Press, 1866), p. 402. This

translation was made by Colonel Probert of Bures and quoted by the late Countess Waldegrave, *Waldegrave Family History* (privately published, n.d.), p. 7.

45 Ibid., pp. 3–6.

46 LaBarge, *A Baronial Household*, p. 66.

47 Price, 'Ralph Lord Cromwell and his Household', Appendix 3.

48 Bailey, 'The Rabbit and the Medieval East Anglian Economy', p. 15.

49 Simone Macdougall, 'Health, Diet, Medicine and the Plague', in C. Given-Wilson (ed.), *An Illustrated History of Late Medieval England* (Manchester University Press, 1996), pp. 82–3.

50 See Theresa McClean, *Medieval English Gardens* (London, Collins, 1981), particularly the chapters on manor gardens, wild flowers and herb gardens.

5. Men at the Table

1   M. Keen, *English Society in the Later Middle Ages 1348–1500* (Harmondsworth, Penguin, 1990), p. 1.

2   See Appendix 2 for references of identified visitors at Acton 1412–13.

3   J.S. Roskell, 'Sir Richard de Waldegrave of Bures, St Mary; speaker in Parliament 1381–2' *Suffolk Institute of Archaeology and Natural History*, 27 (1958), 154–75; Bacon Collection, MS 4357.

4   *The Cartulary of the Augustinian Friars of Clare*, ed. C. Harper-Bill (Ipswich, Boydell Press, 1991), pp. 2, 8, 13; Revd F. Roth, *English Austin Friars 1249–1538* (2 vols, Augustinian Historical Institute, 1966), vol. 1; L.J. Redstone, 'Suffolk Limiters', *Suffolk Institute of Archaeology and Natural History*, 20 (1930), 36–42.

5   *The Oxford Dictionary of Saints*, ed. D.H. Farmer, 2nd edn (Harmondsworth, Penguin, 1987), p. 128; see also *Handbook*

of Dates for Students of English History, ed. C.R. Cheney (London, Royal Historical Society, 1991) for a more accurate dating of the translation of the relics.

6   Lambeth Palace Library, Chicheley, vol. 1, f. 370; J.J. Howard, *The Visitation of Suffolk* (2 vols, London, Whittaker and Co., 1866), vol. 1, p. 29.

7   W. Page, *The Victoria History of the County of Essex* (6 vols, London, Oxford University Press, 1907), vol. 2, p. 180; J.S. Roskell, L. Clark and C. Rawcliffe (eds), *The History of Parliament: The House of Commons 1386–1421* (4 vols, Stroud, Alan Sutton), vol. 2, p. 791.

8   *The Oxford Dictionary of Saints*, p. 182.

9   Ibid., p. 438.

10 J.J. Jusserand, *English Wayfaring Life in the Middle Ages* (London, Fisher Unwin, 1925), p. 300.

11 Ibid., p. 307.

12 *The Oxford Dictionary of Saints*, p. 149.

13 Roth, *English Austin Friars*, p. 316.

14 None of the clergy who visited Alice is mentioned in A.B. Emden's biographical volumes on Oxford and Cambridge.

15 Guildhall Library, Braybroke's Register, f. 410; for Withersfield Church see BL, Add 5806.

16 Norfolk R.O., *Norwich Episcopal Register*, DN4 Book 7, f. 4; DN4 Book 8, f. 35.

17 R. Newcourt, *Repertorium: Ecclesiasticum Parochicale Londinense* (London, 1708), vol. 2, p. 419.

18 *CPR, 1401–5*, p. 372; Norfolk R.O., *Norwich Episcopal Register*, DN4, Book 8, ff. 20, 22; C. Morley, 'Catalogue of Beneficed Clergy of Suffolk, 1086–1550', *Suffolk Institute of Archaeology and Natural History*, 22 (1934–6), p. 40; Bacon Collection, MS 2275.

19 Roskell, 'Sir Richard de Waldegrave', p. 175.

20   *CPR, 1408–13*, p. 278; *CCR, 1419–22*,
     p. 123; Bacon Collection, MS 584;
     Howard, *The Visitation of Suffolk*, vol. 1,
     p. 116; Norfolk R.O., *Norwich Episcopal
     Register*, DN3 Book 6, f. 271, DN4 Book 8,
     ff. 20,22, DN5 Book 9, f. 23.

21   Morley, 'Catalogue of Beneficed Clergy',
     p. 46.

22   PRO, SC6/1245/14,15; Bacon Collection,
     MS 584.

23   PRO, SC2/203/10.

24   P. Coss, *The Knight in Medieval England
     1000–1400* (Stroud, Sutton Publishing,
     1993), pp. 110–17.

25   Roskell, Clark and Rawcliffe, *History of
     Parliament*, vol. 3 , pp. 431–3.

26   Suffolk R.O., Bury St Edmunds,
     458/2/1/1,2, 1417; *CPR, 1408–13*, p. 265;
     CPR, 1429–36, p. 64.

27   BL, Add 19122,3.

28   Roskell, Clark and Rawcliffe, *The History
     of Parliament*, vol. 1, pp. 654–6.

29   Ibid., vol. 2, pp. 790–2.

30   *CPR, 1399–1401*, p. 366; *CPR, 1401–5*,
     p. 372; *CPR, 1405–8*, p. 180; *CPR,
     1408–13*, pp. 311, 355, 414, 485; *CPR,
     1413–16*, p. 423; *CPR, 1416–22*, p. 199;
     PRO, Prob. 11/2b, f. 171, SC6/1245/9;
     Suffolk R.O., Bury St Edmunds,
     H1/5/5/13,17; 458/2/1/2.

31   Roskell, Clark and Rawcliffe, *The History
     of Parliament*, vol. 2, pp. 790–1.

32   Ibid., vol. 3, pp. 475–7.

33   PRO, SC6/989/3.

34   Roskell, Clark and Rawcliffe, *The History
     of Parliament*, vol. 2, pp. 455–6.

35   M.W. LaBarge, *A Baronial Household of the
     Thirteenth Century* (London, Eyre and
     Spottiswoode), 1965, p. 157.

36   J.L. Kirby, *Henry IV of England* (London,
     Constable, 1970), p. 248.

37   Norfolk R.O., Surflete's Register, ff. 64–5.

38   E. Welch, 'Some Suffolk Lollards', *Suffolk

     Institute of Archaeology and Natural
     History*, 29 (1960–1), 154.

39   *The Paston Letters and Papers of the Fifteenth
     Century*, ed. N. Davis (2 parts, Oxford,
     Clarendon Press, 1983), part 2, p. 117.

40   E.D.H. Tollemache, *The Tollemaches of
     Helmingham and Ham* (Ipswich, W.P.
     Cowell, 1949), p. 29; *CIPM*, vol. 19, p. 367;
     BL, Add MS 9672, 9680.

41   Suffolk R.O., Bury St Edmunds, EE
     501/6/47; details of Dame Alice's chantry
     foundation are discussed in Chapter 8.

42   References to Dame Alice's trustees can be
     found in Appendix 2.

43   Morley, 'Catalogue of Beneficed Clergy',
     p. 40; *CPR, 1416–22*, p. 303; K.L. Wood-Legh,
     Perpetual Chantries in Britain (Cambridge
     University Press, 1965), p. 60; Page, *Victoria
     County History of Essex*, vol. 2, p. 150.

44   PRO, SC6/989/10, 17, 18.

45   M.A. Hicks, 'The Piety of Margaret, Lady
     Hungerford (d. 1478)', *Journal of
     Ecclesiastical History*, 38 (1987), 19–38.

46   *The Book of Margery Kempe*, ed. B.A.
     Windeatt (Harmondsworth, Penguin,
     1985), pp. 72, 162–8, 174, 205–6.

47   For example, Katherine de Grandison,
     Lord Bryan's mother-in-law, who mounted
     the defence of her castle at Wark-on-Tweed
     and sent a nephew to Edward III to ask for
     help; R.E. Archer, ' "How Ladies . . . Who
     Live in their Manors Ought to Manage
     their Households and Estates": Women as
     Landholders and Administrators in the
     Late Middle Ages', in P.J.P. Goldberg (ed.),
     *Woman is a Worthy Wight: Women in English
     Society c. 1200–1500* (Gloucester, Alan
     Sutton, 1984), p. 16.

6. *Women at the Table*

1   Judith Bennett, *Women in the Medieval
     English Countryside: Gender and Household*

in Brigstock before the Plague (Oxford University Press, 1987), pp. 6, 22.

2   Once again all sources for material in this chapter relating to Alice's household come from the manuscripts cited in Appendix 1, unless otherwise specified.

3   C. Ross, 'The Household Accounts of Elizabeth Berkeley, Countess of Warwick, 1420–21', *Transactions of the Bristol and Gloucestershire Archaeological Society*, 70 (1951), p. 91.

4   E. Price, 'Ralph Lord Cromwell and his Household' (University of London, unpub. MA thesis, 1948), Appendix 3.

5   P.J.P. Goldberg (ed. and tr.), *Women in England c. 1275–1525*, Manchester Medieval Series, Manchester University Press, 1995, p. 26.

6   Ibid., p. 7.

7   H. Leyser, *Medieval Women: a Social History of Women in England 450–1500* (London, Phoenix Grant, 1996), p. 145.

8   *The Paston Letters and Papers of the Fifteenth Century*, ed. N. Davis (2 parts, Oxford, Clarendon Press, 1983), part 1, p. 339.

9   See, for example, *Kingsford's Stonor Letters and Papers 1290–1483*, ed. C. Carpenter (Cambridge University Press, 1996), pp. 211–6 for the failed courtship between Thomas Stonor and Margery Blount.

10   Doreward's will: PRO, Prob. 11/2b, f. 171, in which he left £20 'to my daughter Elizabeth Chamberlain'.

11   J.S. Roskell, L. Clark and C. Rawcliffe (eds), *The History of Parliament: The House of Commons 1386–1421* (4 vols, Stroud, Alan Sutton, 1993), vol. 2, p. 792.

12   Birdbeak seems a more appropriate surname in view of John's employment and Margaret's apparent need. Brydbek is however the consistent spelling, though the scribe may not have been dyslexic since

brid is an old English variation of bird; see, *The New Shorter Oxford English Dictionary*.

13   Helen Jewell, *Women in Medieval England* (Manchester University Press, 1996), p. 70; and B. Hanawalt, *The Ties that Bound: Peasant Families in Medieval England* (New York, Oxford University Press, 1986), pp. 141–56, on the diffusion of women's tasks in the home economy.

14   S. Penn, 'Female Wage-Earners in Late Fourteenth-Century England', *The Agricultural History Review*, 35 (1987), 1–14.

15   D. Oschinsky (ed.), *Walter of Henley and Other Treatises on Estate Management and Accounting* (Oxford, Clarendon Press, 1971), p. 425.

16   J. Bennett, 'The Village Ale-Wife: Women and Brewing in Fourteenth-Century England', in B. Hanawalt (ed.), *Women and Work in Preindustrial Europe* (Bloomington, Indiana University Press, 1986), pp. 20–36.

17   R.A. Wood, 'Poor Widows, *c*. 1393–1415', in C.M. Barron and A.F. Sutton (eds), *Medieval London Widows 1300–1500* (London, Hambledon Press, 1994), p. 63.

18   Suffolk R. O., Layham Court Rolls for 1413, E/3/1/2, ff. 3,5.

19   PRO, SC6/1297/22.

20   Seg' may have been an abbreviation for *segregatio*, Latin for separation, and would indicate that part of her job was to separate the curds and whey when making cheese and butter.

21   *The Book of Margery Kempe*, ed. B.A. Windeatt (Harmondsworth, Penguin, 1985), pp. 58, 59, 71, 73, 85, 100, 111–16, 141.

22   Ross. 'The Household Accounts of Elizabeth Berkeley', pp. 86–8.

23   Roskell, Clark and Rawcliffe, *History of Parliament*, vol. 4, pp. 545–51 for details of the careers of the Swinburnes. The

Swinburne brass is particularly interesting as the double effigies demonstrate the changing fashion in armoury between Sir Robert's death in 1391 and that of his son in 1412. It appears that at least two of Joan's four sons were also buried at St Peter's in another double tomb, Andrew who died in 1418 and John in 1430. Joan's eldest son William was chiefly responsible for these memorials but he spent most of 1413 in France sorting out his half-brother's affairs.

24   Sir Thomas Swinburne was witness to the deed, together with Alice's stepfather and half-brother, granting the manor of Naylondhalle to Alice's daughter and Henry Lord Scrope around the time of their marriage, *CCR, 1396–9*, p. 216.

25   *The Riverside Chaucer*, ed. F.N. Robinson (Oxford University Press, 1988), pp. 389, 394.

26   R. Hutton, *The Rise and Fall of Merry England: the Ritual Year 1400–1700* (Oxford University Press, 1996), p. 58.

27   J. Bennett, 'Widows in the Medieval Countryside', in L. Mirrer (ed.), *Upon My Husband's Death: Widows in the Literature and Histories of Medieval Europe* (University of Michigan Press, 1992), p. 107.

28   BL, Add Charter 19121, *Suffolk Pedigrees*.

29   PRO, SC6/990/2.

30   *Handbook of Dates for Students of English History*, ed. C.R. Cheney (London, Royal Historical Society, 1991), p. 54; *The Oxford Dictionary of Saints*, ed. D.H. Farmer, 2nd edn (Harmondsworth, Penguin, 1987), p. 231.

31   *The Book of Margery Kempe*, p. 59.

32   Marina Warner, *From the Beast to the Blonde: On Fairy-tales and their Tellers* (London, Chatto and Windus, 1994), pp. 27–50.

33   Leyser, *Medieval Women*, p. 152.

34   M.P. Statham, 'Example of an Oral Will as Accredited by Witnesses; Will of Jone Tetterell, alias Jancks, Proved 22 February 1571/72', *The Suffolk Review*, 1 (1958), 192–3.

35   Lambeth Palace, Chichely's register, vol. 1, f. 370.

36   C. Morley, 'Catalogue of Beneficed Clergy of Suffolk, 1086–1550', *Suffolk Institute of Archaeology and Natural History*, 22 (1934–6), 47.

37   Durham Organization, Registry, *Wills and Inventories illustrative of the History, Manners, Language, Statistics and Culture of the Northern Counties of England*, Surtees Society (2 parts, London, Nichols, 1899), part 1, p. 65.

38   Roskell, Clark and Rawcliffe (eds), *History of Parliament*, vol. 4, pp. 232–3.

7. The Wider World

1   For example: H. Jewell, *Women in Medieval England* (Manchester University Press, 1996), pp. 57–120; H. Leyser, *Medieval Women: a Social History of Women in England 450–1500* (London, Phoenix Grant, 1996), pp. 142–68; B. Hanawalt (ed.), *Women and Work in Preindustrial Europe*, Bloomington, Indiana University Press, 1986); J.C. Ward, *English Noblewomen in the Later Middle Ages* (London, Longman, 1992); C.M. Barron and A.F. Sutton (eds), *Medieval London Widows 1300–1500* (London, Hambledon Press, 1994).

2   Ward, *English Noblewomen*, p. 158.

3   L. Kerber, 'Separate Sphere, Female Worlds, Woman's Place: the Rhetoric of Women's History', *Journal of American History*, 75 (1988), 9–39.

4   *The Paston Letters and Papers of the Fifteenth Century*, ed. N. Davis (2 parts, Oxford, Clarendon Press, 1983), part 1, p. 226.

5   M. Keen, *English Society in the Later Middle Ages 1348–1500* (Harmondsworth, Penguin, 1990), p. 23.

6   PRO, SC6/989/7.

7   Essex R.O., D/DKM 59–61, Court Rolls for Foxearth, Liston and Pentelow 1391–99, 1404–10, 1428–60; D/DQ22/114–118, assorted Court Rolls for Foxearth from 1400; Suffolk R.O., E/3/1/2–8, Court Rolls for Layham 1411–32.

8   PRO, SC6/989/5.

9   Ward, *English Noblewomen*, p. 130.

10 C.M. Barron, 'The Widow's World', in C.M. Barron and A.F. Sutton (eds), *Medieval London Widows 1300–1500* (London, Hambledon Press, 1994), pp. xxxi–xxxiii.

11 PRO, Prob. 11/1, f. 18.

12 *Testamenta Vetusta*, ed. N.H. Nicolas, 2 vols (London, Nichols, 1826), vol. 1, p. 233.

13 E. Rickert, 'Documents and Letters: a Leaf from a Fourteenth-Century Letter Book', *Modern Philology*, 25 (1927), pp. 250–1.

14 Rowena Archer and B. Ferme, 'Testamentary Procedure with Special Reference to the Executrix', *Reading Medieval Studies*, 15 (1989), 3–34.

15 University of Cambridge Library, Hengrave Hall Deposit, MS 20, j, *The Visitation of Suffolk by William Harvey Clarencieux*, 1561 (1837).

16 *CIPM*, vol. 17, p. 294.

17 For some of the outstanding debts owed to and by Lord Bryan see *CPR, 1391–6*, p. 40; *CCR, 1392–6*, pp. 118, 153; *CPR, 1396–9*, p. 296; PRO, CP 40/521, m. 142; CP 40/518, m. 66; CP 40/527, m. 279.

18 PRO, Prob. 11/2a, f. 9.

19 *CCR, 1392–6*, p. 118.

20 *CIM, 1399–1422* (London, HMSO, 1968), p. 177.

21 C.M. Barron, 'The "Golden Age" of Women in Medieval London', in

Medieval Women in Southern England, *Reading Medieval Studies*, XV (1989), pp. 35–52.

22 *The Book of Margery Kempe*, ed. B.A. Windeatt (Harmondsworth, Penguin, 1985), p. 44.

23 Ibid., p. 96.

24 PRO, SC6/833/12.

25 Bacon Collection, MS 4357; ffiona Swabey, 'The Letter-book of Alice de Bryene and Alice de Sutton's List of Debts', *Nottingham Medieval Studies*, xlii (1998), 121–45.

26 Jewell, *Women in Medieval England*, p. 77.

27 PRO, SC6/990/19.

28 Suffolk R.O., EE501/6/47.

29 Bacon Collection, MS 2270.

30 *CCR, 1405–9*, p. 501.

31 *CFR, 1383–91*, pp. 178, 192, 201.

32 *Dorset Inquisitions Post Mortem, 1216–1485*, ed. E.A. Fry (London, British Record Society, 1916), p. 187.

33 PRO, *Coram Rege Notes*, 26/13, p. 486.

34 Christine de Pisan, *The Treasure of the City of Ladies or the Book of the Three Virtues*, tr. S. Lawson (Harmondsworth, Penguin, 1995), pp. 157–8.

35 Rickert, 'Documents and Letters', p. 251.

36 *CFR, 1391–9*, p. 58.

37 *CFR, 1391–9*, p. 69; *CPR, 1391–6*, p. 218.

38 *CFR, 1391–9*, p. 214.

39 PRO, SC6/833/12.

40 *CCR, 1413–22*, p. 453; J.S. Roskell, L. Clark and C. Rawcliffe (eds), *The History of Parliament: The House of Commons 1386–1421* (4 vols, Stroud, Alan Sutton, 1993), vol. 2, pp. 632–4.

41 PRO, C/145/312/5.

42 Bacon Collection, MS 903.

43 J.M.W. Bean, *The Estates of the Percy Family* (Oxford University Press, 1958), pp. 117–27.

44 K.B. McFarlane, *Lancastrian Kings and*

Lollard Knights (Oxford, Clarendon Press, 1992), pp. 51, 67–9.

45   J.H. Wylie, *History of England under Henry IV* (London, Longman, 1896), vol. 1, p. 100.

46   R. Archer, '"How Ladies . . . Who Live in Manors Ought to Manage their Households and Estates": Women as Landholders and Administrators in the Late Middle Ages', in P.J.P. Goldberg (ed.), *Woman is a Worthy Wight: Women in English Society* c. *1200–1500* (Gloucester, Alan Sutton, 1984), pp. 149, 151.

47   N. Orme, *From Childhood to Chivalry: the Education of the English Kings and the Aristocracy 1066–1530* (London, Methuen, 1983), p. 26.

48   E. Rickert, 'Documents and Records', p. 252.

49   PRO, Prob. 11/1, f. 53; *CCR, 1381–5*, pp. 225, 385, 424; *CFR, 1368–77*, p. 222; *CFR, 1377–88*, pp. 57, 143.

50   Swabey, 'The Letter Book of Alice de Bryene', pp. 121–45.

51   H.G. Richardson, 'An Oxford Teacher of the Fifteenth Century', *Bulletin of John Rylands Library*, 23 (1939), 436–57.

52   Helen Suggett, 'The Use of French in the Later Middle Ages', *Transactions of the Royal Historical Society*, 4th series, 27 (1946), 61–83; J. Barnie, *War in Medieval Society: Social Values and the Hundred Years War 1337–99* (London, Weidenfeld & Nicolson, 1974).

53   N. Orme, *English Schools in the Middle Ages* (London, Methuen, 1973), p. 74.

54   S.S.G. Bell, 'Medieval Book-Owners: Arbiters of Lay Piety and Ambassadors of Culture', in M. Erler and M. Kowaleski (eds), *Women and Power in the Middle Ages* (University of Georgia Press, 1988), pp. 149–87.

55   Eileen Power, *Medieval English Nunneries*

circa 1275–1535 (Cambridge University Press, 1922), p. 237.

56   M. Aston, *Lollards and Reformers: Images and Literacy in Late Medieval Religion* (London, Hambledon Press, 1984), p. 195.

57   H. Jewell, *Women in Medieval England*, pp. 138–9.

58   C. Carpenter (ed.), *Kingsford's Stonor Letters and Papers 1290–1483* (Cambridge University Press, 1996), pp. 274, 275.

59   PRO, SC6/1297/22.

60   R. Newcourt, *Repertorium: Ecclesiasticum Parochicale Londinense* (London, 1708), vol. 2, p. 275.

61   C. Woodforde, *The Norwich School of Glass-Painting in the Fifteenth Century* (Oxford University Press, 1950), pp. 72–4.

62   University of Cambridge Library, MS Dd.4.17.

63   Osbern Bokenham, *A Legend of Holy Women*, ed. and tr. Sheila Delany (London and Indiana, Notre Dame Press, 1992), pp. xiii, 138n.

64   F. Prochaska, *Women and Philanthropy in Nineteenth Century England* (Oxford, Clarendon Press, 1981).

8. Considerations for the Afterlife

1   Bacon Collection, MS 4357.

2   C. Platt, *King Death: The Black Death and its Aftermath in Late-Medieval England* (London, University College Press, 1997), pp. 97–119.

3   B.L. Manning, *The People's Faith in the Time of Wyclif* (Cambridge University Press, 1919), p. 119.

4   *The Westminster Chronicle 1381–1394*, eds L.C. Hector and B. Harvey (Oxford, Clarendon Press, 1982), pp. 453, 475, 477.

5   PRO, SC6/833/12.

6   PRO, SC6/1249/2.

7   PRO, SC6/1249/3.

8   E. Price, 'Ralph Lord Cromwell and his Household' (University of London, unpub. MA thesis, 1948), p. 198.

9   E. Duffy, *The Stripping of the Altars: Traditional Religion in England c. 1400–c. 1580* (Yale University Press, 1992), pp. 16–22.

10 C. Ross, 'The Household Accounts of Elizabeth Berkeley, Countess of Warwick, 1420–21', *Transactions of the Bristol and Gloucestershire Archaeological Society*, 70 (1951), 92.

11 PRO, SC6/990/19.

12 William Langland, *The Vision of Piers Plowman*, ed. A.V.C. Schmidt (London, J.M. Dent, 1995), p. 39.

13 E. Duffy, 'Women Saints in Fourteenth and Fifteenth Century England', in W.J. Shiels and D. Wood (eds), *Women in the Church* (London, Basil Blackwood, 1990), pp. 175–96.

14 The Benedictine Monks of St Augustine's Abbey, Ramsgate, *The Book of Saints: a Dictionary of Servants of God canonized by the Catholic Church*, 6th edn (London, A.C. Black, 1989), pp. 57, 74.

15 The Benedictine Monks, *The Book of Saints*, pp. 74 , 263.

16 Duffy, *The Stripping of the Altars*, pp. 200–5; see also M. Gill, 'The Saint with the Scythe: a Previously Unidentified Wall Painting in the Church of St Andrew, Cavenham', *Suffolk Institute of Archaeology and History*, 38 (1995), 245–55.

17 The Benedictine Monks, *The Book of Saints*, pp. 19, 67–8, 174, 210, 574.

18 See Duffy, *The Stripping of the Altars*, p. 23 for a description of the Palm Sunday festivities. The steward's account, SC6/1297/22, in which these expenses are specified is undated but internal evidence suggests it was later than 1417. In 1422 Sir Guy would have been dead thirty-six years, and it was not uncommon to mark such occasions with people to represent years. In A. Simpson, *The Wealth of the Gentry 1540–1660* (Chicago University Press, 1967), p. 25, there is a description of the funeral of Sir Nicholas Bacon, whose son married Anne Butts, the sixteenth-century Acton heiress: sixty-eight poor men followed his funeral procession 'according to the years of his Lordship's age'.

19 G.M. Gibson, *The Theater of Devotion: East Anglia Drama and Society in the Late Middle Ages* (University of Chicago Press, 1992), p. 84.

20 *The Oxford Dictionary of Saints*, ed. D.H. Farmer, 2nd edn (Harmondsworth, Penguin, 1987), p. 452.

21 K.L. Wood-Legh, *Perpetual Chantries in Britain* (Cambridge University Press, 1965), pp. 49, 60; Suffolk R.O., EE 501/6/47.

22 M. Rubin, *Charity and Community in Medieval Cambridge* (Cambridge University Press, 1987), pp. 289–96.

23 PRO, EE301/45/13.

24 *The Journal of William Dowsing*, ed. Revd C.H.E. White (Ipswich, 1885), pp. 16, 22.

25 For the brass on the double-tomb chest, J. Blatchly, 'The Lost Cross Brasses of Suffolk, 1320–1420', *Transactions of the Monumental Brass Society*, 12 (1975–9), 37.

26 *Register of Henry Chichele, Archbishop of Canterbury 1414–1443*, ed. E.F. Jacob (4 vols, Oxford University Press, 1937), vol. 2, p. 535.

27 In analysing wills with lollard features, K.B. McFarlane cites Beauchamp's as a marginal case because of its puritanical features as evidenced by such phrases as 'my symple and wrecched body', while acknowledging her interest in ceremony and gold cloth: K.B. McFarlane,

Lancastrian Kings and Lollard Knights (Oxford, Clarendon Press, 1972), p. 214.

28   F.J. Furnivall (ed.), *The Fifty Earliest English Wills, 1387–1439*, Early English Text Society, 78 (London, Trübner and Co., 1882), p. 8.

29   N.H. Nicolas (ed.), *Testamenta Vetusta* (London, Nichols, 1826), vol. 1, p. 223.

30   PRO, Prob. 11/3, f. 171.

31   J.C. Ward, *English Noblewomen in the Later Middle Ages* (London, Longman, 1992), pp. 160–2.

32   C.M. Woolgar, *Household Accounts from Medieval England* (Oxford University Press, 1992–3), p. 709.

33   C. Carpenter (ed.), *Kingsford's Stonor Letter and Papers 1290–1483* (Cambridge University Press, 1996), pp. 127–9.

34   Furnivall, *The Fifty Earliest English Wills*, pp. 116–17.

35   Nicolas, *Testamenta Vetusta*, vol. 1, p. 85.

36   V. Sekules, 'Women's Piety and Patronage', in N. Saul (ed.), *Age of Chivalry: Art and Society in Late Medieval England* (London, Collins and Brown, 1992), p. 124.

37   R. Davies, 'Religious Sensibility', in C. Given-Wilson (ed.), *An Illustrated History of Late Medieval England* (Manchester University Press, 1996), p. 113.

38   J. Blair, 'Purbeck Marble' in J. Blair and N. Ramsey (eds), *English Medieval Industries, Craftsmen, Techniques, Products* (London, Hambledon Press, 1991), pp. 41–56.

39   M.W. Norris (ed.), *Monumental Brasses: the Portfolio Plates of the Monumental Brass Society 1894–1984* (Woodbridge, Boydell Brewer, 1988), p. 7.

40   J.C. Ward, 'Sir Robert de Bures', *Transactions of the Monumental Brass Society*, 10 (1965), 149.

41   Norris, (ed.), *Monumental Brasses*, p. 7.

42   'Here lies Alice de Bures, daughter and heir of Sir Robert de Bures who once was the wife of Sir Guy de Bryan, junior, who died 11 January 1434 [1435 by modern reckoning]; God have mercy on her soul. Amen.' J. Blatchly, 'The Lost Cross Brasses of Suffolk', p. 39.

43   *The Paston Letters and Papers of the Fifteenth Century*, ed. N. Davis (2 parts, Oxford, Clarendon Press, 1983), part 1, p. 384.

44   Carpenter, *Kingsford's Stonor Letters and Papers*, p. 312.

Bibliography

Manuscript Sources

Chicago

Bacon Collection, Department of Special Collections, University of Chicago Library:

MS 584, 585, bailiff's reports for Foxearth, 1401/2, 1411/2

MS 903, Copy of Court decision relating to land in Suffolk, Essex, Devon, Dorset, Gloucestershire, Somerset and Kent held by Sir James Ormond and Amice, his wife, 1447

MS 2227, Sir Robert de Bures receives the advowson of the church at Foxearth, 11 July 1361

MS 2250, Gift of land in Cockfield and Foxearth, Robert Bere to Sir Guy Bryan, 11 November 1375

MS 2256, Gift of land, Oxenhall, Sir Guy Bryan, junior, 1381; cf. BL, Add Charter 54192

MS 2270, Appointment by Dame Alice of John Folour of Foxearth as her attorney, 10 February 1394, seal attached

MS 2275, Grant and reversion to Andrew, son of Andrew Bures, Margaret his wife, then Alice de Bryene, by John Brook, Ralph Chamberlain and John Reydon, 1402

MS 2358, Gift to the use of Robert de Bures and his heirs of property in Foxearth, 1498

MS 2371, Robert, lord of the manor of Foxearth, and Jane de Bures lease Pentelow, 1508

MS 2903, obligatory bond, Robert de Bures to Sir James Ormond, 1507

MS 3173, William Bures 60s fine to Sir Thomas Ormond, Foxearth and Brookhall, 1488

MS 4357, list of debts of Lady Alice de Sutton, 13 January 1389

Cambridge

University of Cambridge Library, Hengrave Hall, Deposit 2, Collection of the Babergh Hundred:

Copy will of Sir Guy de Bryene, transcribed by John Gage

MS 20, j, Visitation of Suffolk by William Hervy 1561 (1837)

Dorset

Record Office, Dorchester:

D/WLC T296, Concord of agreement between Joan and Sir Richard Waldegrave and Alice and Sir John de Sutton, 1365

Essex

Record Office, Chelmsford:
D/DKM 59-61, Court rolls for Foxearth, Liston, Pentelow, 1391–9, 1404–10, 1428–60
D/DQ22/114-118, assorted Court rolls for Foxearth from 1400

London

British Library:
Additional MS 5806, f. 126, Withersfield church
Additional Charters 9672, 9678, Talmache family, 1396, 1400
Additional Charter 18671, Thorp Morieux, 1385
Additional Charters 19115, 19121-4, Suffolk Pedigrees
Additional Charter 26693, Account rolls of St Gregory's College, Sudbury, 1538
Egerton 8333, Account rolls of Sir James Ormond's property, West Country, 1438/9
Egerton 8548, Account rolls of Sir James Ormond's property, East Anglia, 1438/9

Guildhall Library:
Braybroke's Register: f. 410, will of Thomas Grey, rector of Withersfield, 1395

Lambeth Palace Library: Arundel Register, vol. 1, f. 163–4, Eleanor Bohun, Duchess of Gloucester,
    1399; vol. 2, f. 49, Sir Richard Waldegrave, senior, 1410
Chichely Register, vol. 1, f. 370, John Rokewode, 1415

Public Record Office:

C139-45	Chancery, Inquisitions Post Mortem
C47	Chancery, Miscellanea
CP40	Common Pleas, Plea Rolls
DL29	Duchy of Lancaster, Minister Accounts
E301	Exchequer, Chantry Certificates
Prob. 11/1, 2a, 2b, 3	Prerogative Court of Canterbury, Registered copy wills
SC1, 2, 6	Special Collections and account rolls, see Appendix 1

Norfolk

Record Office, Norwich:
Norwich Episcopal Registers:
DN3 Book 6, 1370–1406; DN4 Book 7, 1407–15; DN4 Book 8, 1416–25; DN5 Book 9, 1425–36;
    DN5 Book 10, 1437–45
Surflete's Register, ff. 64–5, Sir Andrew Boteler's will, 1430

Suffolk

Record Office, Bury St Edmunds:
458/2/1/2, grant of Assington manor, Sir Robert Corbet, 1417

651/8-11, various deeds relating to Robert Cavendish, serjeant, 1434–5

A1/2/16/1,16, deeds relating to Ralph Chamberlain and Thomas Milde

E/3/1/2-8, Court rolls for Layham, 1411–32

EE501/6/47, Alice de Bryene's chantry trust deed, 6 September 1434

EL13/12/4, relating to Thomas Milde, bailiff of Bury St Edmunds, 1430

FL509/13/11, notes on the history of the Clopton family (1972)

HD/749/2/41, Quitclaim, Hemel Hempstead, to Andrew and Margery Bures, 1398

HI/5/5/13,17, John Doreward acts as trustee

Printed Primary Sources

Calendar of Close Rolls, London, HMSO 1902–54

Calendar of Fine Rolls, London, HMSO 1911–61

Calendar of Inquisitions Miscellaneous, London, HMSO 1916–66

Calendar of Inquisitions Post Mortem, London, HMSO 1904–95

Calendar of Papal Letters, London, HMSO 1895–1960

Calendar of Patent Rolls, London, HMSO 1901–71

Blagg, T.M. (ed.). *Inquisitions Post Mortem for Gloucestershire 1359–1413*, 6 vols, London, British Record Society, 1914

Brie, F.W.D. (ed.). *The Brut*, Early English Text Society, Old Series, 131, 2 vols, London, Oxford University Press, 1908

Carpenter, C. (ed.). *Kingsford's Stonor Letters and Papers 1290–1483*, Cambridge University Press, 1996

Christine de Pisan. *The Treasure of the City of Ladies or the Book of the Three Virtues*, tr. S. Lawson, Harmondsworth, Penguin, 1995

Davis, N. (ed.). *The Paston Letters and Papers of the Fifteenth Century*, 2 parts, Oxford, Clarendon Press, 1983

Durham Organization, Registry, *Wills and Inventories Illustrative of the History, Manners, Language, Statistics and Culture of the Northern Counties of England*, 2 parts, Surtees Society, London, Nichols, 1899–1929

Froissart: *Chronicles*, ed. G. Brereton, Harmondsworth, Penguin, 1968

Fry, E.A. (ed.). *Dorset Inquisitions Post Mortem 1216–1485*, London, British Record Society, 1916

Fry, E.A. and G.S. (eds). *Dorset Feet of Fines 1327–1485*, London, British Record Society, 1910

Furnivall, F.J. (ed.). *The Fifty Earliest English Wills 1387–1439*, Early English Text Society, 78, London, Trübner and Co., 1882

Galbraith, V.H. (ed.). *The Anonimalle Chronicle 1333–81*, Manchester University Press, 1970

Hector, L.C. and Harvey, B. (eds). *The Westminster Chronicle 1381–1394*, Oxford, Clarendon Press, 1982

Hingeston-Randolph, F.C. (ed.). *The Episcopal Register of Thomas Brantyngham 1370–94*, 2 parts, London, Bell, 1906

Holmes, G. (ed.). *Rymer's Foedera, conventiones, literae et cuiscunque generis acta publica*, 3rd edn, 10 vols, The Hague, 1740

Howard, J.J. (ed.). *The Visitation of Suffolke made by William Hervy*, 2 vols, London, Whittaker and Co., 1866

Jacob, E.F. (ed.). *Register of Henry Chicele, Archbishop of Canterbury 1414–1443*, 4 vols, Oxford University Press, 1943–7

Julian of Norwich. *Revelations of Divine Love*, ed. C. Wolters, Harmondsworth, Penguin, 1966

Kirby, T.F. (ed.). *Wykeham's Register*, 2 vols, London, Simpkin and Co., 1899

Kirk, R.E.G. (ed.). *Feet of Fines for Essex*, 6 vols, Colchester, Essex Archaeological Society, 1949

Nichols, J.B. (ed.). *Collectanea Topographica et Geneaologica*, 8 vols, London, Nichols, 1834–43

Nichols, J. (ed.). *A Collection of wills known to be extant of the Kings and Queens of England from William the Conqueror to Henry VII*, London, Nichols, 1780

Oliver, G. (ed.). *Monasticon Dioecesis Exoniensis*, London, Longmans, 1846

Power, E. (tr.). *The Goodman of Paris: a treatise on moral and domestic economy by a citizen of Paris c. 1393*, London, Routledge and Sons, 1928

Redstone, V. (ed.). *The Household Book of Alice de Bryene*, Suffolk Institute of Archaeology and Natural History, Ipswich, 1932

Reyce, R. *Suffolk in the Seventeenth Century: the Breviary of Suffolk (1618) with notes by Lord Francis Hervy*, London, J. Murray, 1902

Rickert, E. 'Documents and Letters: a Leaf from a Fourteenth-Century Letter Book', *Modern Philology*, 25 (1927), 249–55

Riley, H.T. (ed.). *Annales Johannes de Trokelowe*, Rolls Series, London, Oxford University Press, 1866

——(ed.). *Thomas Walsingham: Historia Anglicana 1272–1422*, 2 vols, London, Longman, 1863–70

Robinson, F.N. (ed.). *The Riverside Chaucer*, Oxford University Press, 1988

Sharpe, R.R. (ed.). *Calendar of Letter Books, preserved among the Archives of the Corporation of the City of London, 1275–1498*, 11 vols, London, J.E. Francis, 1899–1912

Thomas, A.H. (ed.). *Calendar of Select Pleas and Memoranda of the City of London 1381–1412*, Cambridge University Press, 1932

Thompson, E.M. *Chronicon Angliae 1328–1388*, London, Longman, 1874

——. (ed.). *Chronicon Adae de Usk 1377–1421*, 2nd edn, London, Henry Frowde, 1904

Tolkien, J.R.R. *Sir Gawain and the Green Knight, Pearl and Sir Orfeo*, London, Allen & Unwin, 1975

Vivian, L. (ed.). *The Visitations of the County of Devon, Comprising the Heralds' Visitations of 1531, 1564 and 1620*, Exeter, Henry Eland, 1895

White, Revd C.H.E. (ed.). *The Journal of William Dowsing*, Ipswich, 1885

William Langland. *The Vision of Piers Plowman*, ed. A.V.C. Schmidt, London, J.M. Dent, 1995

Windeatt, B.A. (ed.). *The Book of Margery Kempe*, Harmondsworth, Penguin, 1985

SECONDARY SOURCES

Alexander, J. and Binski, P. (eds). *Age of Chivalry: Art in Plantagenet England 1200–1400*, London, Weidenfeld & Nicolson, 1987

Alexander, J.J. 'Early Owners of Torbryan', *Transactions of the Devonshire Society*, 68 (1936), 197–214

Allmand, C.T. *Henry V*, London, Methuen, 1992

Archer, R.E. '"How Ladies . . . Who Live in their Manors Ought to Manage their Households and Estates": Women as Landholders and Administrators in the late Middle Ages', in P.J.P. Goldberg (ed.), *Woman is a Worthy Wight: Women in English Society c. 1200–1500*, Gloucester, Alan Sutton, 1984

——. 'Rich Old Ladies: the Problem of Late Medieval Dowagers', in A.J. Pollard (ed.), *Property and Politics: Essays in Late Medieval History*, Stroud, Alan Sutton, 1984

——. and Ferme, B. 'Testamentary Procedure with Special Reference to the Executrix', *Reading Medieval Studies*, 15 (1989), 3–34

Aston, M.E. *Lollards and Reformers: Images and Literacy in Late Medieval Religion*, London, Hambledon Press, 1984

Baigent, J. 'Thomas Burgh and his Wife with a Few Words on the Benediction of Widows', *Surrey Archaeological Collections*, 3 (1865), 208–17

Bailey, M. 'The Rabbit and the Medieval East Anglian Economy', *The Agricultural History Review*, 36 (1988), 1–20

Barnardiston, K.W. *Clare Priory: Seven Centuries of a Suffolk House*, Cambridge, Heffer, 1962

Barnie, J. *War in Medieval Society: Social Values and the Hundred Years War 1337–99*, London, Weidenfeld & Nicolson, 1974

Barron, C.M. 'The "Golden Age" of Women in Medieval London', in *Medieval Women in Southern England, Reading Medieval Studies* XV (1989), 35–58

——. and Sutton, A.F. (eds). *Medieval London Widows 1300–1500*, London, Hambledon Press, 1994

——. 'Centres of Conspicuous Consumption: The Aristocratic Town House in London 1200–1550', *London Journal* 20 (1) (1995), 1–16

Bean, J.M.W. *The Estates of the Percy Family*, Oxford University Press, 1958

——. *From Lord to Patron: Lordship in Late Medieval England*, Manchester University Press, 1989

Bell, S.G. 'Medieval Women Book-owners: Arbiters of Lay Piety and Ambassadors of Culture', in M. Erler and M. Kowaleski (eds), *Women and Power in the Middle Ages*, University of Georgia Press, 1988, 149–87

The Benedictine Monks of St Augustine's Abbey, *The Book of Saints: a Dictionary of the Servants of God Canonized by the Catholic Church*, 6th edn, London, A.C. Black, 1989

Bennett, H.S. *Life on the English Manor: A Study of Peasant Conditions 1150–1400*, Cambridge University Press, 1971

Bennett, J. 'The Village Ale-Wife: Women and Brewing in Fourteenth-Century England', in B. Hanawalt (ed.), *Women and Work in Preindustrial Europe*, Bloomington, Indiana University Press, 1986

——. *Women in the Medieval English Countryside: Gender and Household in Brigstock before the Plague*, Oxford University Press, 1987

——. 'Medieval Women, Modern Women: Across the Great Divide', in D. Aers (ed.), *Culture and History 1350–1600: Essays on English Communities, Identities and Writing*, New York, Harvester Wheatsheaf, 1992

——. 'Widows in the Medieval Countryside', in L. Mirrer (ed.), *Upon My Husband's Death: Widows in the Literature and Histories of Medieval Europe*, University of Michigan Press, 1992

Blair, J. 'Purbeck Marble', in J. Blair and N. Ramsey (eds), *English Medieval Industries, Craftsmen, Techniques, Products*, London, Hambledon Press, 1991

Blatchly, J. 'The Lost Cross Brasses of Suffolk 1320–1420', *Transactions of the Monumental Brass Society* 12 (1975–9), 21–45

Bolton, J.L. *The Medieval English Economy 1150–1500*, London, Dent, 1980

Campbell-Klease, J. *A History of Hazelbury Bryan*, privately published, 1983

Cheney, C.R. (ed.). *Handbook of Dates for Students of English History*, London, Royal Historical Society, 1991

Claxton, A.O.D. *The Suffolk Dialect in the Twentieth-Century*, Ipswich, Boydell Press, 1968

Cook, G.H. *Medieval Chantries and Chantry Chapels*, London, Phoenix House, 1948

Copinger, V.A. *The Manors of Suffolk: Notes on the History and Devolution*, 6 vols, London, Fisher Unwin, 1905

Coss, P. *The Knight in Medieval England 1000–1400*, Stroud, Sutton Publishing, 1993

Crossley-Holland, N. *Living and Dining in Medieval Paris: the Household of a Fourteenth-Century Knight*, Cardiff, University of Wales Press, 1996

Davies, R. 'Religious Sensibility', in C. Given-Wilson (ed.), *An Illustrated History of Late Medieval England*, Manchester University Press, 1996

Delany, S, (ed. and tr.). *Osbern Bokenham: A Legend of Holy Women*, Indiana and London, University of Notre Dame Press, 1992

Dorling, E. 'A Montagu Shield at Hazelbury Bryan', *The Ancestor* 8 (1904), 215–8

Du Boulay, F. *An Age of Ambition: English Society in the Late Middle Ages*, London, Nelson, 1970

Duffy, E. 'Women Saints in Fourteenth and Fifteenth Century England', in W.J. Shiels and D. Wood (eds), *Women in the Church*, London, Basil Blackwood, 1990

——. *The Stripping of the Altars: Traditional Religion in England c. 1400–1580*, Yale University Press, 1992

Dyer, C. *Lords and Peasants in a Changing Society – the Estates of the Bishopric of Worcester 680–1540*, Cambridge, Past and Present Publications, 1980

——. *Standards of Living in the Late Middle Ages: Social Change in England c. 1200–1520*, Cambridge University Press, 1989

——. 'The Consumer and the Market in the Later Middle Ages', *Economic History Review*, 2nd Series 42 (1989), 305–27

Erler, M.C. 'Three Fifteenth Century Vowesses', in C. Barron and A. Sutton (eds), *Medieval London Widows 1300–1500*, London, Hambledon Press, 1994

Farmer, D.H. *The Oxford Dictionary of Saints*, 2nd edn, Harmondsworth, Penguin, 1987

Gibbs, V. (ed.). *The Complete Peerage*, 13 vols, London, St Catherine's Press, 1910–59

Gibson, G.M. *The Theater of Devotion: East Anglia Drama and Society in the Late Middle Ages*, University of Chicago Press, 1989

Gill, M. 'The Saint with the Scythe: a Previously Unidentified Wall Painting in the Church of St Andrew, Cavenham', *Suffolk Institute of Archaeology and History*, 38 (1995), 245–55

Given-Wilson, C. *The Royal Household and the King's Affinity: Service, Politics and Finance in England 1360–1413*, Yale University Press, 1986

——. *The English Nobility in the Late Middle Ages: the Fourteenth Century Political Community*, London, Routledge and Kegan Paul, 1987

Goldberg, P.J.P. *A Woman is a Worthy Wight: Women in English Society c. 1200–1500*, Stroud, Alan Sutton, 1984

——. (ed. and tr.). *Women in England c. 1275–1525*, Manchester Medieval Series, Manchester University Press, 1995

Hammond, P.W. *Food and Feast in Medieval England*, Stroud, Alan Sutton, 1993

Hanawalt, B. *The Ties That Bound: Peasant Families in Medieval England*, New York, Oxford University Press, 1986

Hardy, T. *The Trumpet Major*, Oxford University Press, 1986

Harper-Bill, C. *Clare Priory: the Cartulary of the Augustinian Friars of Clare*, Ipswich, Boydell Press, 1991

Harrod, H. 'On the Mantle and Ring of Widowhood', *Archaeologia* 40 (1866), 307–10

Herlihy, D. *Medieval Households*, Harvard University Press, 1985

Hicks, M.A. 'The piety of Margaret, Lady Hungerford (d. 1478)', *Journal of Ecclesiastical History*, 38 (1987), 19–38

Hieatt, C.B. and Butler, S. (eds). *Curye on Inglysch*, Early English Text Society, Oxford, University Press, 1985

Hodson, W.W. 'Sudbury College and Archbishop Theobald', *Suffolk Institute of Archaeology and Natural History*, 7 (1891), 23–33

Holmes, G.A. *The Estates of the Higher Nobility in Fourteenth Century England*, Cambridge University Press, 1957

——. *The Later Middle Ages 1272–1485*, London, Nelson, 1962

Hutchins, J. *History of Dorset*, 4 vols, London, Nichols and Sons, 1861

Hutton, R. *The Rise and Fall of Merry England: the Ritual Year 1400–1700*, Oxford University Press, 1996

Jacob, E.F. *The Fifteenth Century 1399–1485*, Oxford, Clarendon Press, 1961

Jewell, H. *Women in Medieval England*, Manchester University Press, 1996

Jusserand, J.J. *English Wayfaring Life in the Middle Ages*, tr. L.Toulmin-Smith, London, Fisher Unwin, 1925

Keen, M. *English Society in the Later Middle Ages 1348–1500*, Harmondsworth, Penguin, 1990

Kerber, L. 'Separate Spheres, Female World, Woman's Place: the Rhetoric of Women's History', *Journal of American History*, 75 (1988), 9–39

Kirby, J.L. *Henry IV of England*, London, Constable, 1970

LaBarge, M.W. *A Baronial Household of the Thirteenth Century*, London, Eyre and Spottiswoode, 1965

——. *Women in Medieval Life*, London, Hamish Hamilton, 1986

Leach, A.F. *The Schools of Medieval England*, London, Methuen, 1915

Leyser, H. *Medieval Women: a Social History of Women in England 450–1500*, London, Phoenix Grant, 1996

Lobel, M.D. (ed.). *The City of London from Prehistoric Times to c. 1520*, The British Atlas of Historic Towns, 3 vols, Oxford University Press, 1991

McClean, T. *Medieval English Gardens*, London, Collins, 1981

Macdougal, S. 'Health, Diet, Medicine and the Plague', in C. Given-Wilson (ed.), *An Illustrated History of Late Medieval England*, Manchester University Press, 1996

McFarlane, K.B. *Lancastrian Kings and Lollard Knights*, Oxford, Clarendon Press, 1972

———. *The Nobility of Later Medieval England*, Oxford, Clarendon Press, 1973

McKisack, M. *The Fourteenth Century 1307–99*, Oxford, Clarendon Press, 1959

Maddern, P. 'Honour Among the Pastons: Gender and Integrity in Fifteenth Century English Provincial Society', *Journal of Medieval History* 14 (1988), 357–71

Manning, B.L. *The People's Faith in the Time of Wyclif*, Cambridge University Press, 1919

Mathew, G. *The Court of Richard II*, London, John Murray, 1968

Mertes, K. *The English Noble Household 1250–1600: Good Governance and Political Rule*, Oxford, Basil Blackwell, 1988

Morley, C. 'Catalogue of Beneficed Clergy of Suffolk, 1086–1550', *Suffolk Institute of Archaeology and Natural History*, 22 (1934–6), 29–85

Newcourt, R. *Repertorium: Ecclesiasticum Parochicale Londinense*, 2 vols, London, 1708

Nicolas, N.H. (ed.). *Testamenta Vetusta*, 2 vols, London, Nichols, 1826

———. *The Controversy between Sir Richard Scrope and Sir Robert Grosvenor*, 2 vols, London, Nichols, 1832

Norris, M.W. (ed.). *Monumental Brasses: the Portfolio Plates of the Monumental Brass Society 1894–1984*, Woodbridge, Boydell Brewer, 1988

Orme, N. *English Schools in the Middle Ages*, London, Methuen, 1973

———. *From Childhood to Chivalry: the Education of English Kings and Aristocracy 1066–1984*, London, Methuen, 1984

Oschinsky, D. (ed.). *Walter of Henley and Other Treatises on Estate Management and Accounting*, Oxford, Clarendon Press, 1971

Page, W. (ed.). *The Victoria History of the County of Essex*, 6 vols, London, Oxford University Press, 1907

———. (ed.). *The Victoria History of the County of Suffolk*, 2 vols, London, Constable, 1911

Payne, P. and Barron, C. 'The Letters and Life of Elizabeth Despenser, Lady Zouche', *Nottingham Medieval Studies*, xli (1997), 126–56

Penn, S. 'Female Wage-earners in Late Fourteenth-Century England', *Agricultural History Review*, 35 (1987), 1–14

Platt, C. *King Death: the Black Death and its Aftermath in Late-Medieval England*, London, University College Press, 1996

Plucknett, T.F.T. 'The Medieval Bailiff', *The Creighton Lecture in History 1953*, University of London, Athlone Press, 1954

Power, E. *Medieval English Nunneries c. 1275–1535*, Cambridge University Press, 1922

———. *Medieval Women*, Cambridge University Press, 1975

Price, E. 'Ralph Lord Cromwell and his Household', University of London, unpub. MA thesis, 1948

Prochaska, F. *Women and Philanthropy in Nineteenth Century England*, Oxford, Clarendon Press, 1981

Pugh, T. 'The Southampton Plot 1415', in R.A. Griffiths and J. Sherborne (eds), *Kings and Nobles in the Later Middle Ages*, Gloucester, Alan Sutton, 1986

Rawcliffe, C. 'Baronial Councils in the Later Middle Ages', in C. Ross (ed.), *Patronage, Pedigree and Power in Later Medieval England*, Gloucester, Alan Sutton, 1979

Redstone, L.J. 'Suffolk Limiters', *Suffolk Institute of Archaeology and Natural History*, 20 (1930), 36–42

Richardson, H. 'An Oxford Teacher of the Fifteenth Century', *Bulletin of John Rylands Library* 23 (1939), 436–57

Rickert, E. (ed.), *Chaucer's World*, Columbia University Press, 1948

Rosenthal, J. *Nobles and Noble Life 1295–1500*, London, Allen and Unwin, 1976

——. 'Aristocratic Marriage and the English Peerage 1350–1500: Social Institution and Personal Bond', *Journal of Medieval History* 10 (1984), 181–94

——. 'Aristocratic Widows in Fifteenth-Century England', in B.J. Harris and J.K. McNamara (eds), *Women and the Structure of Society*, Durham, NC, 1984

——. '"Other Victims": Peeresses as War Widows 1450–1500', in L. Mirrer (ed.), *Upon My Husband's Death: Widows in the Literature and History of Medieval Europe*, University of Michigan Press, 1992

Roskell, J.S. 'Sir Richard Waldegrave of Bures St Mary; Speaker in Parliament 1381–2', *Suffolk Institute of Archaeology and Natural History* 27 (1958), 154–75

——. Clark, L. and Rawcliffe, C. (eds), *The History of Parliament: The House of Commons 1386–1421*, 4 vols, Stroud, Alan Sutton, 1993

Ross, C. 'The Household Accounts of Elizabeth Berkeley, Countess of Warwick, 1420–21', *Transactions of the Bristol and Gloucestershire Archaeology Society*, 70 (1951), 81–105

Roth, Revd F. (ed.), *English Austin Friars 1249–1538*, 2 vols, Augustinian Historical Institute, 1966

Rubin, M. *Charity and Community in Medieval Cambridge*, Cambridge University Press, 1987

Saul, N. *Scenes from Provincial Life: Knightly Families in Sussex 1280–1400*, Oxford, Clarendon Press, 1986

——. *Richard II*, London, Yale University Press, 1997

Sekules, V. 'Women's Piety and Patronage', in N. Saul (ed.), *Age of Chivalry: Art and Society in Late Medieval England*, London, Collins and Brown, 1992

Simpson, A. *The Wealth of the Gentry 1540–1660*, Chicago University Press, 1961

Stanes, R.G.F., 'Sir Guy de Brian, K.G.', *Transactions of the Devonshire Association*, 91–2 (1959–60), 249–77

Statham, M.P., 'Example of an Oral Will Accredited by Witnesses: Will of Jone Tetterell, alias Jancks, Proved 22 February 1571/72', *The Suffolk Review*, 1 (1958), 192–3

Stone, L. *The Family, Sex and Marriage in England 1500–1800*, London, Weidenfeld & Nicolson, 1977

Suggett, H. 'The Use of French in the Later Middle Ages', *Transactions of the Royal Historical Society*, 4th series, 27 (1946), 61–83

Swabey, ff. 'The Letter-book of Alice de Bryene and Alice de Sutton's List of Debts', *Nottingham Medieval Studies*, xlii (1998), 121–45

——. 'Life in the Household of Alice de Bryene: There's No Such Thing as a Free Lunch', in M. Carlin and J. Rosenthal (eds), *Food and Eating in Medieval Europe*, London, Hambledon Press, 1998

Swanson, R.N. *Catholic England: Faith, Religion and Observance before the Reformation*, Manchester University Press, 1993

Tanner, N. 'Reformation and Regionalism in Norwich', in J.A.F. Thomson (ed.), *Towns and Townspeople in the Fifteenth Century*, Gloucester, Alan Sutton, 1988

Tollemache, E.D.H. *The Tollemaches of Helmingham and Ham*, Ipswich, W.P. Cowell, 1949

Tout, T.F. *Chapters in the Administrative History of Medieval England: the Wardrobe, Chamber and Small Seals*, 6 vols, Manchester University Press, 1920

Upham, E. *Index to the Rolls of Parliament 1278–1503*, London, imprint, 1832

The Countess Waldegrave, *Waldegrave Family History*, privately published, n.d.

Walker, S. *The Lancastrian Affinity 1361–1399*, Oxford, Clarendon Press, 1990

Walker, S.S. 'Widow and Ward: the Feudal Law of Child Custody in Medieval England', in S. Stuard (ed.), *Women in Medieval Society*, University of Pennsylvania, 1976

Ward, J.C. 'Sir Robert de Bures', *Transactions of the Monumental Brass Society* 10 (1965), 144–50

——. *English Noblewomen in the Later Middle Ages*, London, Longman, 1992

Warner, M. *From the Beast to the Blonde: On Fairy-tales and their Tellers*, London, Chatto & Windus, 1994

Welch, E. 'Some Suffolk Lollards', *Suffolk Institute of Archaeology and Natural History* 29 (1961–3), 154–65

Wood, R.A. 'Poor Widows *c.* 1393–1415', in C. Barron and A. Sutton (eds), *Medieval London Widows 1350–1500*, London, Hambledon Press, 1994

Woodforde, C. *The Norwich School of Glass-Painting in the Fifteenth Century*, Oxford University Press, 1950

Wood-Legh, K. L. *Perpetual Chantries in Britain*, Cambridge University Press, 1965

Woolgar, C.M. *Household Accounts from Medieval England*, 2 parts, Oxford University Press, 1992–3

——. 'Diet and Consumption in Gentry and Noble Households', in R.E. Archer and S. Walker, (eds), *Rulers and Ruled in Late Medieval England*, London, Hambledon Press, 1995

Wright, T. *History of Domestic Manners and Sentiments in England during the Middle Ages*, London, Chapman Hall, 1862

Wylie, J.H. *History of England under Henry IV*, 4 vols, London, Longman, 1896

Yallop, H. J. 'Slapton College', *Transactions of the Devonshire Association*, 91–2 (1959–60), 138–48

——. 'Sir William de Bryan', *Transactions of the Devonshire Association*, 98 (1966), 386–97

Index

Generally only people who are referred to in printed sources or manuscripts, other than those relating to Alice de Bryene's estates, are indexed. Numerals in *italics* indicate black and white illustrations, those in **bold** indicate colour illustration numbers.

DATE DUE

HIGHSMITH #45115